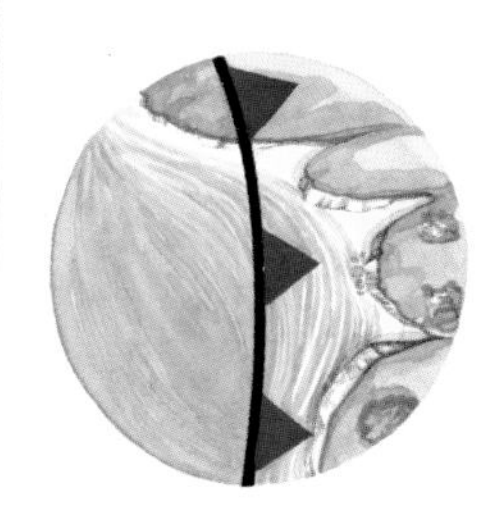

Cold front on a weather map

Lightning strikes a tall building.

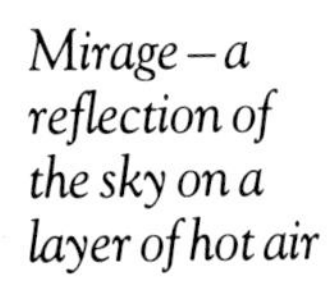

Mirage – a reflection of the sky on a layer of hot air

Thunderclouds overhead

Leaf with dew

Weather

Written by
JOHN FARNDON

DORLING KINDERSLEY
London • New York • Stuttgart

A DORLING KINDERSLEY BOOK

Project editor Christine Webb
Art editors Thomas Keenes, Carol Orbel
Senior editor Susan McKeever
Senior art editor Jacquie Gulliver
Production Catherine Semark

Editorial consultant Ron Lobeck

This Eyewitness ® Explorers book
first published in Great Britain in 1992 by
Dorling Kindersley Limited
9 Henrietta Street
Covent Garden
London WC2E 8PS

A CIP catalogue for this book is available from the British Library.

ISBN 0 86318 825 7

Colour reproduction by Colourscan, Singapore
Printed in Italy by A. Mondadori Editore, Verona

Contents

What is weather?

Weather is just the way the air around you changes all the time. It can be still, moving, hot, cold, wet, or dry. Most importantly, weather is the way water changes in the air. Without water, there would be no clouds, rain, snow, thunder, or fog. In fact, weather plays a big part in our lives and affects many of the things that we do.

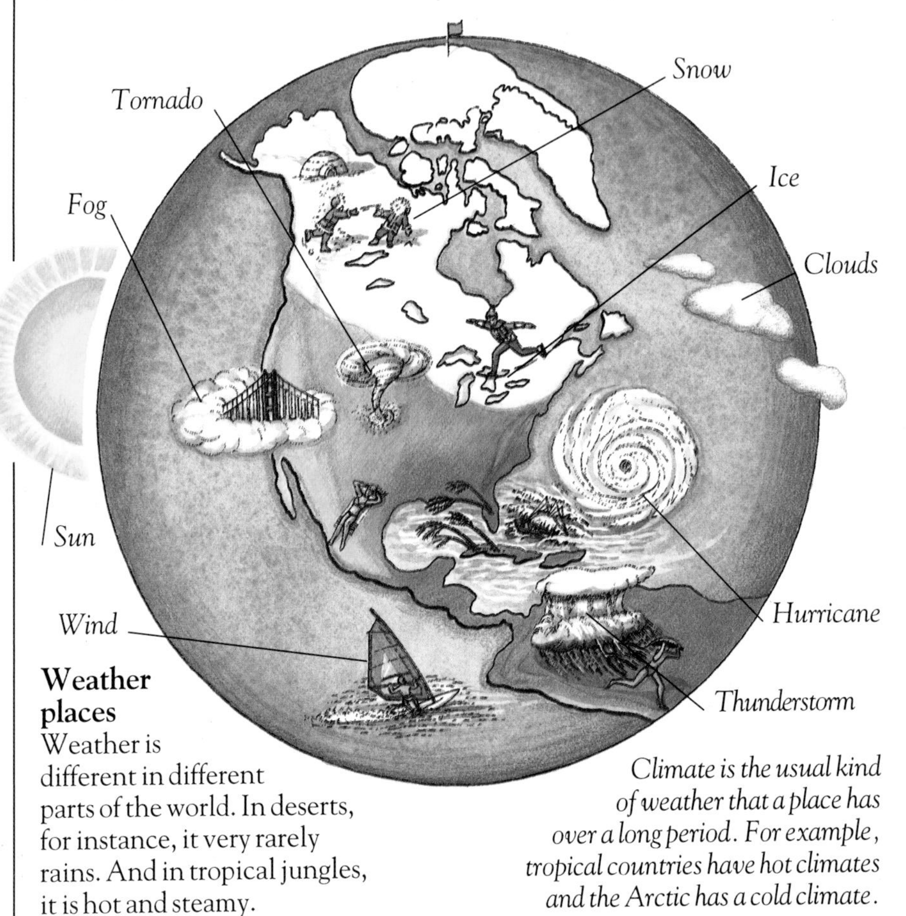

Weather places
Weather is different in different parts of the world. In deserts, for instance, it very rarely rains. And in tropical jungles, it is hot and steamy.

Climate is the usual kind of weather that a place has over a long period. For example, tropical countries have hot climates and the Arctic has a cold climate.

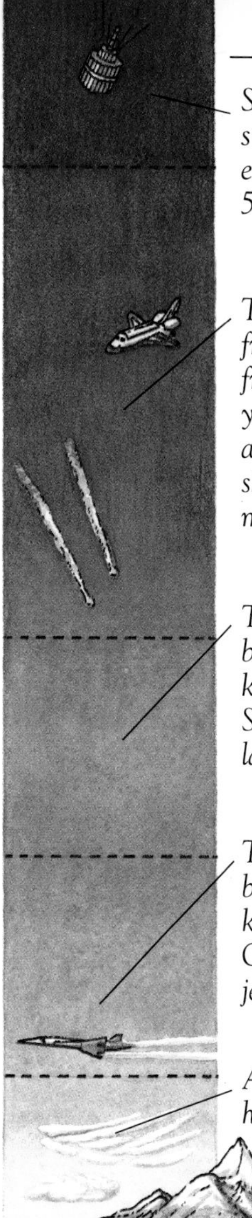

Mighty puff

The Ancient Greeks used to think that wind was the Earth breathing in and out. Now we know it is simply air on the move.

The atmosphere

Our planet is surrounded by a thin blanket of gases called the atmosphere. Weather only happens in the very lowest layer, the troposphere.

Weather forecasts

Weather experts now use modern equipment such as satellites to help them make more accurate forecasts. This satellite photograph shows the direction that a storm is travelling in.

Winter sleep
Many animals like mice sleep away the winter to save energy. This is called hibernation.

The seasons

You can expect a certain kind of weather at certain times of the year. Winter days are often cold or stormy, while summer days may be warm and sunny. It all depends on the season. Some places have just two seasons, a wet one and a dry one. Other places have four: spring, summer, autumn, and winter.

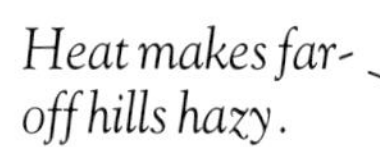

Heat makes far-off hills hazy.

Spring
Once winter is over, the sun climbs higher in the sky and the days get longer. Nights are cold but days can be warm.

Summer
The sun is high in the sky at noon and days are long and warm. Hot weather may be broken by thunderstorms.

Hot Christmas

Because of the way the seasons work, winter happens in the United States when it is summer on the opposite side of the world, in Australia.

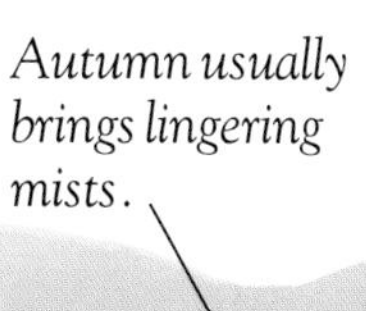

High and low

The seasons occur because the amount of sunlight reaching you varies. In summer you will see that the sun is much higher than in winter. This means that your "part" of the Earth is tilting towards the sun.

Autumn

During autumn the nights get longer and cooler again. Mornings are often misty. Sometimes they are frosty.

Winter

Winter is the coldest time of year. The days are so short and the sun hangs so low in the sky that the air barely warms up.

The three clouds

Clouds come in all kinds of shapes and sizes, but they are all made of billions of tiny water drops or even ice crystals floating in the sky. There are three basic types – fluffy white "cumulus" clouds, huge blankets of "stratus" clouds, and wispy "cirrus" clouds.

What makes a fluffy cloud?
Cumulus clouds are made when sunshine warms up bubbles of moist air and causes them to rise quickly. As they get higher, they swell and are cooled so that the moisture turns into a mist of water droplets.

Cumulus clouds are about 500 metres above you.

This cloud's fluffy shape shows how the bubble of warm, moist air billows out.

Cumulus clouds
Fluffy cumulus clouds are the clouds you usually see in fine weather, when the sky is blue. They look like heaps of cotton wool and are always changing shape.

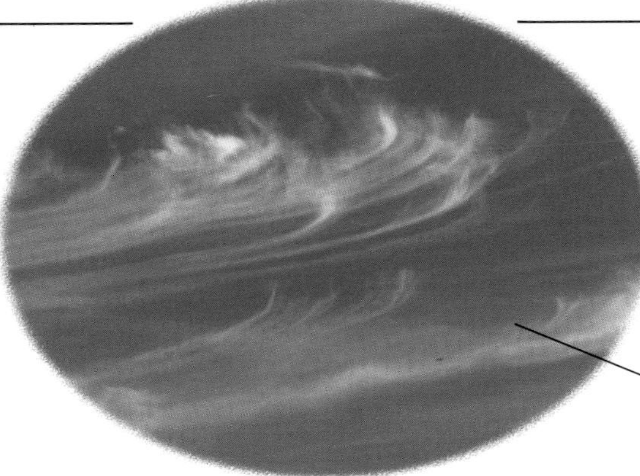

Cirrus clouds

Feathery cirrus clouds form very high up in the sky. It is so cold up there that they are made not of water droplets, but of tiny ice crystals.

Cirrus clouds high up in the sky often signal bad weather.

Mare's tails

Cirrus clouds are often called mare's tails because strong winds high in the air blow them into wispy curls – just like the tail of a horse.

Stratus clouds build up when warm, moist air rides up slowly over a bank of colder air.

Stratus clouds

The word "stratus" means "layers" in Latin, but you rarely see the layers in a stratus cloud. You just see a huge grey sheet of low cloud that can stretch for hundreds of kilometres.

Cloudspotting

Clouds come in many shapes and sizes – some large and fluffy, some small and wispy. It all depends on whether they are formed from water droplets or ice crystals. Weather experts identify clouds by how high they are in the sky, and whether they are layered (stratus) or heaps (cumulus).

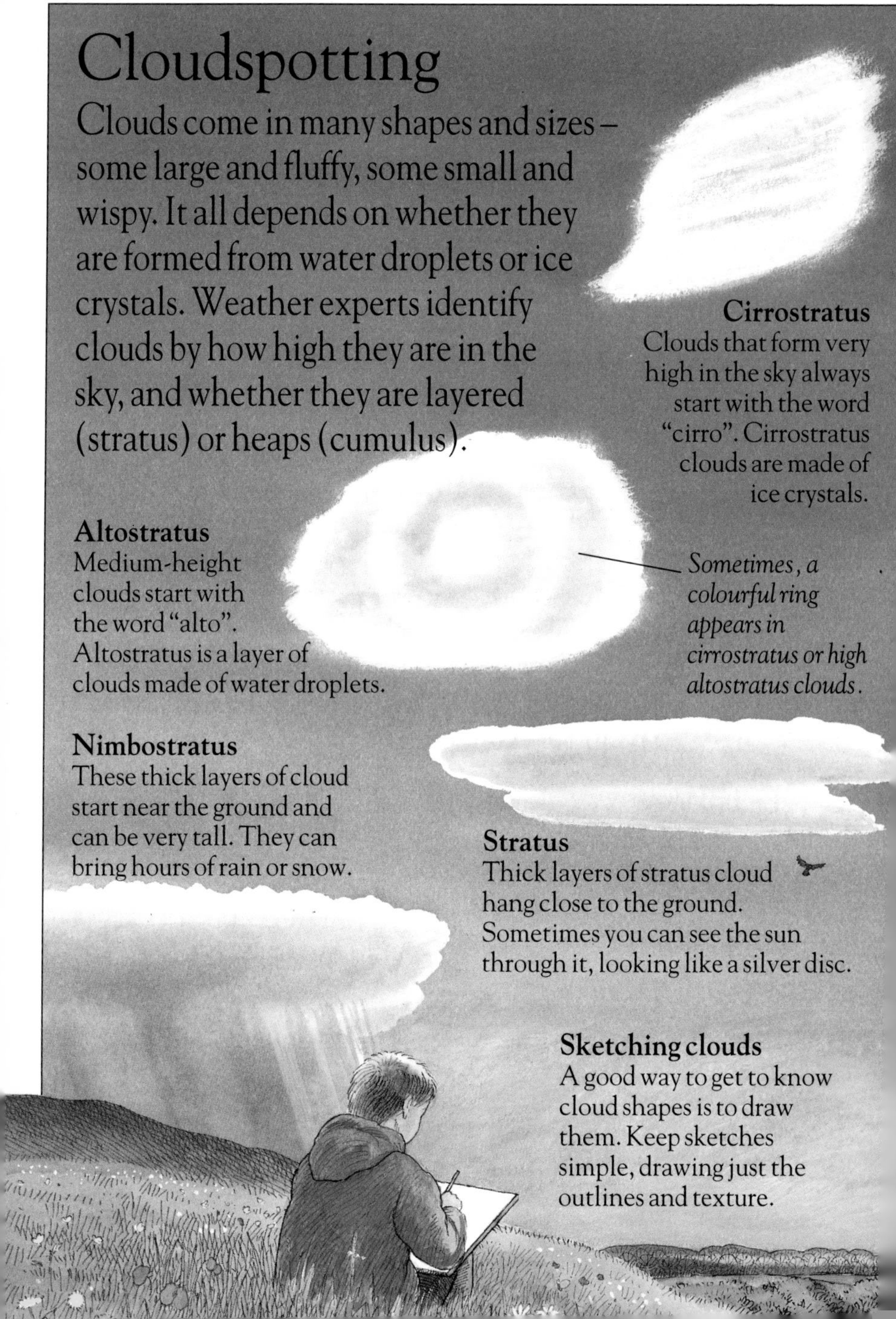

Cirrostratus
Clouds that form very high in the sky always start with the word "cirro". Cirrostratus clouds are made of ice crystals.

Altostratus
Medium-height clouds start with the word "alto". Altostratus is a layer of clouds made of water droplets.

Sometimes, a colourful ring appears in cirrostratus or high altostratus clouds.

Nimbostratus
These thick layers of cloud start near the ground and can be very tall. They can bring hours of rain or snow.

Stratus
Thick layers of stratus cloud hang close to the ground. Sometimes you can see the sun through it, looking like a silver disc.

Sketching clouds
A good way to get to know cloud shapes is to draw them. Keep sketches simple, drawing just the outlines and texture.

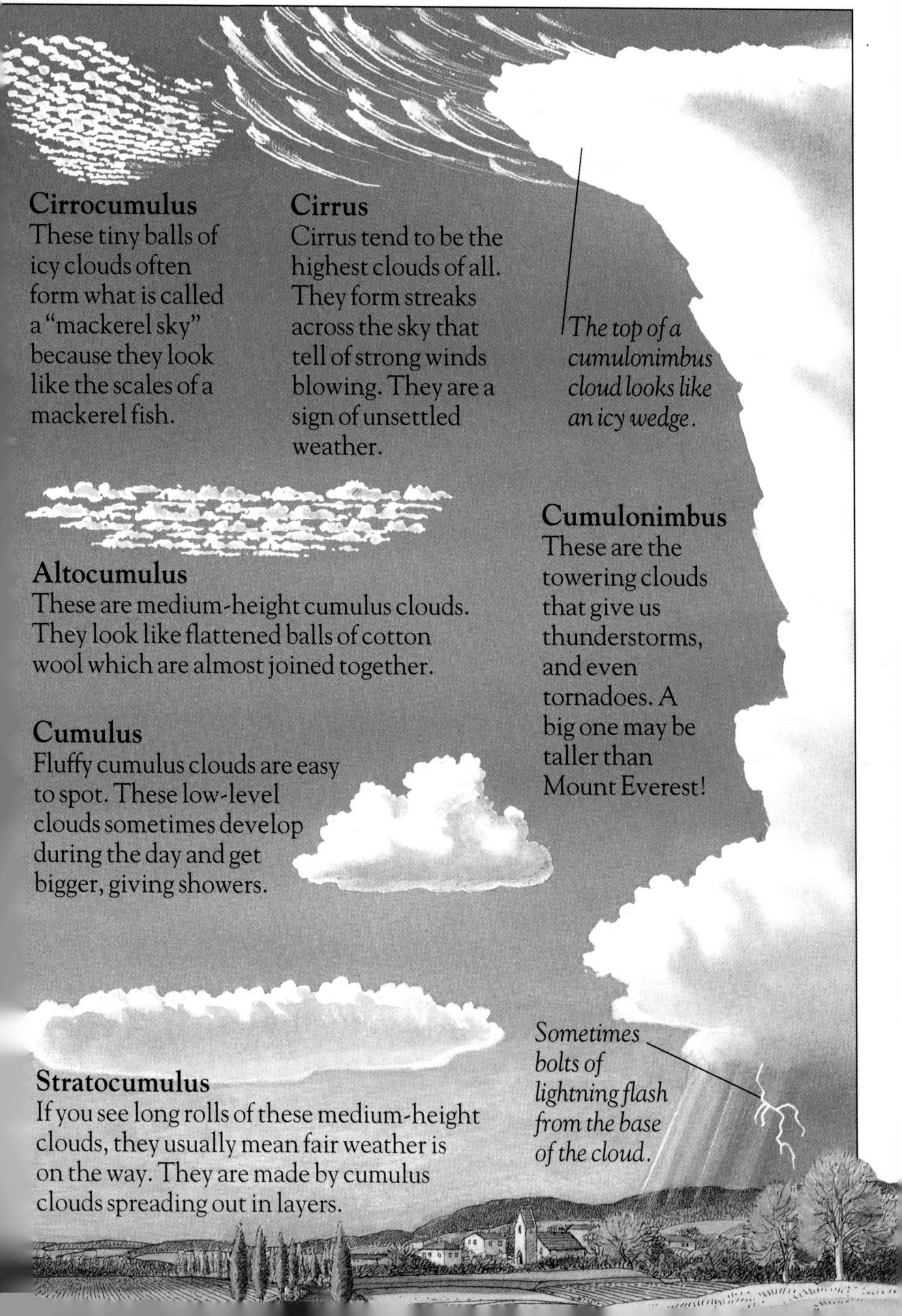

Cirrocumulus
These tiny balls of icy clouds often form what is called a "mackerel sky" because they look like the scales of a mackerel fish.

Cirrus
Cirrus tend to be the highest clouds of all. They form streaks across the sky that tell of strong winds blowing. They are a sign of unsettled weather.

The top of a cumulonimbus cloud looks like an icy wedge.

Altocumulus
These are medium-height cumulus clouds. They look like flattened balls of cotton wool which are almost joined together.

Cumulonimbus
These are the towering clouds that give us thunderstorms, and even tornadoes. A big one may be taller than Mount Everest!

Cumulus
Fluffy cumulus clouds are easy to spot. These low-level clouds sometimes develop during the day and get bigger, giving showers.

Stratocumulus
If you see long rolls of these medium-height clouds, they usually mean fair weather is on the way. They are made by cumulus clouds spreading out in layers.

Sometimes bolts of lightning flash from the base of the cloud.

Wet air

You might not know it, but you're sitting in a sea of water. Like a sponge, air soaks up invisible water vapour. All air contains water vapour, but how much it holds – the air's "humidity" – depends on how hot and dry it is where you are.

Dew wonder
If air cools down, it can hold less water. After a cool night, leaves and grass are often covered in drops of water, or dew, that the air could not hold.

Wet breath
When you breathe out, you fill the air with water vapour. If the air is very cold, the vapour turns into millions of tiny water droplets and your breath looks "steamy".

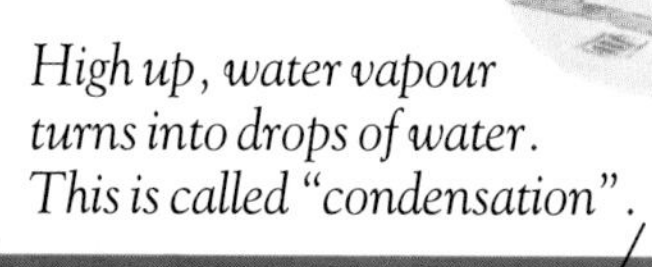

High up, water vapour turns into drops of water. This is called "condensation".

1 Damp air
Water gets into the air because the sun heats up oceans and lakes. Millions of gallons of water then rise into the air as invisible water vapour. This is called evaporation.

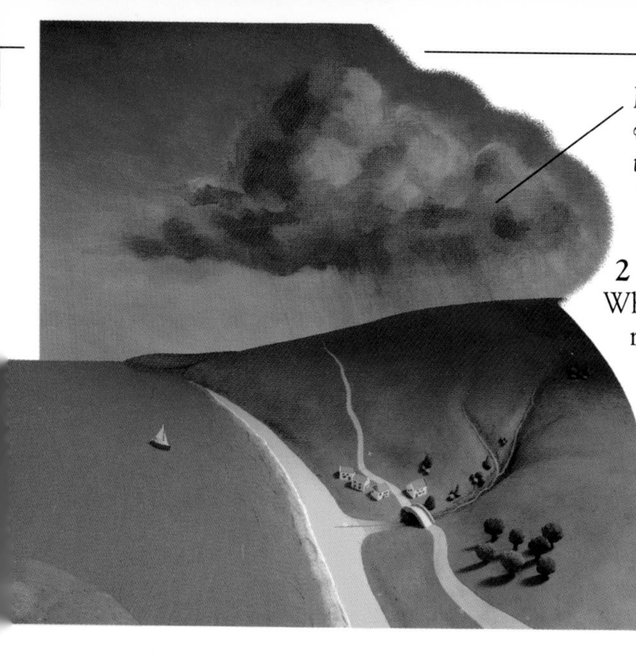

Big clouds are so full of water that some falls to the ground as rain.

2 Falling rain

When some clouds get really big, the tiny droplets of water in them bump into each other and grow. Soon they are so big that they fall to the ground as rain. This is called precipitation.

Once they have lost some of their water as rain, clouds begin to vanish.

Rain is the same water going round and round in a never-ending circle called the water cycle.

Some rainwater seeps through the ground before reaching rivers.

3 Running away

Some rain falls straight into the sea. Rain falling on the ground fills up rivers and streams, which run back to the sea. And so the cycle can begin all over again.

Rain and drizzle

Without clouds, it wouldn't rain. Rain is simply drops of water falling from clouds filled with water. Clouds get full because draughts carry air up until it cools, and the water vapour turns into drops of water, which fall as rain. When the raindrops are very fine, they fall as drizzle.

Raining cats and frogs
Rain sometimes brings other things apart from water – such as maggots, fish, and even frogs!

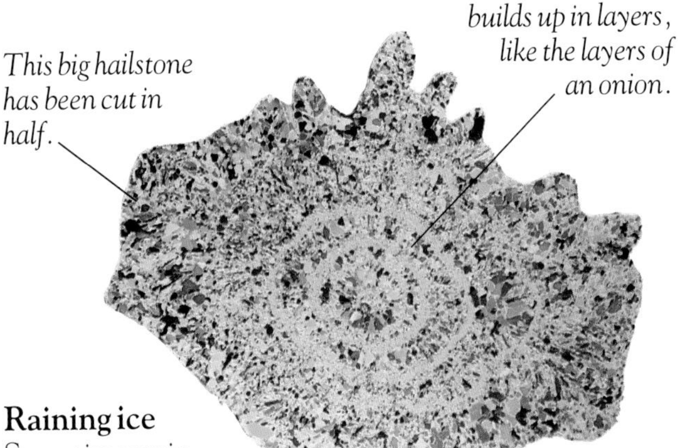

This big hailstone has been cut in half.

See how the ice builds up in layers, like the layers of an onion.

Raining ice
Sometimes rain falls as solid chunks of ice, called hailstones. These are made when raindrops are tossed high up in huge clouds, and freeze into ice. As they are bounced up and down inside the cloud, they grow into big hailstones.

Deep end
The wettest place in the world is a mountain in the Hawaiian Islands, where well over 11m of rain falls every year.

Rain approaching

This picture shows a heavy rainstorm over America's Grand Canyon. Short, heavy showers like this are common in warm places, because the warmth can make air rise rapidly to create big rainclouds.

Weather moos

According to some country folk, you know rain is on its way when cows are all lying down in a field. Unfortunately, the cows sometimes get it wrong!

Raindrops

Every cloud holds millions of water drops and ice crystals. They are so tiny that they are held up by air alone. Some big clouds have water drops at the bottom and ice crystals at the top. Before rain falls, the droplets grow much bigger. Some grow by bumping into one another and joining together. Others grow by condensation.

Tiny water droplets bump into each other and cling together as they fall.

See how they grow
When water drops grow by condensation, water vapour freezes onto ice crystals, and they grow into snowflakes. Then they fall from the cloud. As they fall through warmer air, they melt into raindrops.

Raindrop sends up a splash of water.

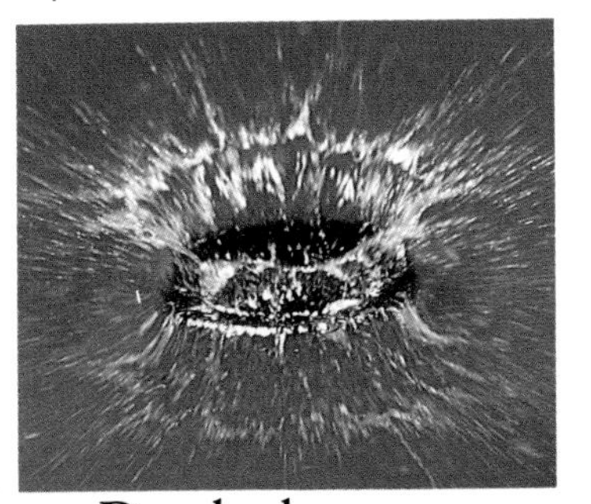

Drop by drop
As a raindrop falls, it gathers up smaller ones below, growing all the time. The biggest raindrops are about 5 mm across. But drizzle measures less than 0.5 mm across.

Drizzle does not make splashes on water.

Make a rain gauge

If you want to keep a record of how much rain falls, why not make yourself a simple rain gauge like this? You will need a large plastic soft drink bottle, scissors, sticky tape, a heavy flower pot, and a notepad and pencil.

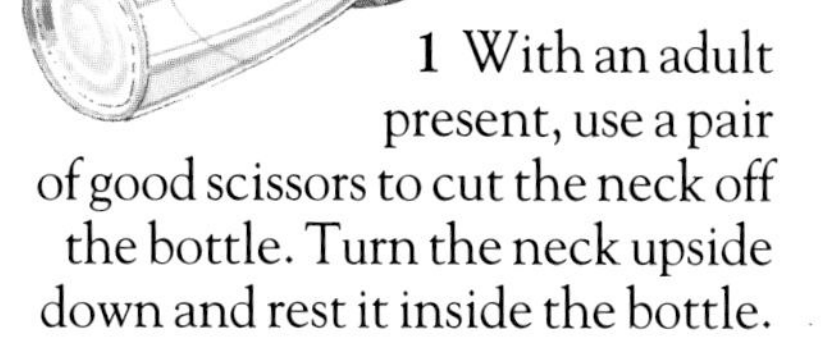

1 With an adult present, use a pair of good scissors to cut the neck off the bottle. Turn the neck upside down and rest it inside the bottle.

If necessary use masking tape to hold the "funnel" in place.

2 Stick strips of tape 10 mm apart up the side of the bottle.

If the bottle is 125 mm across, every 10 mm of water in the bottle shows 10 mm of rain.

Before you start, fill the bottle with water up to the first mark.

3 Set your gauge outside in a heavy flowerpot (to stop it blowing over). Then every day, or week if you prefer, make a note of how much water there is in the bottle, using the marks to help you.

4 Every time you measure the water, you can plot the result on a graph like this.

Fog and mist

On a clear day, you can see for miles if you are high enough. But at other times the air may be so thick with fog that you can barely see across the road. Fog and mist look like smoke, but they are just tiny drops of water floating in the air. In fact, they are clouds that have formed at ground level.

Fog cuts visibility (the distance you can see) to less than 1000 m.

Souper fog

Dust and smoke make fog much worse. Before coal fires were banned in the 1950s, London had some of the world's worst fogs – called "pea-soupers" because they were so thick and green!

Night fog

It gets foggy when the air is too cool to hold all its moisture, or water vapour. At night when the sky is clear, the ground gets cold. It cools the air close to it, making water droplets form in the air. The thickest fogs form when the air holds a lot of moisture.

Golden mist

San Francisco's Golden Gate Bridge is often wrapped in mist because the warm California air is chilled by cold sea currents.

Morning mists are often seen in valleys, where cold air collects in the night.

Morning mist

Mist is made in the same way as fog, but is not as thick as fog. It clings close to the ground, and you can see over the top of it. Long, clear autumn nights often bring misty mornings – especially in valleys, because cold air drains down into a valley during the night.

Mist is thickest just above the ground, because it is the ground that cools the air.

Frost and ice

In winter, the days are short and the sun hangs low in the sky, so we barely feel its warming rays. On clear nights there is no blanket of clouds to keep in even this warmth. In some countries, it gets so cold that moisture in the air freezes, covering the ground with sparkling frost.

Keeping the cold out
People used to say that frost was the icy touch of evil Jack Frost.

Frosty fingers
Sometimes, plants get so cold that moisture in the air freezes on them instantly in spiky fingers. This is called hoar-frost.

When moisture in the air freezes, it becomes frost.

Pretty cold!
If you live in a country where it gets very cold, you may see lovely patterns of fern frost on your windows. This is made when tiny water drops on the glass turn into ice. As more moisture freezes on top of these icy drops, feathery fingers of frost begin to grow.

Rime frost looks like icing around the edge of petals.

All white

Frost coats the ground and plants with thousands of tiny ice crystals. This may happen because the ground is icy cold. Sometimes, though, a damp icy wind makes frosty bands form on the edge of flower petals and leaves. This is called rime frost.

Winter sports

It is lucky for us that ice floats on water. Even when it is really cold, ponds and lakes are covered with just a thin layer of ice. If ice sank, not only lakes but all the sea would slowly turn into solid ice!

Be careful! Never walk on water that is covered with ice.

Ice is frozen water.

Snowy weather

High up where the air is below freezing (0°C), clouds are made up of tiny ice crystals. These crystals grow into large snowflakes, which drift downwards and melt into rain if the air gets warmer. But if it is near or below freezing all the way down to the ground, we get snow instead.

Winter sports

Snowy, freezing weather can have its benefits! Skiing and tobogganing down a snow-covered slope are popular winter sports.

It snows the most when the temperature is at freezing point.

White blanket

Once snow has covered the ground, it may not melt for a while, because the white snow bounces away warming sunlight. If it melts and then refreezes, the crisp, frosty blanket will last even longer.

Snow wonder

Put some snowflakes on a coloured surface and look carefully at them under a magnifying glass. You will see that they are all hexagons, which means they have six sides. But just as no two people are exactly the same, so no two snowflakes are identical.

Avalanche!

Snow can be destructive. When spring arrives, the snow on mountainsides starts to melt and may cause an avalanche. Tons of ice and snow crash down into the valley below, burying everything in their path.

All sorts of snow

When it is below freezing, snow is powdery and "dry" and is useless for making snowballs! But when the temperature is just about freezing, snowflakes are large and the snow is "wet". It is easily crushed into heavy, icy snowballs.

From breeze to gale

Winds are simply the air around us moving. Sometimes the air moves so slowly that the wind is too weak to lift a feather. At other times it moves so fast that trees and walls are blown down, and even cars may be swept into the air.

Force 2: Light breeze
When a light breeze blows, the weather is usually clear. You can feel air on your face, hear leaves rustle, and see plumes of smoke gently drifting.

Force 5: Fresh breeze
During a fresh breeze, clouds often start to scud across the sky, and small trees sway. Crested waves form on lakes.

Wind force
In 1805, a British sea captain called Francis Beaufort began to measure winds by counting how many sails his ships could safely use. He divided winds into 13 "forces", from calm to hurricane. Later, his idea was adapted for use on land.

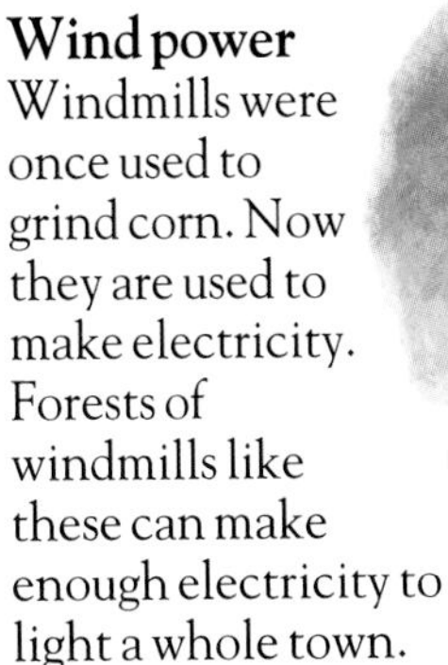

Wind power

Windmills were once used to grind corn. Now they are used to make electricity. Forests of windmills like these can make enough electricity to light a whole town.

Blown away!

The world's windiest place is Antarctica, where winds blow at more than 100 km/h five months a year!

Force 7: Near gale

During a near gale, the sky may be dark and stormy. Large trees sway and it becomes hard work walking against the wind.

Force 9: Strong gale

When the wind blows at strong gale force, the sky may be covered in thick cloud. Large branches snap and chimneys and roof tiles can be blown off.

Under pressure

You can't feel it, but the air is pushing hard on you all the time. This push is called air pressure. Sometimes pressure is high; sometimes it is low. Changes in air pressure bring changes in the weather and make winds blow.

Ups and downs

Changes in air pressure are measured on an instrument called a barometer. When pressure is low, the weather is often wet and cloudy. When it is high, the weather is usually dry and clear.

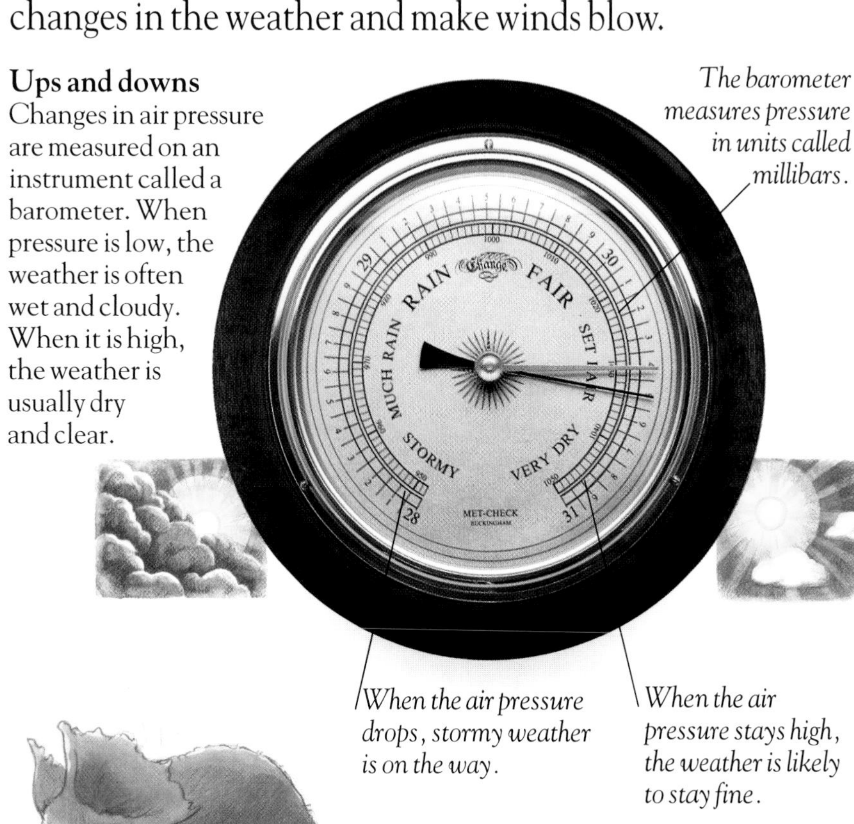

The barometer measures pressure in units called millibars.

When the air pressure drops, stormy weather is on the way.

When the air pressure stays high, the weather is likely to stay fine.

Jumbo force

On average, air presses with the same force as an elephant balancing on a desk! But rather than in elephants, air pressure is usually measured in millibars (mb). For example, 1050 mb is high pressure, and 900 mb is low pressure.

Make a barometer

This barometer will help you predict the weather. Make it on a rainy day when the air pressure is low, or it will not work. You will need a jam jar or straight-sided glass, a long-necked bottle, water mixed with food colouring, and a marker.

When the water is high in the bottle, pressure is high and it should stay fine.

When the water is low in the bottle, pressure is low and it will be stormy.

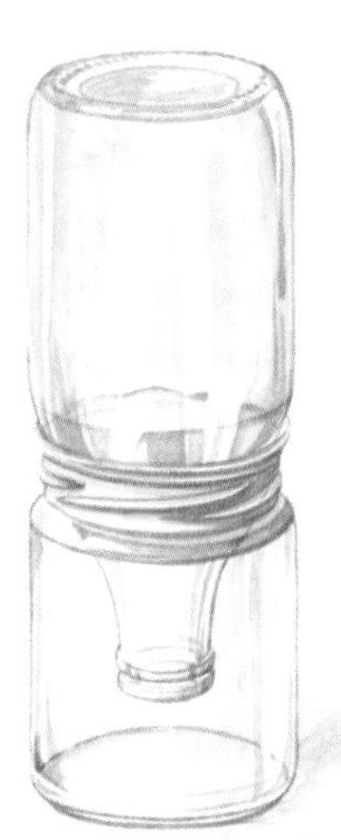

1 Set the bottle upside down in the jar so that it rests on the rim. The top of the bottle should not quite touch the bottom of the jar.

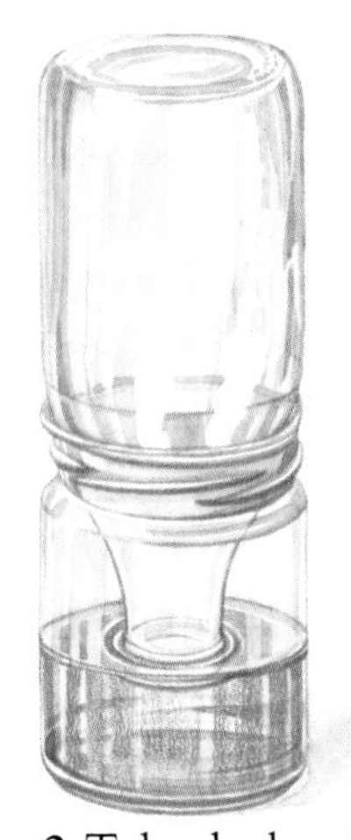

2 Take the bottle out and pour enough coloured water into the jar so that it just covers the neck of the bottle when it is in place.

3 On the jar, mark the level of water in the bottle. Set your barometer in a place where the temperature is fairly constant. Mark any changes in the water level over the next few weeks.

Right windy

Because the world is spinning, winds spin too – out of high and into low pressure areas. Try standing with your back to the wind. If you live north of the equator, high pressure will be on your right. South of the equator, it will be on your left.

Superwinds

In summer, tropical places are hot and sunny. But during autumn, the skies darken and storms sweep in from the sea, bringing fierce winds and lashing rain. These storms are called hurricanes, typhoons, or cyclones, depending on where you live.

Picture of a hurricane taken from a satellite in space.

An eye for a storm

A hurricane starts when hot tropical sunshine stirs up moist air over the sea. It then whirls over the ocean in a giant spinning wheel of cloud, wind, and rain.

Stormy people

Every hurricane is given a name. Once, only girls' names such as Jane and Diana were used, but now they use boys' names too.

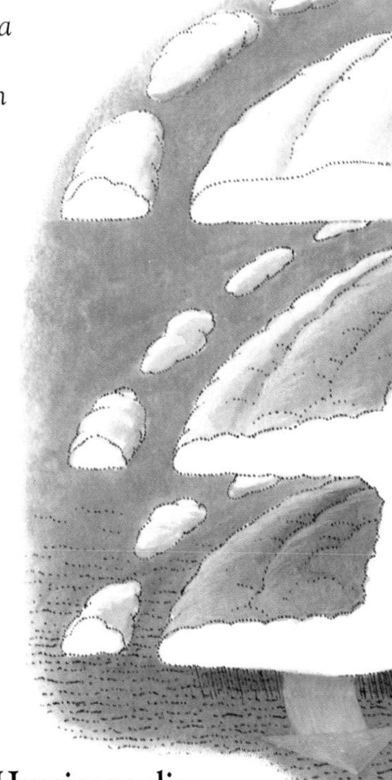

Hurricane slice

What goes on inside a hurricane? Fierce winds hurtle around the bottom of the storm, but the centre is dead calm. The air that spirals up around the centre builds up tall rain clouds.

Blown away

Howling hurricane winds can do terrible damage. On the coast, huge waves raised by the winds can swamp the shore.

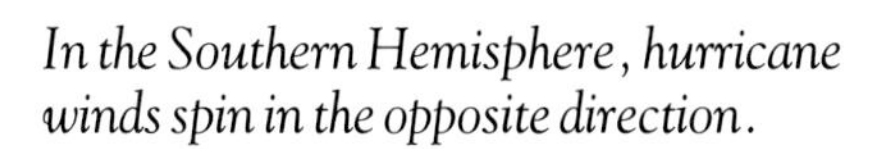

In the Southern Hemisphere, hurricane winds spin in the opposite direction.

Warm, damp air spirals up around the centre of the storm, making huge clouds.

Hurricane winds blow around the base of the storm at 300 km/h or more.

The air in the very centre or eye of the storm is clear and calm.

Hurricanes may be 1500 km across and 12 km or more high.

Twisters

Twisters, or tornadoes, are whirling funnels of air. They hang down from thunderstorm clouds which form in very hot and humid weather. Twisters usually last about fifteen minutes, but if the bottom of a funnel touches the ground, it will suck up and smash everything in its path instantly.

Twister alert
If you see thunderclouds with small, rounded "lumps" beneath them, they are a good sign that a tornado is on the way. These bulging clouds are called mammatus.

Twisters are like the funnel that forms when water is sucked down a plug-hole.

White column
Inside a tornado, air is sucked upwards and starts to spin at enormous speed. This approaching tornado is white, because it has not yet touched the ground and picked up dust and debris. If the train is not in the tornado's path, it will be safe.

Waterspout

When a tornado develops over calm seas, it is called a waterspout. Mist, spray, and water are sucked up into the twisting funnel.

Tornadoes are most common in the United States.

Strange but true

Tornadoes have been known to whirl objects high up into the air, and then set them down, unharmed, nearby.

At the centre of the tornado, wind speeds can reach 400 km/h. They are the fastest winds on Earth.

On target

As the bottom of the tornado touches the ground, it sucks the bridge, dust, debris, and train carriages, high into the sky. Then it hurls them back to the ground.

A tornado makes a deafening roar as it passes by.

Hot weather

In places where the sun sits high in the sky at midday, the days are long and the weather is hot. Hot weather often comes with high pressure areas, because they bring clear skies and light winds. High pressure can last for a long time, making hot, sunny weather last for days on end.

Mirage
Sometimes, on a very hot day, you may see a mirage – a pool of water on the road ahead. Then, as you approach, it disappears. What you are actually seeing is the reflection of the sky on a layer of hot air just above the ground.

Thermometer
Thermometers help us to measure the temperature. Sealed inside a glass tube is a silvery liquid metal called mercury. Mercury swells as the temperature rises and shrinks as it gets colder.

Glass tube holding mercury.

The power of the sun
The sun gives off energy, which we feel as heat. Its energy can be trapped by solar panels and made into electricity. Solar-powered cars run on the sun's trapped energy.

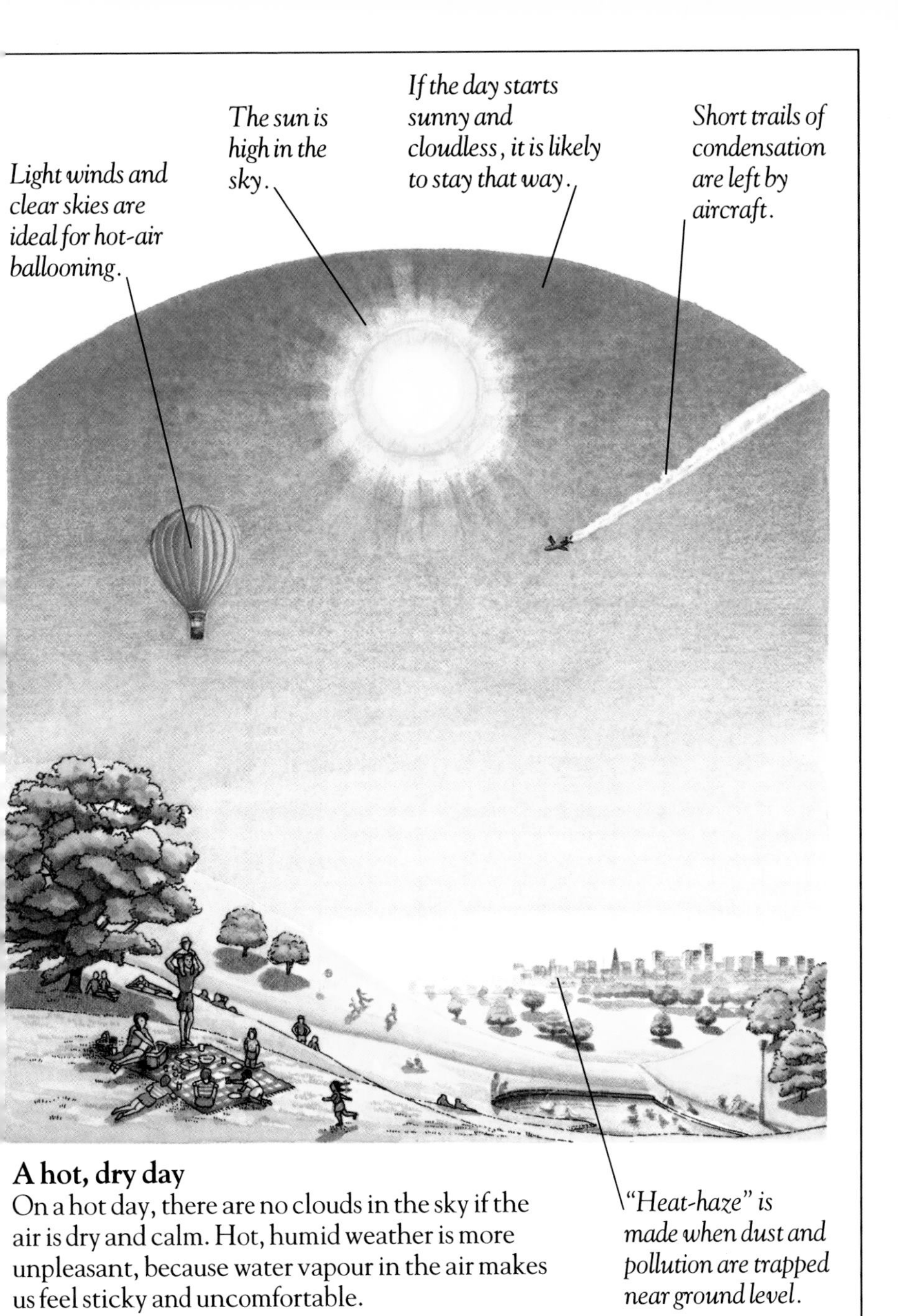

A hot, dry day

On a hot day, there are no clouds in the sky if the air is dry and calm. Hot, humid weather is more unpleasant, because water vapour in the air makes us feel sticky and uncomfortable.

Dry weather

Some countries have plenty of water and shortages are rare. But in some parts of the world water is scarce, and people can never be sure when it will rain next. Droughts happen when for months – or even years – on end, the Earth's surface loses more water than it collects. In some places, called deserts, rain hardly ever falls at all.

During a drought, the land becomes parched and cracked, and food crops die.

Drought
If droughts last for a very long time, animals die of thirst, crops wither in the hot sun, and people have to go without food – they may even die of starvation.

In true deserts, plants and animals can only live near oases, which are areas of open water.

Desert scene
You'll often find deserts inland, next to mountain ranges. The mountains act as a shield and keep rain-bearing clouds away. Semi-deserts like this one in Arizona, in the United States, have a little rainfall – enough to support plants that can store water, like cacti.

Death Valley
One of the driest and hottest places in the world is Death Valley, in the United States. In the past, people have died of thirst in the extreme heat.

Not all deserts are hot. Central Antarctica is one of the driest places on Earth.

Dust bowl
Drought can affect many people's lives. In the 1930s, The Great Plains of North America suffered from a disastrous drought that created a "Dust Bowl". Terrible dust storms buried crops and houses, and many people were forced to leave their homes.

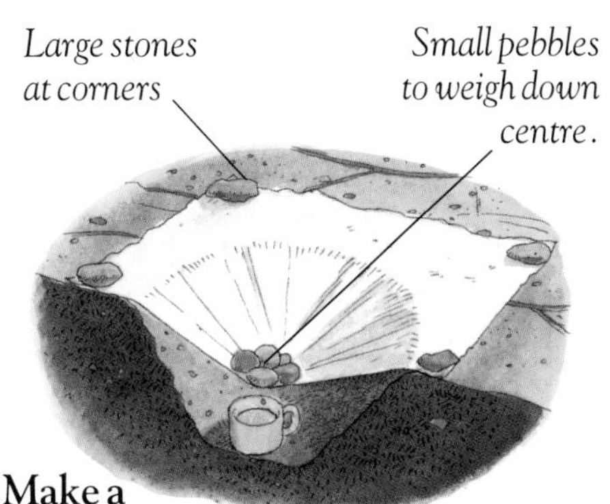

Make a garden moisture trap
Dig a hole and put a bowl in the centre. Cover it with plastic, held down by stones. The next day, you'll see water in the bowl. This happens because water evaporates from the soil and condenses on the plastic, running off into the bowl.

Monsoon

A monsoon is a seasonal wind that blows for about six months in one direction, then turns around and blows in the other direction for six months. In summer, moist winds from the ocean bring dark, rain-bearing clouds to the land. In winter, the cycle is reversed. Wind blows the air from the land to the sea, bringing cool, dry weather.

Dragon slayer
The ancient Hindus thought that a dragon stopped the monsoon from coming. The welcome rains would not appear until the dragon was killed by the god Indra.

Before the monsoon
During the early summer, the hot sun heats up the dry tropical land, while the oceans stay cooler. As warm air rises above the land, cool moist air from the sea rushes in to fill its place. The winds blowing the sea air bring heavy rainfall. This rainfall is the summer monsoon.

Rice crops cannot grow on the parched land, so a monsoon is most welcome.

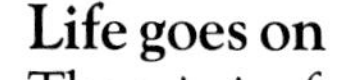

Life goes on
The rain is often so heavy that it washes away crops and floods the streets. Violent thunderstorms can also occur. But whatever the monsoon brings, life goes on.

Where the wind blows

The monsoon is best known in Asia. But monsoon winds also bring rain to other places in the tropics, including Africa, South America, the southern United States, and Australia.

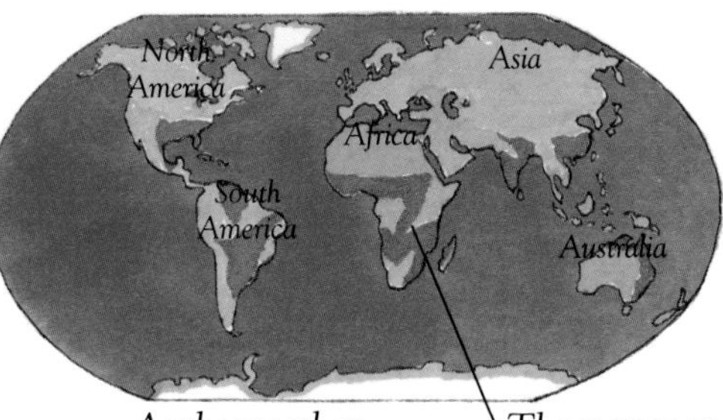

As the weather calms down, people reap the benefits of the monsoon.

The monsoon areas are coloured red.

Monsoon in action

Monsoons are vital for agriculture. Once the monsoon begins, the wet conditions are ideal for farmers. They start ploughing and planting young rice plants in the flooded fields.

After the rain

For six months, showers sweep across the land. Finally, the wind and rain die down. The cool air flows back towards the sea and the land begins to dry.

A warm front

If weather forecasters say a "front" is on its way, then expect the weather to become wet and windy. A front is where a mass of warm moist air bumps into a mass of colder, drier air, creating clouds and rain. Fronts move along with areas of low pressure, and the winds blow stronger as they pass by – like a speeding lorry stirring up litter by the roadside.

Wisps of cirrus cloud.

Curly warning

When you see wisps of feathery cirrus clouds in the sky, you can be sure a warm front is on its way.

Altocumulus clouds

Clouding over

After a while the sky gets hazy and the clouds thicken. Fluffy altocumulus clouds appear, looking like streaks of cotton wool. The wind grows stronger, making the sea very choppy.

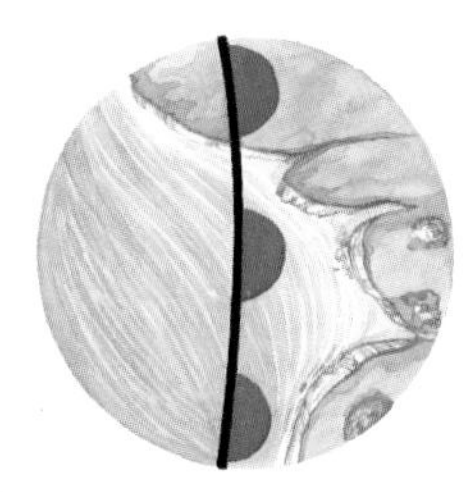

Hot line
On weather maps, a warm front is a line with red bumps on it.

Wet and windy
Soon the sky is dark with thick nimbostratus clouds. It begins to rain steadily and goes on raining for several hours. If it is cold enough, it may even snow.

A cold front

Fronts usually come in pairs. Often there is only a brief gap between one front passing and the next arriving. The first is a "warm" front because it brings warmer air. The second is a "cold" front, and brings colder air and sometimes even stormier weather than the warm front.

Stratocumulus clouds bring occasional drizzle.

On the move
On a weather map, a cold front is a line with blue spikes. The spikes show which way the cold air is moving.

Brief relief
As the warm front moves away, the rain (or snow) stops and it gets warmer. Near the coast it stays cloudy, and there may be drizzling rain.

In summer inland, the sun comes out and it can get hot after the warm front has moved away.

Thundercloud

Storm overhead
You know the cold front is on its way when the wind becomes stronger, giving gusts that rattle windows. The sky may fill with huge dark thunderclouds that lash the countryside with rain or even hailstones.

The sea is very rough.

Cumulus clouds

Patches of blue sky appear.

The sea is calmer.

It's all over
The worst of the storm is soon over. It feels colder as the clouds clear, leaving a blue sky with fluffy cumulus clouds – although there may still be more violent showers to come.

Thunder and lightning

Hot, sticky summer days often end in violent thunderstorms. Dark, towering thunder-clouds send forks of lightning flashing across the sky, and booming thunderclaps fill the air. The electricity from just one bolt of lightning could light a small town for a whole year!

Holy thunder

Some American Indians believed that the sacred thunderbird made thunder by beating its enormous wings, and that lightning flashed from its beak.

Each fork of lightning is many lightning flashes running rapidly up and down the same path.

How near is it?

You can work out how far away a storm is by counting the seconds between a flash of lightning and a thunderclap. For every three seconds you count, the storm is one kilometre away.

Strike

Lightning always takes the quickest path to the ground. So tall trees and buildings are most likely to be struck. The world's tallest buildings are struck by lightning hundreds of times each year.

Thunder is the sound of air bursting as it is heated rapidly by lightning.

Lightning and thunder happen at the same time, but you see lightning first because light moves faster than sound.

Lightning flashes between the bottom of the thundercloud and the ground.

Flash and crack

Inside a storm cloud, violent winds swirl snow, hailstones, and rain up and down. Electricity builds up in the cloud and escapes as a flash of lightning.

Strange strikes

An American park ranger was struck by lightning seven times, and survived! Over the years, he lost a toenail, and his eyebrows, and his hair was set on fire twice!

Colours in the sky

The sky isn't always blue, even when it's fine. Near sunset it can be purple or even red. This is because sunlight is made up of the seven colours of the rainbow, all jumbled up together. As sunlight bounces in different ways off dust and other particles in the air, some of the colours appear.

Rainbow serpent
Australian Aborigines worship a spirit known as the Rainbow Serpent. He lives in water and is the great creator who has made the features of the Earth. He can appear as a rainbow.

Rainbows are curved because of the way light hits the round raindrops.

Curving colours
When sunlight passes through raindrops in the air, the light splits into seven colours – red, orange, yellow, green, blue, indigo, and violet. Many raindrops help to create the pattern.

Make a rainbow

You can make your own rainbow with just a glass of water and bright sunlight. Stand the glass on white paper, facing the sun. The paper must be in shadow; the glass in bright sun. The sunlight will shine through the glass and split into the seven colours.

Ring around the sun

When the sun shines through thin icy cloud, a coloured halo may appear. This is caused by ice crystals in the cloud splitting sunlight into the seven colours, just as raindrops do. But never look directly at the sun, as it will damage your eyes.

To see a rainbow the sun must always be behind you.

If there is a second bow, its colours are always the other way round.

You always see the colours in a rainbow in the same order, from red through to violet.

Changing weather

The world's weather has changed many times. About 10,000 years ago, great sheets of ice covered a third of the Earth. That was the last Ice Age. Today we live in a much warmer climate. Many scientists think we have harmed the atmosphere so much that the world is getting even warmer.

Giant elephants
In the last Ice Age, woolly mammoths, giant elephant-like animals, wandered the frozen land. Their long, hairy coats kept them warm in the icy winds.

Prehistoric weather
Millions of years ago, when dinosaurs roamed the land, much of Europe and North America was covered in forests. The climate was hotter and more humid than it is today.

Sun trap
Only a small portion of the sun's heat reaches the Earth. But the Earth stays warm because gases, such as carbon dioxide, trap the heat – just like the glass in a greenhouse. In the right amount, these gases keep the world nice and warm.

Carbon dioxide is made when we burn wood, coal, or oil. If we produce too much, the Earth may get too warm.

A big umbrella

When volcanoes erupt, they throw large amounts of dust and smoke high into the atmosphere. This cuts off sunlight, shading the ground like a big umbrella. If enough smoke and dust are produced, the Earth could get colder.

Some people believe that the last Ice Age was caused by a volcanic eruption.

Tropical rainforests are vital in removing excess carbon dioxide from the air.

Save the trees

Trees take in carbon dioxide and release oxygen and moisture, which is turned into rain. Cutting down and burning trees may lead to less rainfall and the build-up of carbon dioxide. This could raise the Earth's temperature.

In the Amazon rainforest, an area the size of Britian is cut down every year for farming.

Pollution

You may find it hard to believe, but many things people do every day create pollution – which affects us today and in the future. Too much pollution can cause changes in the weather. It may get too hot in some places, and cause floods or drought in others. Cutting down on pollution now means a cleaner world tomorrow!

Acid rain, carried by wind, can destroy pine forests thousands of miles away.

Pollution problems
Smoke and gases from factories pollute the air and may form smog. This is a mixture of smoke and fog which can make people sick. Car exhausts give off poisonous gases that not only affect our lungs but can block out the sunlight.

Acid rain
Power stations that burn coal or oil to generate electricity release the waste gases into the air. The gases float with the wind until raindrops dissolve them, making "acid rain". This eats away at buildings and kills trees, plants, and life in rivers and lakes.

Test for acid rain

Here is an experiment you can try to test for acid in rainwater. You will need two finely chopped red cabbage leaves, distilled water (from a pharmacist), rainwater, a bowl, two glass jars, a measuring jug, and a sieve.

2 Strain the cabbage juice into a measuring jug. The liquid should be a dark purple colour.

1 Put the leaves into the bowl. Get an adult to pour hot distilled water over them. Then let them stand for an hour.

3 Pour 20ml of distilled water into one jar, and 20 ml of rainwater, collected from your garden, into the other.

4 Add the same amount of cabbage juice to each jar. The water will change colour. Compare the colour of the distilled water (this stays the same) and the rainwater. If the rainwater turns red, it is acidic.

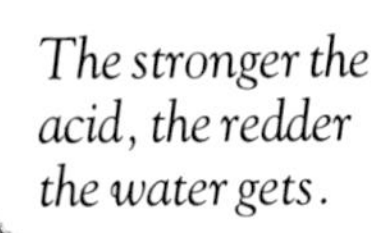

The stronger the acid, the redder the water gets.

The Earth's blanket

The ozone layer of our atmosphere protects us from the sun's harmful rays. But some spray cans that we use contain chemicals that can destroy it. Holes have appeared in the ozone layer, allowing some harmful rays to reach the Earth's surface. This could damage many living things.

The pink, purple, and black areas in this satellite photograph show the hole in the ozone layer over the Antarctic.

Weather lore

Nowadays, weather forecasters use satellites and radar to tell us what the weather holds. But before this, people used to look for clues in nature to predict the weather. They didn't just look at the skies – they also watched how animals, birds, plants, and insects acted. Some of the signs are reliable, but others aren't foolproof!

Frog-cast
One way to tell if it's going to rain soon is to look out for frogs. They love to come out when it's damp. As the air usually becomes humid before it rains, when you see more frogs about, you will know to expect rain.

Aches and pains
The weather affects the way we feel, so it's natural to expect that the way we feel can help predict the weather. Some people suffer aches and pains when damp, cold weather is on the way; others feel strange when thunder is near.

Red sky at night
People used to say a red sunrise meant bad weather to come, and that a red sunset meant good weather to come. Try to watch the sky at sunrise and sunset to see if this saying is always correct.

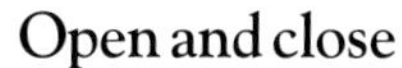

Open and close

Pine cones are traditionally used to forecast the weather. Put a pine cone outdoors and watch what happens. It will open out in very dry weather and close up when it is damp.

The pine cone's scales open in dry weather.

Scales are tightly shut in wet weather.

Groundhog forecast

In the United States, people say that if you can see a groundhog's shadow at noon on the second of February, there will be six more weeks of winter. Fortunately, the groundhog isn't always right!

Flower power

When you want to know what the weather will be like, look for the magic carpet flower. It grows in South Africa and other hot, dry places. Its petals stay wide open in fine weather, but they close up when the sky grows dark.

Weather forecasting

To work out what weather is on its way, forecasters take measurements from weather stations all over the world. They also study photographs of the Earth taken from satellites in space. Then, huge computers print out weather maps that show what the conditions are now and what they will be like in a few hours or a week from now.

Weather map
This picture shows some of the features you might see on a weather map, along with the kind of weather you might expect. Look for the warm front, which will bring stormy weather.

The warm front is moving from right to left on this map, so the weather will stay fine here longer than in the town. Fronts usually travel eastwards, so move from left to right on weather maps.

The weather is fine here now, but it will turn for the worse as the warm front (bumpy red lines) moves in.

The barometer indicates changeable weather here. It will soon begin to drop, showing that a front is on its way, bringing rain.

Feathery cirrus clouds high up show that a front is on its way.

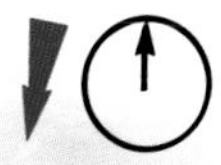

Stratus clouds

Mountain tops are often covered in cloud, while valleys are clear. This is because the air high up is colder and can hold less water.

Air pressure is high here.

Isobars are lines drawn on the map to link up places where air pressure is the same. So isobars tell you where pressure is high and where it is low.

A change in the wind direction warns of a change in the weather.

The wind changes direction and gets stronger.

Cirrostratus clouds

Altostratus clouds

Nimbostratus clouds give steady rain.

A red line with bumps shows where a warm front touches the ground. It is moving from right to left.

The weather will improve for a while after the front has passed.

The day

During the course of each day there are changes in the weather. On fine days, you can almost tell the time by the way the weather changes through the day – from the cool chill of dawn through the heat of the afternoon to the clear, calm evening.

Daily record
Why not make a note of the way the weather changes through the day? You may learn to predict when to expect the sun to come out, or when it will rain.

Warm days and cool nights often bring morning mists.

Clouds are small and may fade away as quickly as they form.

Sun rise
Dawn is usually chilly, as the ground loses heat steadily all night. It is often misty too, for the cool of the night makes water condense in the air.

Midday
As the sun climbs in the sky, morning mists fade away and it gets warmer. By midday, a few fluffy cumulus clouds appear, made by rising warm, moist air.

Why is the sky blue?

Sunlight contains all the colours in the rainbow – but mixed up it seems white. Sky is blue because only blue light bounces off the gases in the sky. When we look at a blue sky, we simply see the blue bit of sunlight reflected off the gases towards our eyes.

Towards sunset

As the sun drops lower towards sunset, its power to stir up the air gets less and less. So the end of the day is often calm and clear, with barely a cloud in the sky.

Mid-afternoon

Mid-afternoon is the warmest time of day. Often, though, the morning's fluffy cumulus clouds can build up and up until they interrupt the afternoon with brief but heavy showers of rain, or even thunderstorms.

Night

Once the sun has dropped below the horizon it gets steadily colder – especially if there are no clouds to keep the heat in.

Index

Lying in the sun

Mist

Snowflake

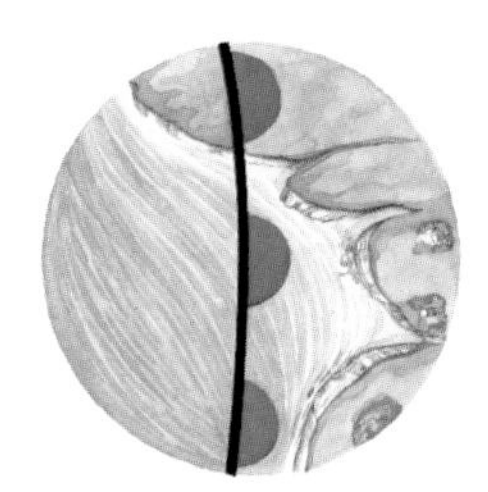

Warm front on a weather map

Wind power

Raindrop

Acknowledgments

Dorling Kindersley would like to thank:
Simon Battensby for photography on pages 16-17, 22-23, 28-29, 34-35, 42-43, 44-45.
Donks Models for models on pages 16-17, 22-23, 28-29, 34-35, 42-43, 44-45.
Carl Gombrich, Gin von Noorden and Kate Raworth for editorial assistance and research.
Sharon Grant for design assistance.
Ron Lobeck for help with writing text.
Jane Parker for the index.
Jim Sharp for help with authenticating text.

Illustrations by:
John Bendall-Brunello, Julia Cobbold, Louis Mackay, Richard Ward.

Picture credits
t=top b=bottom c=centre l=left r=right
Frank Blackburn: 16tl.
Bracknell Weather Centre 24bl.
Bruce Coleman Ltd: 38br; /Chris James 26b; /Kim Taylor 20bl, 20bc, 20br; / Roger Wilmshurst 24cr.
Frank Lane Picture Agency: 32tl, 51t; /L.West 13tl, 25t.
R.K. Pilsbury: 13b, 24b.
Quadrant Picture Library: 36bl.
Science Photo Library: 5, 9br; /Martin Bond 54br; / John Mead 12b; /NASA 53b; NCAR 18c; / Nuridsany & Perennou 26t; /Dr.M. Read 51b.
Zefa: 39l, 47t; /K.L. Benser 19t; /Kalt 10bl, 10br, 11bl, 11br.

R.W. Connell, D.J. Ashenden, S. Kessler, G.W. Dowsett

Making The Difference

SCHOOLS, FAMILIES AND SOCIAL DIVISION

GEORGE ALLEN & UNWIN
SYDNEY LONDON BOSTON

First published in 1982 by
Allen & Unwin Australia Pty Ltd
An Unwin Hyman company
8 Napier Street
North Sydney NSW 2059 Australia
Ninth impression 1989

National Library of Australia
Cataloguing-in-Publication entry:

Making the difference: schools, families and social division.
ISBN 0 86861 124 7.
ISBN 0 86861 132 8 (pbk.).
1. Education — Australia — 1965–. 2. Educational sociology — Australia. I. Connell, R. W. (Robert William).
370. 19′0994

Set in 10 on 11 pt Times by
Colset Private Ltd., Singapore
Printed in Malaysia by SRM Production Services Sdn Bhd

Contents

Preface

What this book is

A report on a research project, some reflections on theory and method in the sociology of education, and a discussion of several current practical issues of school reform. The project was called the 'School, Home, and Work' project; our theme is the interplay of school, family, and workplace — and the larger social structures that shape them. But our theme is also individual lives, hopes, fears, and sometimes passions. There is nothing abstract about these questions. We consider individual lives can only be understood by understanding social processes on the largest scale; but equally, those processes can only be understood through the way they affect particular lives. So this book is partly biography, partly history, and partly the intersection of the two, which is politics and sociology. Research is about learning from experience. We think the experiences discussed here are both fascinating and important, and we hope other people will also find them useful.

The title

The book was originally going to be called 'Equal rights, to a certain extent', a quote from one of the interviews. We thought the present title was an improvement. If it were not too clumsy, we would have liked to stress in the title that the book is about social *relations* quite as much as social *differences*.

Authorship

We would like to make a statement at the start of the book about its authorship. The four people whose names appear on the title page have worked together now for four years. Two are academics, two are school teachers; two were joint grantees for the research, two were research assistants employed on the grant.

The process of our working together has been complicated, to say the least. Academic work tends to be organized hierarchically; decision-making remaining in the hands of those at the top, with acknowledgement duly given for help received from those below.

In the course of our work — and partly because of the issues being studied — we were led to challenge this division of labour, this method of decision-making, and this way of working together. Among other things, we wished to continue working together after the day the funding ran out.

We call ourselves a collective; we have operated on that basis from very early on. We have all taken a substantial part in the detailed planning of the study, in the interviewing, in the analysis of the results, and in the preparation of reports, through a constant sharing-out of the work and an endless mutual debate about what we were doing and how we were doing it.

In the course of this we have grappled with a series of difficulties in the path of collective work, which are worth listing: differential abilities to do 'academic' work; pre-conceived status and conventional ways of valuing different skills, knowledges and talents; our differences in certification; and, quite important, the need for economic survival for two of us who relied on the research grants to pay our wages.

When we started writing articles on sections of our work about two years ago, the question of authorship arose. What constitutes authorship of a literary work? There are various principles to which we could appeal. One is skill at the craft of setting words on paper till they make sense. Another is the power to employ research assistants and organize the collection of data. Another is the fact of having contributed one's efforts to a project over a long period. To choose any one of these principles is to take a political stand.

There is, then, a politics of collective authorship. We wished to stress collectivity. But we have different skills — at writing especially — just as some have clearer thoughts and wittier jokes. Yet, what skill, idea, or argument could be of value by itself, without interacting with other skills or ideas residing in the collective?

We decided to make the point of collective authorship by listing our names alphabetically, and then rotating them in each article or paper. We explained that this was designed to counter ideas of 'seniority' or special kudos.

To confuse librarians, and affront staid minds, was fun for a while. But 'the book' loomed as a different proposition — and perhaps the inverted commas are the problem itself. For this book is the project's key academic product, and the hardest of all our attempts to disseminate our findings. Old conversations, deep fears about integrity, and loss of confidence, surfaced again, and focussed on the number and kind of words produced by each of us — that is, on authorship in the narrow sense.

We compromised. Authorship in the narrow sense is represented by the order of names on the title page. The fact that all our names appear there implies a more genuine collective authorship. It is a true reflection of what has been an intense and immensely productive collective enterprise. By the way, the person who wrote least of the words in this book wrote this preface.

Acknowledgments

Our main acknowledgments are to the students, parents, teachers, and principals who gave us interviews. This often meant a real commitment of time and emotional energy; some of the interviews were by no means easy going. We deeply appreciate the contribution these people made to the project, and hope they feel it has resulted in a worthwhile contribution to educational thought and practice. To maintain the anonymity of all our material, they, like the school secretaries, deputies, form teachers, and others who helped us in the field, must remain unnamed.

Funds for the project were granted by: the Education Research and Development Committee (now abolished by the 'Razor Gang'); Macquarie University; Sturt CAE; Kuring-gai CAE; the Society for the Production of Really Useful Knowledge. Permissions were granted by the NSW and SA Departments of Education, and the principals of all schools involved in the study, state and Independent.

Over the past four years, literally scores of people have helped the project in various ways: reading and commenting on drafts and papers, discussing the research plan and case studies as they were done, lending space and other facilities, and doing the massive task of typing and transcription, much of it highly specialized. It would be invidious to single out individuals, and impossible to list them all, but we would particularly wish to mention: Heather Williams, Robyn King, Jill Wright, Julie Tsolakis, Bernie Pearce, Jill Jenner, Beryl Fisher, Jan Porteous, Jenny Thomson, Clive Dorman, Sue Nash, Pat Thomson, Ken Bridge, Sylvia Kinder, Greg Brown,

Cynthia Bridge, Jan McMahon, Kevin Hamilton, Steve Smart, Peter Bicknell, Miranda Roe, Mary Mortimer, Janet Kossi, Barbara Bee, Sally Sayer, Jim Campbell, Russell Darnley, Lorraine Mortimer, Brian Abbey, Jean Blackburn, Pam Benton, Carol O'Donnell, Bill Connell, Margaret Connell, Doug White, and Clare Burton.

Conventions and abbreviations

To preserve anonymity, we have changed all proper names — of people, families, schools, and suburbs — that might identify people in our study. For the same reason, we have frequently combined elements from different stories to make composite 'cases', both of families and schools, though with careful regard to the real dynamics. We would stress that no detail mentioned in the book is made up; everything comes from the interviews.

Proper names not connected with the identity of interviewees are of course unchanged. For example, when in Chapter Five we refer to schools in Brunswick, the actual suburb of Brunswick in Melbourne is meant.

We use the term 'Matric' to refer to the examinations at the end of Year 12, which have different names in different states.

The term 'Independent schools' refers to non-Catholic private schools plus the elite Catholic colleges. In this study we are concerned mainly with those which service the most powerful and affluent clientele, and we sometimes refer to this subset of Independent schools as 'ruling-class schools'. There is, especially in Victoria, a significant number of protestant private schools with a distinctly less affluent clientele, which are interesting but fall outside the main concerns of this study.

The character of the text

We hope, rash as the thought may be, that the material in this book is of interest to several groups: teachers concerned with the causes of the problems they face; parents and parent organizations concerned with educational reform; academics and students interested in the sociology of education; teacher unions and other people concerned with educational policy. We have tried to write the book in a way that will be accessible (for the most part) to all of these groups. But there are passages here and there directed to one group of readers which others may find of little interest.

The book deals with a set of issues that are both complex and tightly interwoven. In writing the first drafts, we found ourselves repeatedly covering the same points in different contexts and from different angles. We have cut out most of these reprises, and replaced them with references forward or back to sections or chapters in which particular issues are mainly dealt with. We realize repeated cross-references can be annoying to the reader, but we can think of no other way of doing justice to the interconnectedness of the issues without a great deal of repetition.

So as not to burden the text with apparatus, we have kept footnotes to a minimum. We thought it would be more useful for most readers to have a select bibliography in the form of a guide to further reading, rather than an alphabetical list of all works we consulted or used. Our technical analysis of the academic literature is contained in several articles listed at the end of this reading guide.

1

Inequality and education

This book is written at the end of an era in Australian secondary education.

We began our research intending to study one aspect of the social background of educational success. We now find ourselves grappling with questions about curriculum reform, school organization, and how the system as a whole can be reshaped to meet profoundly changed conditions. Though this was unintended and unexpected, we can now see why it should have happened: partly the problem we started with, and partly the nature of the times. Before presenting our research findings, then, we must discuss their context. This chapter introduces the problem of inequality, the school system in which it arises, and the way it has been usually discussed — and misunderstood.

Before the Second World War, the secondary school system was a small device sitting on top of a mass primary system. High schools and private colleges took the 'cream' — the small number of boys (and fewer girls) who were going to get on — while technical schools trained some of the workers' children for trades. Most pupils left at or about the minimum legal age. Social inequality was hardly a problem: it was built in to the system from the start.

With the war's end there was an abrupt shift. Secondary schooling expanded with dramatic speed. It was widely argued that secondary education was the right of all, and that every child would have equal access. Not only to the secondary school, but through it to the university and the privileges beyond.

Thirty years later, the schools were still being criticized as giving working-class youth a separate and inferior education, and much less than equal opportunity. For a time, in the early 1970s, it looked as if there would be still more expansion (especially of tertiary education) in pursuit of the goal, and extra help for the 'disadvantaged' as well. It is now clear that that will not happen for the foreseeable future.

Growth has ended. Programmes like the Disadvantaged Schools Programme were small and weak when they began and have not become any stronger. Central government policy now tends to increase educational inequality rather than reduce it. The relationship of schools to the labour market has changed. A programme for a drastic reform of schooling in a socially conservative direction is emerging. Secondary education has reached a turning point that looks as abrupt as that of 1945.

This is not just the stuff of history. It is the circumstance of everyday experience for people like Wilma Roberts and Sophie Phelan. Sophie and Wilma are both 15 years old and both in Year 10: Sophie at Auburn College, one of the country's most prestigious girls' Independent schools, and Wilma at Rockwell High, a government school built, like the suburbs around it, in the 1950s.

Wilma has always enjoyed school, and done reasonably well. She has usually been among the top four or five in her class, and is now in the 'A' stream in a large and (by the standards of the system) well-equipped and properly-staffed school. Her parents want her to get the education they missed out on. Wilma's father, Dave Roberts, is a tradesman's assistant and knows that

> I have missed many opportunities because I did not have the papers.

He left school thirty years ago, when he was Wilma's age, after 'wagging' most of his last two years. He wants Wilma to go on to Year 12 so that she can have her pick of any kind of job. Judy Roberts left school, like her husband, on the day she turned 15, and was in a factory job the next day. She doesn't push as hard as he does, but she too gives Wilma support for going on at school as long as necessary to get the job she wants. When Wilma watches TV, Mum tells her:

> That won't help you. Homework will. You're losing marks!

It's just what the educational sociologists ordered; but somehow it's not quite working. Wilma is, as her Dad puts it, 'browning off' and 'losing interest' in school. She wants to leave at the end of the year. Most of the kids at Rockwell do. 'They can do it', says Wilma, 'why can't I?' The school is glad to see the back of many of them. 'So undisciplined, so noisy, so rude!', as one shell-shocked young teacher put it. Wilma wants to do a secretarial course.

In the meantime Sophie Phelan, and her school, are flying.

Auburn College has had its ups and downs, but at the moment it has a long waiting list for places. Around 90 per cent of its girls take Matriculation and a good proportion of them get straight A's in the 'hard' subjects of maths, physics and chemistry. Sophie is likely to be one of them. Her teachers say that she is even brighter than her two older sisters. Both of them went through Auburn and both are at university doing professional degrees. James and Mary Phelan, their parents, did well at school too. James is a successful barrister and Mary was, until her marriage, a teacher. Sophie has always taken her schoolwork seriously, but now that Year 11 is looming, she is really starting to stretch out. 'I can't be anything', she says, 'unless I do well at school'. Her parents are amazed, even a little troubled, at the way their daughters work — *much* harder than they did. While Wilma wavers and Rockwell High struggles, Sophie and Auburn College accelerate away.

We met the Roberts and the Phelans in 1978, in the course of the research project which forms the basis of this book. We worked in twelve schools in two cities, and talked at length with a hundred 14 and 15 year olds, their parents, their school principals, and many of their teachers. Half of those hundred students were the sons and daughters of tradesmen, factory workers, truck drivers, shop workers; the other half were the children of managers, owners of businesses, lawyers, doctors. We wanted to find out why the relationship between home and school worked so much better for one group than for the other; and we were guided by a mass of research evidence which showed that Wilma Roberts and Sophie Phelan are not exceptions.

Here are some examples from recent Australian studies.[1] In 1974 Martin and Meade began a survey of about 3,000 state high school Year 9 students in Sydney, whom they followed through the Higher School Certificate (HSC) in 1977. Among other things they asked about fathers' jobs, which were then divided into two groups representing higher and lower 'socio-economic status'. Here are the percentages of students in each group who stayed in school to the final year to do the HSC:

Higher status	43 %
Lower status	28 %

About the same time as Martin and Meade began their study, the Australian Government Commission of Enquiry into Poverty did a smaller but more intensive survey of 150 18 year olds in Melbourne, looking back at the level of education they had reached. This group too were classified according to their fathers' jobs. Here are the percentages of each group who remained to the HSC:

Fathers	%
professional, managerial	52
clerical, sales	27
skilled workers	30
semi-skilled, unskilled	6

In 1978 the Schools Commission and the Australian Bureau of Statistics compiled a volume of statistics on 'Australian students and their schools'. Curiously they didn't compile any statistics on the effects of occupation, income, or wealth; but they did calculate the overall percentages going through to the Matriculation or HSC year (apparent retention rates to Year 12) for the different school systems:

Schools	%
Independent	86
Catholic	43
State	30

Facts like these have turned up in every study of school retention and social background that has been done in Australia for the past thirty years. Facts like these have piled up in all the advanced industrial countries; and they are even piling up in third-world countries as they develop education systems on the Western model.[2] Social class inequality is a massive fact of our system of secondary education. It has persisted through a transformation of schooling that many hoped would abolish it. Why? To begin to answer that, we must look at the transformation of schooling itself.

THE SHORT HISTORY OF MASS SECONDARY SCHOOLING[3]

The growth of secondary schooling in the decades after the war was extraordinary. Several hundred high schools were created, many of them newly-built in the suburbs of the cities and in new towns (eventually provoking a revolution in school architecture). The total of secondary students in the country rose from about 181,000 in 1945 to

771,000 in 1965, and to 1.1 million in 1975. The number of secondary teachers rose from about 6,000 in 1945 to 74,000 in 1975. Before the war, half of Australian children did not go to secondary schools at all; by the early 1970s a large majority were getting four years in secondary schools, and about a third were getting six.

This growth, which was paralleled in many other countries, was not the product of a major policy decision by Australian governments, nor of organized public agitation for more schooling. In fact it was all done remarkably quietly. Its main architects were not premiers or prime ministers but bureaucrats such as Robertson in Western Australia and Wyndham in New South Wales in the 1950s, supported by a very diverse coalition of interests, and a groundswell of popular feeling that there should be more education, for all.

The coalition favouring growth had a number of elements. People of a liberal mind had long been urging that more education meant social uplift. Critics and researchers in the 1940s pointed out the class biases in the education system, and a natural response was to eliminate them by extending more schooling to those who had been excluded. Advocates of economic growth believed that more education meant a more efficient workforce and hence more rapid national 'progress'. This was a period of industrialization, and businessmen, while supporting the rapid expansion of the workforce by immigration, could also see the virtue in having it more highly trained. Both Liberal and Labor parties were converging on broadly similar strategies of expanding the action of the state into 'welfare' areas like health, social services and education. Both took credit for any rise in enrolments or buildings completed in the annual Education Department reports.

Above all, there was popular support. For most people in the 1940s, more education was one of the hopes they had for a better and more equal postwar world. It was not (as many commentators have supposed) that the masses entertained large ambitions and tripped over each other in the rush for tickets into the middle class. Rather, Depression memories saw education as a protection against unemployment. With full employment, massive immigration and economic expansion in the 1950s, it was more a case of getting left behind if you didn't join in. This was the lesson Dave and Judy Roberts learnt. They aren't pushing Wilma to become a professional; they do want her to stay at school longer than most of her schoolmates, so she can avoid getting the jobs that most of them get, in factories and shops.

When this is combined with the specific and very strong desire in immigrant families for their children to use the schools to maximum advantage, it can be seen how the independent actions of millions of people cumulated and confronted each other as a 'social pressure'. Governments removed some barriers to it: high-school fees and qualifying exams were abolished in most states during the war, and the age of compulsory attendance was raised (partly out of fear of unemployment for returned servicemen). The trickle of students through the high schools became a flood.

With expansion came reform of organization. The main vehicle of the boom was a new kind of school: the comprehensive, coeducational, urban area high school. The move to comprehensive area schools for the most part eliminated the distinctions between full selective highs and junior or domestic-science highs. In most states it also spelt decline for the technical school system, which for 40 years had been the educational pride of the labour movement. The move to coeducation was uneven, as a good many of the new schools were built segregated. (For example: in the northern beach suburbs of Sydney in the 1950s, a new boys' high was built at Brookvale and a new girls' high a few miles north at Narrabeen; as population continued to grow, a new separate girls' high was built across the road at Brookvale and a new separate boys' high at the other end of the same block of land at Narrabeen.) But in due course coeducation became general policy in the state system.

Yet in other ways the organization of schooling was not significantly changed. First, the dominant position in the whole system held by the competitive academic curriculum. Originally defined and administered by university academics through the public exam system, and the special province of the selective high schools, it was not in fact rejected as those institutions declined in weight. The reform of curricula proposed by progressive educators was far slower in winning acceptance than the reform of school organization.

Rather, the academic curriculum was internalized by the new mass schools, and became the province of their top streams. As a result the 'comprehensive' schools became, informally, 'multilateral' schools, with several programmes running within the same walls, the academic programme having most prestige and influence. There is evidence that the children of more affluent parents tended to be concentrated in the academic streams and the children of poorer parents in the non-academic streams.

Second, there was no change in the division of Australian school children among three systems: state, Catholic and Independent (mostly Protestant). The Catholic system, a microcosm of the whole with its own rank-and-file schools for the children of the workers and elite colleges for the children of the affluent, also attempted to expand at a great pace. It consequently found itself in dire straits economically, until pushed into alliance with the Protestant private schools to win state aid in the 1960s.

The Protestant and Catholic elite schools, as a group, had dominated academic secondary education and university graduation before the war; their only serious competition coming from a small group of selective state schools. (A South Australian study found that 86 per cent of Medicine and Honours Arts graduates, in the 1930's, and 78 per cent of Law graduates, had come from private schools.) Wealth was a simple discriminator — and that was why James and Mary Phelan, who went to private schools in the 1940s, hadn't had to work terribly hard to keep up their position. This situation came under increasing pressure as the growth of state schools produced more and more claimants for academic honours. The private schools shifted their concerns further towards academic pursuits — and that is registered in how much harder Sophie Phelan works. They not only survived, but in due course flourished, as a specialized sector of the secondary system.

So the educational 'revolution' of the postwar decades was by no means as thoroughgoing as some of the rhetoric suggested. And as expansion continued, results began to appear which were very different from what its sponsors hoped for.

One has been a deepening problem of authority in the schools. The failure to renovate curricula meant that more and more children encountered knowledge which they found of little use or relevance and which led them nowhere in particular. Teachers were increasingly faced with dilemmas about content and motivation; some fought for socially-relevant curricula and student-centred classes, some fought for established standards and teacher control. Problems of 'discipline' in the non-academic streams became endemic.

At the same time, the experience of growing up was changing. The transition from child to adult became more extended; 'the teenager' as a social category appeared. With it came adolescent peer groups, and a kind of youth culture with its own music, clothing, and amusements ('sex and drugs and rock and roll', to quote the title of a recent rock song), fed by specialized businesses. The authority of adults was weakened, in families and in schools. Both the Roberts and the Phelans are worried about this — though more about other peoples' children than their own. The schools, especially suburban state schools like Rockwell High, had to cope not only with increasing scepticism about their syllabuses, but also with a new disrespect for teachers.

On another front, those looking to the schools to train the workforce in useful skills and techniques were also to be disappointed. Technical education was increasingly marginalized, and avoided by successful students. The main school system established a rather different relationship with the labour market: it was used, not so much to increase the usefulness of employees, as to increase their market price and to make a social selection among them. Employers, who had long used 'coming from the right school' as a qualification for recruitment into management, increasingly used school achievement as a criterion for recruitment to other kinds of work — even where it was of little technical relevance. On their side, the members of more and more occupations stressed 'qualifications' to validate their claim to special expertise and demand a higher price for it. The more prestigious the credentials (that is, the more schooling consumed in getting them), the higher the price.

People like Dave Roberts, who acquired a wide range of practical skills on the job, had more than a suspicion that this was going on and therefore had a healthy scepticism about credentials based only on book learning. They found, nonetheless, that they had to urge their children to get more of it. The pressure on schooling increased as the credibility of its knowledge declined. In the economic recession of the late 1970s, the two trends combined with youth unemployment to produce a breakdown in the relationship between school and labour market.

As for the teachers themselves, they were more youthful than before, almost as awkwardly placed between the worlds of children and adults as the newly-created 'teenager'. They too were drawn into the competition for credentials as a profession, but with limited means to win a higher price for their services. (The expansion of teaching was so rapid that it resulted in dilution — the percentage with university degrees actually fell after the war.) Worse, their uncertain professional self-images were insulted by conditions of work that routinely included overcrowded classrooms and staff rooms, temporary buildings, and bureaucratic control by their employer. Secondary teachers in particular became a volatile, unpredictable lot — and increasingly militant. The first widespread teacher strikes came in Victoria in 1965, in NSW in 1968.

So schooling became, for the first time since the late nineteenth century, a major source of difficulty for the state. Teacher unions had become powerful and articulate. Parent organizations ceased to be content with running fetes and barbecues, linked up across states, and demanded to be heard. Even students began to organize, in the wake of student mobilization in the universities. A flurry of agitation surrounded the schools in the late 1960s and early 1970s. The famously monolithic and uniform Departments of Education moved in different directions. In Victoria central control was strenuously challenged; in NSW the Department and the Federation both clung doggedly to their traditional methods; in South Australia the Department tried to coopt criticism and lead the way into community participation, decentralization, relevant curricula and progressive teaching methods.

A stream of official enquiries on education attempted to find a stable policy for mass education — and couldn't. The central problem they were wrestling with, but rarely named, was what to do about education for the working class; or, more broadly, what to do about education in a stratified society. No strand of opinion had a clear solution to the dilemmas this question raised; but up to the time of the Karmel Report of 1973, the general drift had been to incorporate working-class kids in a common programme with an academic rationale, and trust to expansion to look after problems of unequal access.

The Karmel Report of 1973 is best known for its attachment to the idea of equality. Indeed it was the first major official acknowledgment that the strategy of expansion hadn't worked: that many children were disadvantaged, and needed to be given special support. But the report also urged teachers to make curricula 'relevant' to different groups of children, and often talked of 'differences' instead of inequalities. In these arguments it was at one and the same time endorsing and abandoning two ideas which had helped to launch and sustain mass secondary education: that there could be common schooling, and that education could make opportunity equal.

In these respects, the Karmel Report was the first sign of a sea-change in secondary schooling. Only a few years later growth had stopped, the teacher shortage had turned into teacher unemployment, and the focus of central government policy had shifted from what to do about inequality to how to make the schools serve industry more efficiently. Critics of the system began to say the schools couldn't do anything about inequality anyway. Those who had been active in the pursuit of equality looked around with dismay. David Bennett, the first chairperson of the Schools Commission's Innovations Programme, remarked in 1979

> a good school system would be one in which all students become socio-economic successes and that is why there are no good school systems.[4]

THE PROBLEM OF INEQUALITY IN EDUCATIONAL RESEARCH[5]

There is not much comfort in this story for educational researchers. Despite a mountain of research, the social sciences have so far failed to come up with a convincing explanation of Sophie Phelan's success and Wilma Roberts' troubles. Perhaps more important, researchers have done little about changing that state of affairs or helping people in the schools who have tried to. It seems important to understand why, if we are to do any better.

Part of it has to do with the way the problem has been set up — with the kinds of ideas and methods current in educational research. The first of the social sciences to have a significant impact on the issue was educational psychology, which gained a foothold in Australia in the 1930s through the research and guidance branches of the Education Departments, and the Australian Council for Educational Research. This development drew on a very peculiar kind of psychology, which claimed to show that each individual was endowed with a more or less fixed mental capacity, usually called 'Intelligence', and that this was distributed in more or less fixed proportions, with a few very bright, many in the middle, and a few subnormal. As the Vice-Chancellor of the University of Melbourne concluded at the time, psychology provided 'official' confirmation that some people are stupider than others, and that schooling ought to be organized around the differences.[6]

This kind of doctrine, then, implied a tiered educational system; and was usually taken to imply secondary schools organized to cream off the most able, and direct them towards university and the professions. And it easily slipped into thinking that that was how things really *did* work — that the problem with people like Wilma was that their IQs were lower than people like Sophie's. In short, it led to the belief that educational inequality was basically a question of innate individual brains and talent. That belief is still far from dead.

It had come under criticism, nevertheless, as early as the 1930s and 1940s. Another group of researchers pointed out that the amount of schooling children got closely corresponded to the size of their parents' incomes. Once it was seen that educational inequality was associated with social patterns which were themselves under strong criticism at the time, it was not a large step to suggest that education ought to become more equal. At this stage, however, there was little criticism of the idea of 'ability' inherent in educational psychology. La Nauze, the author of the major critique of educational inequality in the 1940s, accepted the ACER's estimate that only ten per cent could go into university, demonstrated that only one per cent of state school students did, and argued that the balance should. From various quarters the argument converged on the idea that there ought to be an expansion of secondary schooling, not to produce equal outcomes (which were forbidden by the natural inequalities of talent), but to equalize opportunities to move up an educational ladder which remained competitive and stratified.

For the next 25 years, while the school system expanded at a tremendous pace, educational research added very little to this picture. A few studies continued to be done, with improved methods as survey techniques became familiar, which demonstrated continuing inequalities to anyone who cared to dig them out. But they had not the slightest impact on educational policy. It was not until the troubles of the later 1960s came upon the school system that the issue was taken up again. Once more the demand for equality had popular appeal and force. A summary of the accumulated evidence of inequalities, Roper's book *The Myth of Equality*, gained wide attention. All of a sudden, educational sociology was in demand — and was asked to produce, not just statistical maps of inequality, but also explanations of it.

The sociology which attempted to respond to this demand was heavily influenced by the approach to inequality which had flourished in American sociology in the 1950s. All modern societies were taken to be 'stratified', that is, divided like layer-cakes; and enormous ingenuity and uncounted computer hours went into measuring the number of layers and the thickness of the cream between them. Further, it was assumed that the recipe for each layer of the cake was different — people in different 'social strata' had different attitudes, values, child-rearing methods, personality problems, and so on. This was the kind of answer sociologists first gave to the question 'why educational inequality?'. Members of lower-status groups (Wilma Roberts) failed because their homes (Dave and Judy) weren't up to it. There wasn't enough ambition, or stimulation, or loving-kindness, or patience, or whatever, in the homes of the lower strata. 'Deficit theory', as this has been called, naturally enough implied that the home circumstances of the disadvantaged should be improved, enriched, or compensated for.

Apart from being insulting, such accounts of the matter were conspicuously lopsided. It really is difficult to explain educational inequality without bringing in the school. Once the school came into focus, it seemed that the problem was less the Roberts' deficiencies than the difference between their styles and values and those of Rockwell High — or even the conflict between them. Researchers got busy trying to measure an ever-increasing list of 'dimensions' of home and school, and to compute the relative contribution of home and school to educational success.

This was an improvement on 'deficit' accounts, but shared a number of difficulties with them. Most research in this vein used questionnaires to collect a few simple facts about largish numbers of people — the only thing orthodox survey methods can do well. A cult of statistics developed in educational research, as elsewhere, at the expense of understanding. This was useful when the task was to map inequalities, disastrous when the problem was to explain them. A mass of research discovered little that wasn't already known and produced almost no new ideas about the social relations and processes impinging on education. The weakness of the research was a major reason why the explanations offered by educational sociology were so thin; and why the Karmel committee and the Schools Commission, when they came to frame the Disadvantaged Schools Programme, had so little to draw on apart from overseas analogies.

Those analogies were mostly remedial programmes like Headstart in the USA and the Educational Priority Areas in Britain, and that raises the second key problem. Notoriously, sociologists look 'down' and not 'up'. A good deal of research was done on what was going wrong with Rockwell High and the Roberts, very little on what was going right with Auburn College and the Phelans. (No-one seems to have thought of an *Advantaged* Schools Programme, to cure inequality by eroding the advantages of the rich.) While social scientists were focussing on homes and schools and their linkages, they were *not* looking at the larger social arrangements that made them the way they are. Very few researchers even posed the question of why we have a hierarchical schooling system in the first place.

With social hierarchy taken for granted, remedial action was pointed firmly towards the disadvantaged and their schools. And that led back to dilemmas reminiscent of the 1940s. If their schools were singled out, it implied a separate education for the disadvantaged, and abandonment of the ideal of common schooling. And if state-organized education was part of the problem, could it be the means to the solution? The dilemmas are plain, and unresolved, in the Karmel Committee's report.

These linked difficulties of theory and practice were the context of a great change that came over educational sociology in the 1970s. The old kind of research continued to be done, but its assumptions and methods came under increasing scrutiny, especially in a long-running debate in the pages of the *Australian and New Zealand Journal of Sociology*. The importance of schools as active producers of inequality was argued. Other forms of inequality, notably inequality between the sexes, were brought into the picture. Confusions in the concept of 'status' were found.

These approaches arose from problems of Australian research and politics, but they were also linked with similar debates in other countries. The problem of inequality lurched suddenly towards clarity — or what seemed like clarity — under the influence of scholars in the USA, Britain and France. A new doctrine swept the field, with the central argument that schooling *reproduces* the structure of inequality itself. As a recent local version puts it,

> the whole education system operates to ensure that inequalities fundamental to capitalist production — in particular those based on class and sex — are constantly being reproduced. Social stratification in Australia does not exist despite the provision of 'free, secular and compulsory' schooling, but essentially because of it.[7]

Labels can be misleading, but we think the conceptual shift here is so substantial that it needs one. Accordingly we will call the basic assumptions of the approaches sketched up to this point — psychologistic, economic, deficit and difference theories alike — the 'Inequality Approach'. They all focus, though in different ways, on the reasons for the unequal chances of individuals to climb up the educational ladder. The approach being discussed now we will call the 'Reproduction Approach', from its central argument that the school system as a whole reproduces an unequal society.

The focus of research here has been shifted from the careers of individuals to the ordering of society as a whole. In place of the layer-cake is a piece of heavy machinery, a structure of class domination and control. Instead of blaming the victim, one blames the system. The lack of social mobility through education was scarcely mysterious, and certainly not a rallying-point for action. Instead of collecting bits of information by surveys and doing rigorous statistics on them, the researcher should do rigorous theorizing about the nature of society, especially about capitalist economies, and work out the character of schooling from there.

In the first fine flush it all seemed to fit. In 1976 the leading American exponents of this line of thought, Bowles and Gintis, addressed large and enthusiastic audiences around the country. The largest and most enthused of them carried a motion to establish a movement 'based on the analysis of Bowles and Gintis'. Educational sociology not only had come up with some answers — it had suddenly become a political movement in its own right.

Unfortunately no-one seemed to follow. The new paradigm ran into difficulty at a familiar point: practice. If indeed inequality is ordained by the structures, just what, exactly, could be done? Teachers, however hard they try, can't overthrow the whole economic and political system. The kind of social theory that lay behind 'reproduction' arguments about education was coming in for strong criticism anyway for being too rigid and too pessimistic.

More troubling, reproduction theory repeatedly implied, and sometimes stated openly, that most people could not truly understand what was happening to them. It suggested that they were blinded by ideology (which was why they went on reproducing the structures); and that only intellectuals who understood proper theory really knew what was going on. This is no happier a position for social scientists to be in than proposing deficit theory. And the contradiction between democratic purposes and implicit elitism seems to have been sensed by many teachers. The reproduction paradigm wrought a revolution in theory, but has had rather thin effects on practice.

OUR RESEARCH

That was the state of play when we planned the research on which this book is based. Our thinking was much influenced by reproduction theory: one of the authors was a speaker at the Bowles and Gintis conference, another was among the audience, and a third wrote an article criticizing inequality research with the aid of reproduction arguments. But we were bothered by the increasing abstractness and dogmatism of this literature, and thought that 'a good dose of awkward facts' was the right kind of cure.

Similarly we were influenced by inequality-approach research, which after all, had done the job of collecting the awkward facts about educational inequality. But we reacted strongly against its dessicated methods. Very often, researchers had never even laid eyes on the people being researched; at best they saw them briefly while handing out questionnaires. Normally they communicated only via ticks on answer sheets handed in by research assistants or part-time interviewers, then processed through computers. Such research was more like manufacturing margarine than like meeting people and learning about their problems.

So we set out to do something a bit different: to get close to the situations people found themselves in, to talk to them at length about their experiences. We thought it was vital to learn what actually happened, and what they actually did, in their working lives and in relation to schooling. In this we were encouraged by a small number of studies from various countries which had used rather similar methods and come up with unusually interesting results. We were particularly impressed with Sennett and Cobb's book *The Hidden Injuries of Class*, from the USA, and Jackson and Marsden's *Education and the Working Class*, from England, both of which showed how much could be learnt by listening to people talking about their own life histories. In other respects, our methods have been very different from theirs.

If a useful study needed to learn vastly more about particular people and particular situations than survey research usually did, it followed that (unless we were given research grants of truly imperial grandeur) we would have to be content with a 'sample' much smaller than surveys usually have. This posed a serious problem: how could we be in a position to generalize, to offer conclusions about the school system as a whole — which, after all, was the point of our project? We took a somewhat unconventional decision. Instead of trying to sample broadly across the population, we would focus the research on two quite specific and carefully-defined groups of families, whose social position and relationship to each other was reasonably well understood, and whose relationship to the school system could be expected to cast a particularly clear light on what was happening generally.

We have already noted the general character of the two groups we talked to: the families of people doing manual or semi-manual work for wages on the one hand; and of managers, businessmen, and professionals on the other. Here we should also note that we chose only two parent, English-speaking families, that half came from Adelaide and half from Sydney, and that half of the teenagers were girls and half boys. We will have a lot more to say about these families and what we learnt about their milieux, in the following chapters. Technical details of the sampling and other aspects of procedure are given in the Appendix at the end of the book.

In another respect also we departed from what was usual. Surveys on these problems have usually involved students or parents or teachers — rarely two of these groups together, still more rarely the interactions between them. We argued that to understand the educational situation of a teenager thoroughly, it was necessary to get to know all the significant people in it: her family, her friends and her teachers, as well as herself. We gave up on the idea of interviewing the friends but we did interview the others. So the research, organized around a 'sample' of 100, was actually based on 100 *clusters* of interviews — each normally consisting of the two parents, the student, and a number of the student's teachers. Looked at another way, we have four sets of interviews:

the students	100
their parents	196
their classroom teachers	118
their school principals	10

making 424 interviews in all.

With the permission of the principals and the Departments of Education concerned, the study was conducted through the schools; and we owe a tremendous amount to the principals, deputies, year teachers and school secretaries who made arrangements, found space, gave us local background, helped us get in touch with the families, and generally looked after us in the field. We will have a lot to say about the schools and their problems in what follows; here there is one major point to be noted. It was clear from the start that the two groups of students we wanted to talk to would be in different schools. We went to the kinds of schools where they are usually to be found: government comprehensives in working-class suburbs on the one hand; Independent fee-charging schools on the other. There are many things these schools have in common, but there are also crucial differences, as will be seen. In writing this report we have adopted the convention of calling schools in the former group 'Such-and-such High', and in the latter, 'Such-and-such College'.

The interviews, plainly, could not be the sort of thing done in Gallup polls — a short list of fixed questions. They had to be detailed, they had to be flexible, they had to give the people being interviewed a real chance to get their ideas and experiences across, and give us a chance, however imperfectly, to get inside their worlds. This meant we could not farm the work out to a large group of part-time interviewers. All the interviews were done by one or other of the four authors. It took us more than a year to do them, from mid 1977 to late 1978.

The content of these conversations will be clear from what follows; but, because this report is concerned with general issues, and quotes only short fragments from any one, the nature of the interviews themselves is not very clearly conveyed. They were, as might be expected, extremely varied. Some people were understandably shy or reluctant to talk about anything that mattered personally. Because the study was organized through the school, and we were in some way associated with school authority, some of the kids were very cagey indeed. We did our best to respect any reservations people had about giving away information. But on the whole, shortage of information was not our problem. Most of our informants, once they were convinced we were serious about trying to understand their situation, talked honestly and at some length. A number of interviews ran for two hours, some for three. The evidence they gave us was rich, complex, and often unexpected.

Some of our respondents found it a welcome and unusual opportunity to reflect on their own lives. 'It's an experience you only have once in a lifetime', one parent told us. In some cases the discussion moved into intimate and difficult areas of personal life and relationships, and the interviewer would come away wondering what was and was not 'data' in a research project. We have tried to respect confidences. But we cannot forget that the issues we are trying to study *are* stressful ones, the dilemmas they pose really can be painful, and that we are dealing with processes that do damage people and distort human relationships. Sometimes the difficulty of handling the interviews may be a sign that they are getting close to the bone.

It has not been easy to interpret all this material. Its sheer bulk has been daunting, to say the least. Our first step was to put the material from each 'cluster' of interviews together, and try to make sense of what was going on in and around each of our students' lives. It took the best part of two years' work to do this systematically for 43 'clusters', and the job is still going on. Only after we had worked through a large part of the evidence this way could we try organizing it in other ways — for instance, putting together the material that spoke to the social processes surrounding a particular school, or the material that spoke to the experiences of the girls as against the boys, and so on.

We have, then, engaged in a fairly active process of digesting the evidence. As we began to formulate preliminary conclusions from it, we spoke about them to several seminars and conferences, mainly of teachers and parents; and reconsidered after hearing their reactions. In the second half of 1981 we took the results back for discussion with the schools and families we had studied three years before.

This is a step that is not usually part of a research design. We recommend it strongly, though it can be stressful for the researchers. It is a severe test of whether the researchers' ideas do make good sense to the people who, after all, know most about the situations being researched. We think that our material stood up reasonably well to this test; that, for instance, we had something useful to say about issues that really were major practical concerns for many teachers. More than that, it brings out new ideas, or themes that were only implicit in the original interviews. One of the central concerns of this book is the degree to which working-class families are disabled by the schooling system. The report-back sessions showed repeatedly how critical discussion of that experience could en-able, could validate peoples' own ideas rather than undercut them.

Wrestling with the evidence has forced us to refine, and in some cases substantially change, conceptions with which the project started. It has also brought into focus issues whose importance was by no means obvious then. So there are unevennesses in our material, and incoherencies in our reasoning, which reflect the development of ideas within the project.

A case in point is the basic sociological concept with which the project began — class. For all their differences, the inequality paradigm and the reproduction paradigm share an approach in which classes or strata are basically understood as categories: sets of individuals who all share the same attributes or possessions (such as level of income, type of occupation, ownership). It was a conception of this kind with which we defined our 'sample', for want of anything better.

This was already somewhat in tension with a view of class we had been developing in other research, and which our interviews in this project were to confirm very strongly. It is not what people are, or even what they own, so much as what they *do* with their resources and their relationships, that is central. (Some of the things done with resources very much concern education.) Classes are not abstract categories but real-life groupings, which, like heavily-travelled roads, are constantly under construction: getting organized, divided, broken down, remade. (Significant parts of this activity occur in and around the schools.) At the same time, classes reflect terrible constraints in the lives of their members, for their making and remaking is done in the course of the intransigent conflicts that arise in a deeply divided and unequal society.

One of the problems pushing us towards this way of thinking was that conventional ideas of class as category practically always defined it via status in the workplace or the marketplace (for example, type of occupation, ownership of capital). People who weren't in either — notably school pupils and housewives — could only be given a class 'location' by labelling them with the status of the nearest adult male. The inadequacy of this became very obvious when we met families that were internally divided along class lines; where, for instance, a wife had a different class identity, was pursuing different strategies, and stood in a quite different relation to the school, from her husband.

This sort of situation also forced us to think very much harder about an issue we had been conscious of at the start of the research but had not seen as central to it: relations between the sexes. The evidence of the interviews is clear that this is a quite central issue for understanding the relations between families and schools in general; and for understanding the issue of class inequality in particular. It has therefore become one of the major themes of this book.

We will be dealing with it in a way that may be unfamiliar to some readers, but is, we hope, consistent with the way we also deal with class. We treat gender not just as a matter of the existence of two categories of people, male and female, but primarily as a pattern of *relations* among people. It is an extensive and complex pattern, woven through all the institutions they live in — families, schools, workplaces — and shapes their lives at every level from public affairs to basic psychological makeup. We hope the point of this approach will be clear in what follows. We will return to the general issue of sex and gender in the final sections of Chapter Four.

Of course we were not doing all this in a vacuum. The debate over educational reform went on. So did changes in the federal government's priorities in education funding, the transfer of resources from public to private schools, the growth of a 'transition education' programme, the squeeze on tertiary institutions — making us despair that we could ever make sense of our material in time to affect a policy debate to which it was centrally relevant. More positively, we began to see connections between some of the arguments emerging from our material and the work of teachers in some innovative inner-city education projects in Melbourne, Adelaide and Sydney.

A number of studies came out overseas which seemed to lend support to our ideas about method, and sometimes theory. We were impressed by Grace's *Teachers, Ideology and Control*, Woods' *The Divided School*, and especially by Robins and Cohen's *Knuckle Sandwich* and Corrigan's *Schooling the Smash Street Kids*. During our fieldwork, also, we read the book which has become the most-discussed example of reproduction theory since Bowles and Gintis, Willis' *Learning to Labour*; this helped us formulate the argument about class and gender, though it sharpened our consciousness of the difficulties inherent in reproduction theory.

As the research proceeded, we became convinced that there were interwoven problems of analysis and evidence, theory and practice, which could not be overcome within the reproduction approach, however refined. It became one of our main concerns to find different ways of thinking through these problems. This re-thinking has been considerably helped by some developments in sociological theory: particularly, work by several European theorists which suggests a much more active relationship between social structures and individual practices than either the inequality approach or the reproduction approach usually admitted. We will discuss this conceptual issue in more detail at the end of Chapter Two. Yet, in a sense, it is the job of the book as a whole to make out an argument about how these questions should be understood. Let us begin where the plan of the project did, with families as the main link between school students and the larger social structure.

2
Families and their kids

WHY FAMILIES MATTER

How does the link between family circumstance and schooling actually work? How do families in practice relate to their children's schooling? What is it about their situations, and their structure, that shapes their relationships with schools? These are the questions we will be addressing in this chapter. We thought it would be useful to start off with a discussion of just one family, which might show in detail how a range of social and economic experiences and dilemmas are tied together in real life, and why it is important to understand them in order to understand a teenager at school.

Kevin Jones is 15, and in Year 10 at Greenway High School, a suburban comprehensive with a working-class 'catchment'. In his own opinion, 'I'm not brainy but I'm not dumb', and certainly that corresponds to the marks he has usually got in tests. 'He just seems to be an ordinary run-of-the-mill type of student', says one of his teachers. He is one of the kind who don't inspire their teachers with enthusiasm but also don't drive them to an early grave.

He is getting a bit bored with school now, it seems constantly the same, though he certainly isn't a troublemaker. He's reaching the age at which most of his schoolmates will leave formal education for good, and he may join them at the end of this year. Not that he has a clear view of where to go. He has about half-a-dozen jobs vaguely in mind, and none very clearly in prospect. So he might stay longer at school, even try for Matric. The school has said he can go up to Year 11 'on probation', which is supposed to mean that he has to show improvement in the first term or he will be put back to repeat Year 10. However, as his class teacher notes, 'probation' is a dead letter at Greenway High, for nobody in fact gets put back. So the reality is that Kevin will be promoted if he wants to stay in school, but will go on under a cloud.

A familiar pattern, it would seem. A conventional view might see here a working-class boy 'finding his level' in the education system, having unrealistic ambitions 'cooled out', and being gradually directed to the appropriate part of the labour market. But if that were really so, we might expect Kevin's teachers to hold a pretty standard view of him. In fact they are strikingly inconsistent. Kevin is described by different teachers as pretty dull and unintelligent, as middling in ability, and as quite bright and needing to be pushed. One teacher found him personally unpleasant, another good-natured. One saw him as 'run-of-the-mill', another called him 'unforgettable'. One said that he is polite, another that he is arrogant. This is much more than the ordinary ambiguity of people's views of each other. Kevin, it would seem, genuinely *is* different in the relationships he constructs with different teachers. And the range of these patterns implies that he simply hasn't found a satisfactory *general* way of relating to the school: he is trying one thing after another, or several at once.

Far from having an educational fate imposed on him by the social system, Kevin is actively constructing a relationship with the school — as his teachers are actively constructing relationships with him. It is likely that he knows of the derogatory opinions about him and resents them. From time to time he demands more attention from his teachers. Because (in the conditions of their job) they are pressed for time, and because Kevin isn't an academic star, this demand comes across to them as 'immaturity', cheekiness, or laziness. One teacher who told us that Kevin was not bright enough to matriculate, also offered the much more perceptive comment that Kevin *tries too hard* to impress his teachers. We'll explore the background of this later, but want to stress it at the outset. The idea of someone actively working on their relation to the school, to the point of 'trying too hard', is a long way from the conventional image of what a run-of-the-mill, bored, not very successful, working-class school boy would be like.

Kevin's attempt to construct a satisfying relationship with the school has obviously run into a good many difficulties. He recalls his primary school experience with some affection, liked the situation where he could learn at his own pace, and dislikes the lock-step classes at high school. Schooling currently is a bit of a struggle, especially in subjects that require written composition. Written work, one teacher put it, is an 'ordeal' for Kevin. Once she realized this, she changed her requirements of him, and got an enthusiastic response. Other teachers haven't, and talk about Kevin's poor spelling, monosyllabic answers, 'badly presented' work, papers handed in with unanswered questions, lack of effort, and so on. He is now spending less time on homework, and more time just kicking about talking with a small group of male friends, or helping his father on construction projects in the garage at home.

Why then is Kevin still at school, given that he could legally have left some time ago, and is even thinking about staying through Year 11 and trying for Matric? One important reason is that he comes from a close-knit family and his parents want him to get as good an education as possible. And there is a specific and strong reason for this: they didn't.

Both Elizabeth and Frank Jones have vivid memories of their schooling — it was brutal, and it was completely alienating. Elizabeth, the daughter of a wharf labourer, was thrashed in school and told she was stupid, as a result of a specific reading difficulty that emerged in Grade 2 and is still with her. She hated school from then on, got through her tests by cheating, and left as soon as she was legally able to. Frank's experience was, if anything, worse:

> I'm a bad speller, I just freeze up if I've got to fill out a form . . . I was a terrible dunce at school, and I was almost expelled because I got that way. I couldn't do it, and the teachers were not like they are today. They just made you do things and if you couldn't do it . . . instead of trying to explain it they would cuff you under the ear. I got frightened and then froze up inside. That's how, I think. And from then on, I didn't care. I don't care what happens from now on, you can belt me, you can. And they used to thrash me, and I would say 'Are you finished Sir?'

Frank was sent to an 'opportunity class' for slow learners — 'a dreadful thing, you were scorned and you were pointed at' — escaped from school the moment he could, and never went near an educational institution again, until he had his own children. The main thing his schooling gave him was a lifelong anxiety about writing, and he has had to pass up several chances for better jobs — seeing apprentices he has trained promoted over his head — because there was no way he could handle the paperwork.

One reaction to an experience like that might be to reject the whole business of education with contempt; another would be to form a strong determination that your children are going to get something very much better. The Joneses have gone the second way. They stress the importance of education to their two children. 'I think it's very important', says Elizabeth, 'because I haven't got any'; and she at least wants to see Kevin go to Matric. Frank is a bit vaguer about what level is appropriate, but certainly wants Kevin to get as far as he can. Both go along to parent-teacher nights, not that they get much information there. They feel that schools are more relaxed and friendly places than they used to be, and have one or two stories of good teachers who have taken a kindly interest in their children's problems. They support the authority of the school in cases of misbehaviour by their kids. This pro-schooling push was interpreted, by the only one of Kevin's teachers who was aware of it, as a case of parents who 'overestimate his ability'.

Why does his parents' schooling, and their reaction to it, matter in Kevin's schooling? Plainly that has to do with nature of his emotional relationship with them; and that in turn grows out of a family history of a definite kind.

Both Frank and Elizabeth left school at 14, and went to work as factory hands, where they met each other. In a close, deeply loyal relationship, they set about building what their schooling had done its best to deny — a sense of pride and achievement. They focussed their energies on their life together rather than on the world outside. They put a small deposit on a block of land even before they were married at 18, and built the house with their own hands, gathering timber and other materials wherever they could. For the past twenty years they have lived in it as they built and extended it. It is now a comfortable fibro house with a room for each of the kids, a garage/workshop for Frank, and a garden featuring a magnificent rockery which Frank built and Elizabeth's green thumb has brought to life. As soon as they could afford it, Elizabeth gave up her job and became a full-time housewife and part-time builder's labourer; since the children arrived, a full-time mother.

Immense emotional energy, then, has gone into house and household, and the emotional ties between parents and children are very strong. 'Until just recently we wouldn't go anywhere without the children', Elizabeth observes. Frank has not only built the house but also a boat, a caravan, and is currently rebuilding a wrecked car; Kevin does a lot of work with him in the garage on these projects. When his employer moved the factory to the other side of the city, Frank gave up the best-paid job he had ever had rather than uproot the family.

Kevin and his sister have thus grown up in a family which responded to the economic and social pressures of working-class life by developing an intense solidarity and a vigorous practice of cooperative coping. For that reason his parents' opinions about education, and their relation to the school, matter a lot to him. But that's far from being the whole story.

For one thing, the Jones family may be closely knit, but that doesn't mean the relationships within it are smooth or easy. Elizabeth accepted early on a thoroughly subordinated place in the household: that's what her meek and retiring mother had been, that's what her religion told her she ought to be, and that's what the logic of Frank's jobs said too. But accepting 'a woman's place' hasn't been all that easy. Children were slow to come after the marriage, and when they did, Elizabeth became extremely anxious about how good a mother she was. She now worries about whether she is over-protecting the two children. She also became increasingly confined to the small haven she and Frank had made, and reluctant to venture outside it:

> I like my four little fences and I don't like the outside world . . . I only go out when I have to . . . People frighten me.

It is Frank who negotiates with the 'outside world' and holds authority in the family. Within this patriarchal arrangement, with its strong division between the sexes, Kevin is very clearly identified with his father. (He even reproduces his father's pattern of being better with figures than with words at school.) But this doesn't mean that the two have an easy-going relationship. Frank lays down the rules in the family very firmly, and if the kids transgress, they get thrashed. There is a good deal of tension too, especially as the adolescent Kevin increasingly wants space of his own.

Through this relationship, perhaps even because of its high-pressure combination of affection and aggression, Kevin has incorporated much of his father's personality and much of his outlook on life. He accepts, for instance, his father's model of masculinity, believes that a woman's place is in the home, and resents the way his teachers at Greenway High seem to favour the girls. All the jobs he has in mind are conventionally masculine ones; all the friends with whom he talks things over are male; and opinion in that little group is pretty contemptuous of women. The opinion seems to be returned: Kevin is having a hard time from the girls in his class at school, who regard him as sexually unattractive and let him know about it. At present he also gets on badly with his younger sister, alternately ignoring her and putting her down.

Even setting psychological processes aside, we can see how Frank's life has structured Kevin's learning. His first job was unskilled work in a factory, and since then he has been a shop assistant, a delivery man, a garage mechanic, an assembly-line worker, a quality controller, a maintenance worker in a refrigeration plant, and a long-distance truck driver. He currently holds a licence to drive every kind of vehicle his employer, a large construction firm, operates. He is unable to get supervisory jobs, as we have already noted, because of the anxiety created by paperwork. What he has done is convert this barrier into a source of creativity, developing a tremendous versatility with his hands, both at work and at home. He notes with some irony how a person classified by his school as a 'slow learner' can pick up trades at the drop of a hat. And it's not just a matter of 'purely manual' skills (if indeed there are any such). He has also *designed* much of the house and the machinery he has built in his garage.

This has an influence on Kevin's schooling that is strong, but also divided. The Joneses' support for formal education meets at least three cross-currents here. One is the plain fact that they *have* made a go of it despite their own poor educational start, and the irrelevance of schooling in Frank's working life since. When Frank tells his kids, in effect, 'stick with school so you won't have to be like me', he is undercutting the authority of his own example.

Second, neither success with the home nor versatility at work has ever wiped out the shame both Elizabeth and Frank feel about their lack of education. They still *feel* outsiders in relation to the school. And of course they have never had the chance to acquire the skills with paperwork, or the knowledge of educational institutions, that would enable them to give Kevin much practical help beyond the most elementary stages of his schooling.

Third, while his parents and teachers have pointed him towards the academic curriculum at school, Kevin has also absorbed a body of knowledge of a very different kind. Over long hours in the garage with his dad, he has been learning not only the specific skills picked up in a varied working life, but also something much more general. He has learned about a kind of competence that exists outside academic curricula, about the importance of versatility as against certification, and about the pleasures of actually creating useful things.

It's not surprising, then, that both Kevin's parents, and the teacher who knows him best, and he himself at times, should think of a trade as the right kind of job for him. We can also see why this is very far from being a settled choice, why Kevin and his mother both have white-collar jobs in mind as well. What is also very clear is that Kevin is not *competing* very hard for advancement in school or in the job market, nor are his parents pushing him to compete. This has a lot to do with the way they have interpreted their life experiences, the view of the world they have constructed.

When Frank and Elizabeth want 'the best' for Kevin and his sister, that doesn't mean that they want them to be rich, or influential, or anything like that. They do believe that there will always be rich and poor in the world, that you have to have bosses and workers. Despite their own financial struggles they have no resentment against the rich ('good luck to them', says Kevin too); equally they have no admiration or deference for them, and Kevin accurately expresses the family sentiment when he criticizes those who rise in the world by treading on others. His mother and father don't see themselves as having risen, as they moved from poverty to security, so much as having come out of the darkness into the light. It is that security, above all else, that they want to hand on to their children and that animates their support of schooling. They want to make sure the kids don't slip back into the kind of struggle they have won through.

It has been a real struggle. For most of their married life they have depended on one wage, and a pretty modest one at that. Frank has never commanded a high rate, and his overtime earnings for years were limited by the demands of work on the house. But they have made ground. They live in a postwar suburb which is about half privately-built homes and half Housing Authority homes, and there is a clear sense in the immediate neighbourhood that the Joneses' end is the place to be. Down at the Housing Authority end is where the no-hoper families are, who don't work and don't care. (Families from those streets, whom we also interviewed, wax satiric about the pointless snobbery of their neighbours up the rise.) The Joneses see their security and respectability as something they have achieved through their own efforts. Frank is very antagonistic to 'dole bludgers', who he insists don't want to work. He is critical of unions as a kind of protection racket and the main cause of inflation; and though he usually votes Labor, he sees Malcolm Fraser as an honest man doing a difficult job.

Kevin, then, is growing up in a milieu which says a lot to him in practice about the importance of individual effort, and has strongly-emphasized ideas about doing the right thing, pulling your weight, and working within the rules. But it's a milieu that places no value on competition or competitive success, and a family that isn't organized to engage in competitive striving — rather, cooperative coping.

Kevin has absorbed this, clearly enough. There was an interesting moment in the interview where he discussed the idea of 'getting ahead'. What this meant to him was not scrambling up some ladder ahead of everybody else, but making enough money to be able to save up and retire early. To the extent that educational 'success' means getting into the business of competitive achievement, it is clear that Kevin's school would have a hard time trying to separate him from his family's characteristic practices and attaching him to its meritocratic programme. And in fact it has not. For all their differences, that's the one point all Kevin's teachers are agreed on.

This is far from being the whole story of Kevin's schooling or his family's experience with the class system; we aren't offering this as anything like a complete account. Nor are we offering it as some sort of paradigm of 'the working-class relationship with education'; there is no such animal. Of course the Joneses do share many experiences with other families we will be talking about. But the main point here is to show that the student's education is tied in with the family's situation and experiences in quite a number of ways.

We will be pursuing these in detail in the following sections, and there is a danger they will be disconnected there. So it is important to remember that in real life they are aspects of one and the same situation — the Joneses have to handle them all together. The way they do it, balance different demands, digest experiences, use their resources, reconstruct their own relationships, and construct a future, we will call their 'collective practice'. In using such a concept we mean to stress that families don't just exist in a static shape, but are constantly grappling with changing situations.

HISTORIES

The link between family and school cannot be understood if it is taken just at one point of time. Each family has a history, each school has a history, and so does the connection between them.

Understanding that connection means understanding the way it has developed.

This is true generally; it is however most vivid where the relationship has reached a point of crisis and we can actually see it changing. This was happening in the Owens family at the time we interviewed them. They have had the same kind of economic struggle as the Jones family, surviving for most of the time on Mr Owens' wage as a labourer. Like the Joneses they have built their own home, in fibro, on a block in a very similar neighbourhood. Mr Owens also had the same kind of experience of schooling — moralizing teachers, boredom, and the cane. He got out as soon as he could (in fact he remembers feeling cheated at age 12 because he had believed he could leave then) and now has no kind of respect for education at all, has nothing to do with his three daughters' schooling, and in particular holds that 'schooling's a waste for girls'.

This opinion doesn't count for much, however, as he has nothing like the authority in this family that Mr Jones has in his. From quite early in the marriage he began to lose his claim to patriarchal authority, partly because he didn't supply housekeeping money regularly, and is now regarded by all the family, himself included, as having failed in his responsibilities as husband-and-father. Mrs Owens has become the strong central figure in the household, making the key decisions, and a close solidarity has developed between her and her daughters. She had a more positive experience of schooling, and when she left at the minimum age it was because her mother forced her to, rather than because she wanted to.

She regrets the lost chance, and has given warm support to her daughters' education, overseeing homework (and helping with it up to the point allowed by her own minimal schooling), keeping up contact with the school, and vigorously contesting her husband's view of education for girls. Ruth, the oldest girl, responded energetically and has been doing very well, getting lots of 'A' grades. She has just completed Year 10 with good marks, wants to become a teacher, and there was every expectation that she would go on to Matriculation and 'teachers' college' (the family's term) thereafter. Ann, who is a year younger, though more of a 'home body' and considered to have less 'brains' than Ruth, was following in her footsteps. She was in no sort of conflict with the school, worked steadily at her subjects, and also contemplated going to Matric. A couple of years ago Mrs Owens went back to work as a packer in a factory twelve miles away, to save enough money to put the girls through.

It so happened that we interviewed the Owens family right at the end of the school year, a time that always provokes thought about futures, and the family was in crisis because Ruth had just decided to give it away. She and her parents had begun to look for a job for her, and in the depressed state of the youth labour market (the area they live in has one of the worst youth unemployment figures in the country), a job wasn't easy to find. Mrs Owens was quite anxious that despite all Ruth's efforts at school, she would now wind up in a shop or a factory.

The reasons for the decision to leave school were not entirely clear to us, though the family offered several justifications. One was the current fact of teacher unemployment. Why make all the effort and sacrifice to stay at school when the job Ruth wanted wouldn't be there at the end anyway? Another had to do with a sense of let-down and disappointment about the school itself. Kids who waste their time still pass, they copy Ruth's work, get homework in late, and aren't penalized. Why try so hard when the system gives so little recognition to conscientious effort?

But if the exact balance of motives is still unclear, there is nothing obscure about the consequences. A whole strategy of life, a collective practice developed by the women of the Owens family, has come unstuck. Ruth's efforts in past years, and her mother's, are going for nothing, both in terms of schooling and employment. A radical reassessment of the value of education is taking place; there is every likelihood now that the younger girls will leave at the minimum age, or at longest stay to Year 10. With this is coming a re-assessment of Ann: she is the one who had always got dinner and done the washing-up while her elder sister stayed in her room reading books. Her best subjects at school were Home Science and Needlework, her presence in the household was cheerful and helpful and dependable. So the crisis of one strategy, centred on Ruth, has meant a bonus for another, centred on Ann. And in this strategy the importance of formal schooling is very much less.

Here we can see family history in the making. Some issues, however, go a long way further back. Both the Jones children and the Owens girls face situations shaped in important respects by their parents' schooling thirty years ago. Let us examine more systematically the kinds of experiences and memories the parents bring to the encounter with their children's schooling.

For a significant number of parents, the memory is of an alienating, sometimes brutal and frightening, experience. This is not a pleasant thing for members of the teaching trade to have to record, but there can be no doubt of its truth; we could multiply examples like Mrs Jones, Mr Jones and Mr Owens. In some recollections the point is not so much about physical brutality as about a social put-down where poor kids were stigmatized. Mrs Roberts recalls this:

> The teachers used to look down on you . . . I only ever clashed with one teacher in primary school . . . he said to me, 'You're like a lot of pigs, you'll be up the backyard with all the pigs' . . . I went to Causeway Girls' High, and I clashed with a teacher there, a library teacher. She used to always pick on us. That's the trouble, you see, coming from big families, you don't have this and you don't have that. 'Cause we couldn't afford to pay the text fees, you know. We used to pay them off, and by the time you finished paying, school was ended. You used to have to borrow books to do your work.

Here we see a definite undercurrent of class hostility in the teacher-pupil interaction. In other instances the feeling could be good but the eventual outcome not very different. Mr McArthur also got defined as 'hopeless', though in the kindest possible way:

> *How did you get on with the teachers at primary school?*
> Quite good. I used to get very upset at tests; not too bad in the year, but when a test came along . . . I still get trouble, like, my brain freezes or something, you know. I can't do a test. I remember in sixth class and the aisles . . . The teacher used to have more quizzes, and the best out of each aisle would go out the front and the other aisle would ask questions. And my aisle, I used to always get picked and go out the front. But when the test came — and these questions [in the aisle quiz] were nearly always on history or geography or something — when the test would come, I'd fail. Because I can't write, properly, you know. And I couldn't write things down and I've always been like that. And I used to get very upset and worried about it. And the teacher knew that and in the end, I don't know if the teacher did the right thing or not, but I don't think he did, he put me on the milk run when spelling was on, because he used to know that I used to get that upset every day. And he put me on the milk run, which we used to have after morning tea or something . . . I didn't learn anything, but at least I didn't get upset.

In a variety of ways, the school operated for these people as a mechanism of exclusion. It passed a hostile judgment upon their abilities, and left some at least with a life-long anxiety about things to do with reading and writing. A significant part of the working-class experience, then, has been that the schooling they got was a positively dis-abling experience.

At the same time, and no doubt in the same schools, something very different was happening to another group of kids. Mr McArthur got sent on the milk run because he had difficulty coping, Mrs Crisp had to make the inspector's tea for the opposite reason:

> *What did the college seem like after the parish school?*
> It wasn't all that much different, I'd say, because the teachers were the same order. I'd say it was better equipped, that would be outstanding; but other than that, very little difference. When I was at the parish school I was the sort of kid who did everything: I answered the phone, I made the inspector's morning tea, you know, one of those? [laughter] When I went to the college I thought I was going to have a nice easy time, I thought 'Good, I'll switch off, and just be myself, and settle down in a corner'. But I didn't get the opportunity, 'cause my reputation was known even if I wasn't known to all of them. So I was reasonably well involved. I was interested in books, and if younger children needed help, reference help or something like that, they would be referred to me.

Mrs Crisp was a beneficiary of the long-established practice of teachers picking out and promoting kids who are like themselves. She won a bursary from the parish school to the fee-charging college, then a scholarship to a teachers' college, and duly became a teacher herself — rising to be a headmistress twenty years later. The fact that *some* working-class children did win social promotion through the schools is nearly as important as the disabling experiences just discussed. It was known about, and represented a possibility which any working-class kid might try to grasp, once identified as 'bright'.

Most memories of working-class schooling, however, were neither as bruising as Mrs Roberts' nor as benign as Mrs Crisp's. The commonest pattern is a mixture of good and bad moments; helpful teachers remembered with warmth, others with annoyance; often increasing boredom; and departure at or soon after the minimum age, because of economic pressure on parents, or a signal from the school that it was time to go, or the kids' own desire to stop being a child and start earning:

> *Did you find teachers difficult to get on with?*
> Some. Not all, but some of them.
> *And what were some of the things that annoyed you about teachers?*
> Some of them were very, very short-tempered. Impatient. When you see some parents and then see teachers, there's not a lot of patience in

> a lot of teachers. I suppose it's from the years of teaching. Some were very patient. Others weren't. In fact I was the favourite with a couple of teachers, but there were others that I wasn't. (Mr Siemens)

> They used to say to me 'You'll end up in a factory!'
> And I always used to say 'Well somebody has to'.
> And that was just my way out of it because I wouldn't let them know that they were getting the better of me . . . I can always remember them saying that, and I always had the same answer. I don't think I'm any less a person because I worked in a factory. My Mum worked in a factory you know. (Mrs Arlott)

> I think that Mum finished school when she was 13. I had to leave school when I was 14, because my Mum was sick. She was pregnant and had very bad varicose veins, she couldn't walk. So I had to leave school then and I only got to second year in school . . . I think she had to leave school when she was about 13, to look after her mother too, the same thing . . .
> *Did you like school?*
> I did like it, yes.
> *Would you say you did well at school?*
> I must have been all right.
> *Why do you say 'must have'?*
> Because I've got a certificate for shorthand, typing, arithmetic, English. I got honours for typing and merits for shorthand . . .
> *So it was a pretty sad thing that you had to leave school?*
> Well, I didn't want to leave. I only had one more year to go anyhow. But, it just had to happen, that's all. My father couldn't look after her, he was working. (Mrs Poulos)

These are only fragments of rich and fascinating biographies which give a remarkable account of working-class schooling in the 1940s and 1950s. Clearly, it was an involving, empowering, experience only for a few. Yet when most left at 14 or 15, it was not so much a product of having 'failed' in an academic competition — most of them were never in it — as of the collective practices of their families and communities in the face of economic need. As Mrs Young put it:

> Things weren't real good, you didn't get a lot of money in those days . . . And so I was offered a job, and of course you know at 15 you left school then; and it was only the rich that seemed to go on.

Leaving at that age didn't need a specific reason. It was just what everybody *did* unless there was clear reason to do something else (such as winning a scholarship).

Still, we should not take too bland a view of this history. Traumas like those of Mrs Roberts, Mr McArthur or Mr and Mrs Jones, may not have been the majority experience, but they were not rare either. And those are magnified versions of experiences that *were* very common. Mrs Arlott's protest about ending up in a factory reflects real hurt as well as a vigorous rejection of a class put-down. There is a tone of disappointment in a lot of these recollections. For all these reasons it is not surprising that when we asked these parents what use they had found their education in the years since they had left school, the usual answer was, quite simply, 'none'.

In Mrs Young's eyes, 'it was only the rich that seemed to go on'. What of them? The first thing we would have to say is that the stories told by some of our Independent school parents show her to be wrong. They weren't rich as children, but rose to wealth or prestige via their schooling. Mr Andrews, for instance, was the son of a small country businessman whose family was left without resources after the father's death. He won a scholarship to a church school in the city, and was eventually placed by the school as a management trainee with the establishment company of which he is now a director.

In most cases in our Independent school sample, however, the situation was much closer to what Mrs Young had in mind. Most of these parents came from families that were already socially-established or wealthy, and most of them went to private schools, themselves. Hardly any of them left before the end of secondary school, and about half went to university or did some other full-time tertiary training. The rich did 'go on'.

Their experience of schooling was not always very different from that of their working-class contemporaries. Mr Middleton, for instance, the child of prosperous capitalists, was sent to the Christian Brothers:

> I think they were good days, looking back.
> *Can you recall how you regarded school when you were there*?
> Well I think it was a very strict upbringing. You know, you performed or you got belted. The Brothers, they didn't muck around. You know, if two or three couldn't answer their questions, it wasn't impossible for the whole class to get a belting! And you know, I think you learnt. [laughter] You had to bloody well learn . . . On the other hand, you know, I can remember well a couple of the Brothers there especially that were as tough as nails in school, in the classroom, and yet the things that they did for people were, you know, to me seemed to be quite the reverse. You know, that they were two — not two-faced — but you know how one minute they could belt the living daylights

out of somebody and the next minute they'd help him like their own son . . . I suppose that the same fellows would get belted up pretty regularly.
Were you one of them?
No, I was very fortunate. I was able to keep out of most of it.

While working-class Catholic lads were flogged on towards the Intermediate Certificate and apprenticeships or public service jobs, he was launched towards university; where, on his father's instructions, he did a Commerce degree so he could go into the family firm.

Dr Williamson (whose daughter's observations on the social networks of private schools will be quoted later), went to a much more exclusive Protestant school, as a boarder, though he found it less than impressive academically:

So I was shoved in the School House with a lot of country boys and had to make my way amongst them. I must say that if you have any potential to be a scholar it soon gets knocked out of you at boarding school . . . First of all sport takes quite a lot of the time in the afternoon, and then you are marched into the dining room and you're marched out again, allowed to mingle for five minutes and then you have to go into the prep room and do your homework. There's usually somebody up there who's no earthly use in helping you anyway, a prefect or a master . . . I remember my maths master was called up in 1942 and because there was nobody to take his place we had the Headmaster land on us, which filled us with absolute horror, because he was a frightening sort of cove and I've never been very keen on maths . . . well I just completed my education in a reasonably satisfactory way and then I matriculated at the university . . .

Mr Chandler, reflecting on the school to which he went and his son now goes, stresses the stability of basic philosophy among staff who stay for thirty or forty years:

There is therefore an in-built tradition in the school which not only applies to the kids but is very strongly transmitted by the staff . . . I think their attitude is to produce academic results which are relevant to the child, because there's not a tremendous emphasis on masters having to achieve results from a particular stream to get promotion or whatever it may be. I think there's a heavy emphasis on participation in things like sports; perhaps, depending on the headmaster current at the time, in some people's view, undue emphasis on sport. From my point of view, I'm not really concerned with sporting excellence, but with the fact that in fact an opportunity is there for every kid to play some sort of sport in whatever capability he may have. And a very

> strong emphasis on character building, basically Christian background, character building in general, and on a very wide range of extra-curricular sort of activities. Virtually any aspect that the kid's interested in, there is an opportunity to take part, and there are staff members who are prepared to supervise that and to put time into doing that.

Mr Napier, a professional who emigrated from England after the war, came from a business family and was sent to 'a very classical school':

> You could choose to go three ways in that school. You could choose to go in what they called 'classical' and that meant Greek; or 'science', in which you did Latin, science and mathematics; or 'modern', in which you did languages and probably science as well, natural science. But still it was quite a practical school. I learnt quite a lot of Latin, I was quite a Latin scholar at one time. And of course in those days you are told that you are the chosen few. You are expected to carry the world on your shoulders as a leader. You are definitely a leader of men, and if you didn't become a leader of men, then you have failed. That was what it was all about.

The women who had been to his sister schools rarely gave quite that impression of having been processed by a powerful though benign machine; their schools seem to have been more personal. For some, indeed, this was the main point. What the school mainly provided for them was the beginnings of a social network. Mrs Graves went to one of the more socially prestigious private schools in her city:

> I was a very gregarious person at school. I was always rushing about having a terrific time with my school friends but . . . .
> *That had an effect on your results*?
> Oh, I didn't ever work terribly hard.

Nevertheless she completed Matriculation and went on from this happy beginning to marry a young lawyer from the boys' private school up the road, to which his family has gone for three generations.

Other girls' private schools, however, were giving more of an academic push, and feeding their charges into the professions or fitting them out for a place in the larger world. Mrs Somerset, who went to university and entered a profession, recalls the technique:

> *What was it like at Maryknoll College*?
> I loved it. Loved every minute of it. I was lucky. I did well at school. We were a small school. We only had one class in each year. A maxi-

> mum of thirty girls per year. Our teachers were old — very old and very strict. And very good . . . Say we went into history. Right. We all had to get out our history books and of course the teacher knew every girl in the school and we knew every girl in the school from this size [gesturing — knee-high] to Leaving. We knew everybody because there was, you know, only 200 or 300 of us. And she'd say 'Right Janey, you start reading'. So Janey would have to stand up and read and we would all have to follow and Mary would follow and so on and so on say for twenty minutes. She'd say 'Right, close your books. Catherine, tell me about what you've just read'. And we would have to stand up and tell it back. Maths was probably the weakest link at that school. Very strong in French, German, English, Ancient History. They always got the four tops. Always.

Obviously enough, this was a very different collective experience of schooling from that recalled by working-class parents. It was markedly less alienating, less violent, and involved fewer oppressive experiences with teachers. There was a much closer correspondence of purposes and manners between the ruling-class homes and schools. And there is a stark difference in the practices surrounding school leaving. In working-class milieux, leaving at 14 or 15 was the normal course of events. To someone like Mrs Somerset, going to university was. Even Mrs Graves rushed about having a terrific time with her school friends right up to Matric. The academic pathways of the school were familiar here, in a way they weren't for workers' children, even for Mrs Crisp. And for most of the Independent-school parents in our study, their own schooling has been of very practical use — getting them into their professions or helping to contract the right kind of marriage.

We have spent some time discussing events of thirty or forty years ago because we think this historical dimension is largely ignored in discussion of contemporary schooling, and does matter. Those experiences form legacies and feed into traditions to which parents and children in the present must respond. They may do this in quite diverse ways, as Mr and Mrs Owens show. But however it is done, the one thing people cannot do is walk away from their histories, be they good or ill.

TRANSACTIONS AND RELATIONS

At the simplest level, home and school are linked by the encounters that family members have with the school's staff. The most important of these, of course, are the daily transactions of the pupil herself. This is the main source of information about the school for other family members, from discussions in the kitchen, over dinner, or around the TV set. Nevertheless there are transactions, formal and informal, which involve other family members.

Some opportunities for this are provided formally. The school is surrounded by a small swarm of auxiliary institutions, most designed to tap the voluntary labour or the pockets of parents — Mother's Clubs, Parents' and Citizens' associations (P & C), working bees, and so on. Some events are intended to inform and involve them with the children's progress — parent/teacher nights, sports days, speech days. And there are bodies with a somewhat wider reach, like Old Boys' and Old Girls' associations, which hardly exist in working-class comprehensives but can be quite important fund-raisers for the Independent schools.

A good deal of the contact, however, is quite informal. A parent may ring up a teacher or principal about a problem of discipline or academic work. Conversely a parent might get summoned for consultation about a delinquency, as Mrs Siemens was when her son Carl was discovered to have artistically carved graffiti in his desk — though this seems to have been more for psychological effect than for mutual information, as the principal rubbed it in to Carl how upsetting this was for her. In the Independent schools, many of the fathers get most of their contact with teachers on the touchlines of football grounds, watching their sons play in the school teams that the teachers coach. Mothers working in the school canteen will talk with teachers and other staff in the course of the day. And at times a teacher may appear at a local organization that parents are members of — a club dinner, or a Sunday School prizegiving.

Transactions, then, are very diverse; but they are far from random. For instance, there are strong conventions about who does what. Work on canteens, and other routine voluntary jobs around infants' and primary schools, are almost entirely done by married women. Most of the contact with school about the kids' academic work is undertaken by their mothers; fathers are more likely to be called in on big decisions or on discipline. Major fundraising committees are likely to be run by men; and fathers who can't find the time for checking homework will often turn out to watch their sons play in school teams.

Links between Independent schools and their families seem to be as strong at secondary level as at primary. Indeed the fathers seem to get more involved as the children move further from infancy and the investment in their education comes closer to pay-off. By contrast, working-class families often tend to lose contact in the transition to high school. Often this is about the point where parents' ability to help with homework ends. Almost always it means a shift from a small institution, the neighbourhood primary school, to a much larger one further away, with a staff of subject specialists and a different way of organizing teaching. We came across a good many parents who had been active in supporting their primary school, but whose involvement fell away almost to nothing after the shift. To the high school staff, the parents therefore appeared to lack interest in their kids' education — one of the commonest complaints we heard in these schools.

Behind the flux of daily transactions, then, we can see more enduring relations that are realized through them. One is a division of labour between parents in child-rearing, in which women are defined as having primary responsibility for child care, which carries over to their relation to the other major child-rearing institution, the school. Both the organization of families (for example, where husband has a job and wife doesn't) and the practices of schools (for example, setting up 'Mothers' Clubs') sustain this sexual division of labour. It naturally becomes important to the kids, most of whom, boys and girls alike, see their mothers as the parent to take school troubles to in the first instance. On their side, married women usually see it as important to be home when the kids get back from school and this affects the kinds of jobs they look for.

There is also a class pattern of involvement and exclusion. Working-class parents who drop out of involvement with their kids' schooling after the transition to high school have rarely lost interest; it is simply that the school is organized in a way that makes that interest difficult to put into practice. As the research went on, we became very familiar with stories told us by parents of the ways they had been frozen out: promises of action not followed up, phone calls not returned, principals retreating behind bureaucratic rules, insinuations of ignorance and uncouthness, and so on. It is hard to miss the parallel with the experience of their own schooling. There were also many stories of helpful teachers and responsive principals, but it is abundantly clear that working-class families face large difficulties in building a relationship with the high school.

Not that processes of exclusion are unknown in the Independent schools. Indeed quite a complex and subtle dialogue can go on between the school and families of different backgrounds. The relationship between St Margaret's College and the Paton family — mother an Old Girl, father a high-ranking professional, both university-trained and Presbyterians — is noticeably closer and more involving than the relationship between St Margaret's and the Carpenters, who are equally rich but whose money comes from business, who went to state schools and have no university training, and who are members of an unfashionable Baptist church. Nevertheless it is broadly true that the Independent schools are much more open to parents' approaches (for reasons we will explore in Chapter Four); and that the parents here find it easier to include the kids' schooling as an integral part of the families' collective practices.

HOW FAMILIES AND SCHOOLS THINK ABOUT EACH OTHER

The pleasures of mutual ignorance

Except for those few cases where they are really activists in the life of the school — office-holders in the P&C, for instance — parents have rather limited chances to learn about what goes on inside classrooms, staffrooms, or playgrounds. Their kids may tell them a lot or a little. If a lot, it is of course filtered by what the kids think is fit for their parents' ears. If a little, most parents have only infrequent contacts with teachers, casual discussion with other parents or kids in the neighbourhood, stories told by siblings, and school reports, to fill out the picture.

The schools we studied had an institution designed to overcome this problem, the parent/teacher night, where all the teachers taking a given grade stay back one evening to talk to the parents. In some places this means parents actually queuing up in front of teachers sitting behind tables for a few minutes' quick consultation, while the teacher flips through her book of marks and the rest of the queue breathes down their necks. Opinion is almost universal, on both sides, that this exercise is of little use as an exchange of information. To the parents, the time is far too short; to the teachers, the parents they really want to see are the ones who never come. Yet there is a steady roll-up. Mrs McArthur suggests the main reason:

> It wouldn't matter if you sat there and talked about flying saucers. It's

of no consequence to the children what you talk about, but it seems to give them confidence . . . Each time I come home, I get the quiz: 'What did the teacher say?' 'What did this one say?' Well you can't tell the children what the teacher said, but it's of no importance . . . you can see an improvement in their work and in their attitude. Particularly if you hit a teacher you can communicate well with. Some teachers couldn't be bothered.

It's a way for parents to show they care; and that really is crucial in everybody's thinking about schools.

Teachers have even less chance to learn about homes than parents do about classrooms. Apart from very thin indications that might be got from parent/teacher nights, or school record cards (for example, parents' occupations, usually out of date), or staffroom conversation, the only way an ordinary teacher has of learning is if the pupil talks about her family in class or in a private consultation. Most kids don't do that — especially working-class kids who are very wary of saying anything that might make them vulnerable. There are a few teachers who make it their business to find these things out, and put a lot of energy into it. But most secondary teachers effectively know nothing about their pupils' families.

Most people in the education business, including most of the teachers and parents we talked to, would regard this state of mutual ignorance as a bad thing. There are, however, some good reasons for it. School and home do exchange enough information for routine purposes — bearing in mind that secondary schooling is a strongly institutionalized activity, and so are many aspects of parenting. Through report cards, marks on exercises, and so on, the school provides the family with enough information to explain its placement and treatment of the child. Through attendance notes, phone calls and so on, parents provide the school with information about medical events, housing crises, or other things that might disrupt attendance.

To go beyond this level would require expending energy beyond what is normally necessary. And there are some more definite reasons why it isn't usually expended. Working-class parents normally aren't very familiar with the way the high school works, and aren't very confident about approaching it or laying demands on it. Nor does the school as an institution do much to overcome their reservations, as we have seen.

The parents at Independent schools normally know more about what goes on inside them than the parents at working-class comprehensives. Even here, however, there are reasons for a degree of mutual ignorance. There are things such families do not care to have known, notably about their financial affairs. While things are going swimmingly on the academic front, as they usually do in these schools, there is no particular reason for the teachers to wonder about the kids' 'backgrounds'. The very success of the teaching encourages parents to think of teachers as professional experts who can be left on their own to perform their craft. As Mrs Andrews put it,

> You don't go to the doctor unless you've got a problem; why go to the teacher unless you've got one?

On the teachers' side, in the working-class comprehensives things are a little more complex; for here academic work normally isn't going swimmingly, and 'home background' is almost universally thought to be a reason why. It would seem that teachers have a strong reason to find out a lot about the families of the kids they work with. But this would be to reckon without the actual conditions of their work. High schools mix pupils and teachers in proportions of about 13 to 1, which seems almost intimate until one thinks about the way the teachers' work is organized. Between 100 and 150 heads go past in an ordinary working day, and the teacher confronts each new batch alone. Faced with a procession of classes and the turbulence that is normal in these schools, the teacher's first, and continuing, problem is survival as a teacher. Len Johnson, one of the staff at Greenway High, describes a common solution:

> The teacher considers that his job is done in the classroom, and then they nick off home. And you really can't blame them . . . You know, that's what it boils down to. Practicality is the whole thing. And there's a lot of people who've been around long enough to know that you don't take on more than you ought to.

It would indeed be crazy, as things are now, for most high school teachers to try to get close to the family circumstances of even half the kids they deal with. It would be physically and emotionally overwhelming, and would disrupt many of their own survival strategies. To make it possible would require major changes of the circumstances in which the job is done.

Views across the school fence

The fact that parents and teachers normally don't know very much about each other is, of course, no bar to their having strong opinions.

The working-class parents' opinions of teachers are, on the whole, not very flattering. Rarely hostile across the board, they are often sharply critical of particular teachers, and see the teaching force as a pretty thorough mixture of good and bad eggs. Mr Grey's comments, if a little acidly expressed, are absolutely typical as to content:

> The two headmasters I speak of have always said it's the kids. It's never the teachers. Well I'm afraid to say it's only this year that I had the same problem, I've had it for a couple of years, with the younger son. And the headmaster still won't own up. Because the young bloke's picked up something fantastic this year; and it was his previous teacher that was the trouble with Mark as well. It was the teacher he had, that wasn't interested. Was only interested in one thing: money. I just had the same trouble with George: the teacher just never liked George for a start. He had it in for George, and that was it. The headmaster, definitely no. He swore black and blue in front of me, and he run this teacher down, in front of me. When I walked out of there, he run down my son, and backed the teacher up . . . As far as I'm concerned, he's no good . . . He's got a teacher that's interested in him this year. Not only is he interested, but he's also a teacher to lift a kid. The one I'm talking about was a young teacher, just come out of — what do you call it? — Advanced Education, he's just taken it on. As far as he's concerned, he's God, and that's it.

Mr Grey, be it noted, praises the teacher who *is* interested in his son and able to 'lift' him. Elsewhere in the interview he praises principals and teachers who will 'go out of their way' for a kid. Mr Poulos, whose son is doing much worse at school than Mark Grey, describes such a teacher in more detail:

> Bill has been going to this school now since he was 13. And I've had one interview with his school teacher. And I'd say he's one of the most dedicated . . . He's the one school teacher who has bothered to call me in to discuss with him the problems of Bill: what he's got, what he hasn't got, why he's so far behind. And I explained to him why. Actually Bill was twelve months behind the other kids, and he's caught up now . . . Even now Mr Riley is the only teacher who will stay back with students, I've never seen anything like it. To stay back with two or three students and try to help them on their weak subject . . .
> *And did that help Bill?*
> It helped him a hell of a lot. He's caught up. I was real pleased with that teacher. But, any other teachers in the school, I don't think they could give a hoot. They just put their lessons forward; and if the kids

> listen, they listen; and if they don't, well, bad luck Charlie, you missed out, and it won't be repeated again.

That's not a fair summary of the attitudes of the teaching force at Rockwell High, but it is obvious how typical survival strategies on the part of teachers could produce that impression on a critical parent. In some cases it comes, literally, closer to home. Mr and Mrs Roberts call a particular kind of teacher 'screamers' because they can hear them screaming at their classes in the school just across the road.

On their side, teachers make quite similar distinctions about homes. They usually see 'good' homes as ones where the parents are interested in the kids, and keep them clean and well-dressed; 'bad' homes as ones where the kids are left to their own devices while mothers have jobs or both parents go boozing at the club, homes which don't support the school's authority and generally are slack and disreputable. The 'bad' home is much the clearer image. Some teachers see the whole neighbourhood in which they are working in these terms, as a cultural desert populated by beer-swilling Dads and mindless Mums. Others don't have such negative overall views, but reach for this category to explain the indiscipline, poor academic performance, or sloppiness of particular kids:

> Well, he's untidy, slightly untidy, unkempt hair, not brushed every day, shirt hangs out sometimes. His teeth, I don't know whether it's a fair indicator, but his teeth don't look well looked after, and perhaps at home it's not something that's pursued, or money spent on them to get them fixed. So I think he probably comes from a poor background, his parents haven't spent much time with him, just haven't encouraged him in areas that we would encourage children.
>
> (Leo Wilson, Greenway High)

Given their lack of concrete knowledge about the homes, it seems likely that these views are in large measure a response to the problems of school life. In short, they are imaginary, but they have a point — which is, again, survival as a teacher: keeping discipline, and getting the kids to learn. Teachers collectively construct images of families that would either help or hinder these tasks, and load them up with quite a lot of responsibility for what happens in the school. On the parents' side, the images of good and bad teachers are also partly imaginary — as is clear from the absolute contradictions that often occurred in different parents' descriptions of the same teacher. Normally their judgments were based on tiny samples of the teacher's behaviour, sometimes just one incident. We suspect they often have more to do with the way the parents are trying to make sense of schooling generally than with the work of the particular teacher.

It is striking, in fact, how rarely working-class parents think of teachers *as workers* — that is, think of what they are doing in terms of the whole pattern of their job and its strains and opportunities, the character of their workplace, its authority relations, and the teachers' economic and industrial problems. In some ways parents seem to perceive teaching more on the model of being a parent than on being a worker. Hence the indignation that can arise when teachers go by the regulations, and don't seem to care about their particular child.

Ruling-class parents do tend to see teachers as workers — from the perspective of employers, which of course many of them are. They don't hire the teachers personally, but they can, if sufficiently dissatisfied with their performance, sometimes cause them to be fired. Their picture of teachers, then, is much more that of technical specialists who are evaluated according to the results they produce in their area of expertise. They usually have a favourable opinion of their abilities, on the assumption that if they aren't good, they won't last. Parents at Independent schools generally think their teaching force is superior to that of the state schools; this is often a reason they give for choosing a private school.

The respective images of parents and teachers are much less strongly drawn at the Independent schools than at the state schools. The two do see more of each other, and so individual characteristics stand out more than group images. No parent at Greenway High could do what quite a number of Independent-school parents did in our interviews — run through the full list of their child's teachers and comment on the strengths and weaknesses of each one. Their interactions, though sometimes abrasive, usually have more of the flavour of consultations between fellow-professionals than negotiations between sharply distinct groups.

Models of education

Even in the most harmonious school, neither parents nor teachers are agreed on educational philosophies. The kids' schooling goes on in the context of an unresolved debate about its purposes and methods; and it is important to see the relationships between home and school in this larger context.

Eighty years into 'the century of the child', none of the working-class parents we interviewed held recognizably child-centred views of education.[8] Most of them clearly supported firm discipline, teacher-centred pedagogy, and job-oriented curricula.

Why is this? One reason is their lack of sources of information about anything else. They never see books about education. Accounts of schooling in the mass media (for instance, commercial TV and mass-circulation papers) rarely get beyond drugs, sex, and the general awfulness of modern youth. The mass organizations of the working class, the unions and the Labor Party, rarely give a clear lead about it. (It has been NSW Labor Party policy for years to abolish selective schools, a minor but obvious reform; the Labor Premier has promised not to do it.) The parents' own experience of schooling was, for the most part, authoritarian and teacher-centred, if not particularly vocational.

Yet that schooling, as we have seen, failed them. Why aren't they looking for alternatives? By and large they are — but alternatives as *they* see them, not as academics (or even teachers) do. Education is still defined as the transmission of an accepted body of knowledge, in every context they know about. The parent who is bitterly regretful in retrospect about having dropped out of school at thirteen, is still very likely to blame him or herself, not the school as an institution. 'The alternative', then, is not something different in quality but more of the same — maybe four or five years more — to supply the knowledge that the last generation missed out on. Thus, in a good many families, a strong push from the parents for the kids to stay on regardless of the trouble they run into.

There is another important reason. Education is also 'socialization', in the old, full sense of making the asocial infant a fully social being. This means, among other things, learning to do what you're told, hold yourself in check, accept the necessity to do things you don't want to do. It also means respecting legitimate authority, deferring to those who are older and wiser than you are, keeping in your proper place. All this was well learnt, often at the end of a cane, by the older generation from their elders. It was, in many respects, a survival skill; and it has been particularly important to those of our families who (like the Joneses) had a long hard haul to establish themselves in modest comfort and security. They have a name for this kind of learning: 'discipline'.

The 'breakdown of discipline' is not a media invention. It is real, and it is experienced by many of these families as their children move through adolescence. Connected with changes in youth employment and with the growth of 'youth culture' (which we will explore in Chapter Four), it is also connected with changes in the schools. For progressive educational reforms have had an impact there: the kids are freer, the schools livelier, less orderly and more creative, than they ever were in the past. Many parents approve of this, as meaning more pleasant and humane learning environments than what they had. Many also see it (and sometimes these views overlap) as a collapse of discipline. They see kids answering back to teachers, classes in uproar, apparently unplanned curricula, no measurable learning; and they are worried. Some see it reacting back on the family and creating discipline problems there. If this is what new ideas in education mean, they could do with less of them.

So there is a constituency here for the 'New Right' in education, and the demand for more traditional pedagogy is one reason for the shift to private schools — in working-class areas, mainly Catholic schools — in recent statistics. (There are other reasons, such as federal government funding policies.) Yet there are serious obstacles in the path of conservatism. The 'back to basics' movement can't deliver jobs, which are in shorter supply than basic skills — and youth unemployment is the background to a lot of what is going on in high schools now. A shift to heavier-handed discipline is a recipe for more conflict, not stabler authority, in the schools.

On the other hand it is difficult to see a constituency for progressive reforms, at least in the form that educational progressivism has taken in the past. By and large it has done little for working-class parents. Wanting the best for their kids, and supporting the expansion of schooling, they accepted reforms like new primary curricula (the 'new maths'), and comprehensive secondary school organization, largely because the professionals said they were best. The increased turbulence in the schools has increasingly called that expertise into question. There remains a good deal of conditional respect for teacher's knowledge, and a fund of goodwill towards schools in general; but we think educators will only be able to draw on that fund by constructing a new kind of relationship with the parents.

The debate about philosophies in and around Independent schools has had a rather different cast. Here the issues revolve around methods of modernization. Some of these schools have long kept a very traditional pedagogy; and this is subject to criticism from two directions — on grounds of liberalism, and on grounds of efficiency. Because principals in these schools have greater personal authority, and because they can mostly take for granted things for which working-class schools must struggle (notably the pupils' attachment to academic learning), there is considerably more room for manoeuvre. The variety of educational theory and teaching practice is probably greater among Independent schools than in the very much larger state system.

The defining fact about private schools is that parents who don't like what a principal is doing can walk away from that school and pick another. So the debate about models of education in this context turns into the working of an educational market, in which there is a complex interaction of consumer preferences with marketers' strategies. We will pick up the debate about modernization when we come to analyze this market in detail in Chapter Four.

At a very general level, a distinction can be drawn between valuing education for what it does to you and for what it does for you. The latter is the instrumental approach, and in a good deal of the literature is supposed to characterize working-class families' approaches to education. It is true that schooling is instrumentally important to them — as a means of avoiding downward mobility especially — though it is hard to see this is any more marked than the instrumentalism of ruling-class families who use schooling to place children in the right jobs and the right social circles.

What seems to us to be missing from most accounts of the matter is the widespread, non-instrumental, respect for education that is also present among working-class families. The teachers who see working-class suburbs as cultural deserts are entirely wrong in this sense. It is difficult for a regard for learning and knowledge to flower there, given the character of the mass media and the fact that adult education reaches less than one adult in twenty in the population as a whole. But there is a vital possibility and resource nevertheless.

WHERE DO FAMILIES COME FROM?

The main conclusion of modern research on the family has been that families are not the closed, self-contained units, the 'haven in a heartless world', they are often supposed to be. On the contrary, they are shaped in quite fundamental ways by larger social structures, and some of these ways are highly relevant to education. Anyone wanting to understand the social context of schooling must try to understand how the students' families come to be the way they are. In this section we will explore three aspects of social structure that clearly have important effects: the organization of work, the organization of cities, and relations between the sexes.

The organization of work

Our sample from Independent schools was evenly divided between families where the father was a manager and those where he was a professional. The kind of work, and the social relationships in which it is done, differ in the two cases.

Consider Mr Walker, the youthful general manager of a company in an expanding high-technology industry, and a high flyer by anyone's standards. He thinks his son Ian is 'too conservative', and by that he doesn't mean right-wing so much as conformist, inclined to wait at a door until other people have gone through it. In Mr Walker's world, that is a good way to get trampled.

> The world's not going to stand still for traditional ways any more, not in my business anyway. We don't sell any product we sold five years ago, they're all gone. In five years' time we won't sell any product we sell today . . . They're going to be lighter, or faster, or quicker, or cheaper or something. And our people can't think the same way, they can't be doing what they did five years ago.

Certainly Mr Walker is not going to get left behind in the rush. He works like a demon — probably puts in a 90-hour week — and makes sure his second-echelon managers also work their guts out. If they don't shape up, he fires them.

As the executive head of the firm, he rarely deals directly with the workers who actually make his products. The people he has most contact with are those who themselves 'head up' a group — personnel manager, finance manager, product managers, and so on. His very diverse workload still embraces industrial relations — keeping *au fait* with the state of the labour market and the attitudes of workers, reorganizing salaries and bonus schemes to maximize the sales staff's performance, negotiating with unions and devising ways of keeping them out of his industry — as well as a host of other problems such as planning, training staff, dealing with other companies, and keeping up with new technology. He has to be, and is, energetic, ruthless, profit-conscious, and extremely well-informed.

A work situation like that plainly has important consequences for the family. First, it means wealth — big salaries, fringe benefits, and a chance to share in profits through bonuses and share options. That enables the family to live in an affluent suburb and buy a private school education. Second, it means a massive absorption of the husband in his work. Not all managers are as fanatical about work as Mr Walker, but it isn't uncommon. In the life cycle of a successful business family, the middle childhood and adolescence of the kids is likely to coincide with a key phase in the father's career, when he is taking off for the top levels and the demands are particularly strong. This forces a sharp division of labour between the husband and the wife, who in all the business families we met was wholly responsible for running the house (sometimes hiring a cleaning woman to help), had much closer contact with the children, and was responsible for monitoring events at school. Father was usually called in only when there was a big decision to be made or big trouble had arisen.

What is not so easy to understand is the very marked gap between the working lives of men like Mr Walker and the kind of education they buy for their children. The conditions he describes — the constant turnover of products, the pressure for change, the urgency of keeping ahead — are, more or less, the general conditions of existence in capitalist industry when there is any significant competition. And it is a long way indeed from the Queen-and-Country conservatism of schools in which the 'A' form still does Latin, where the Cadet Corps or Divine Service are *de rigueur*, where boys and girls are taught proper pronunciation and Christian responsibility, while their fathers are busy axing sales managers who don't reach their growth targets. The tension here may be one reason why progressive educational ideas can sometimes get a grip in this intensely conservative milieu, as a way of modernizing its schools.

This gap is very much less for families where the fathers are professionals: barrister, surgeon, physician, dentist and professor are among those in our sample. Here the job itself is organized around a body of knowledge, and entry to it is via higher education; it is more closely integrated with schooling from the start. The business of controlling other people that looms so large in managers' working lives is here reduced to small dimensions. Where Mr Walker has a couple of thousand subordinates, a barrister who is a father at the same school, and who in point of wealth and influence would certainly be his equal, employs exactly half a typist.

Professional practice also means greater control over working hours, so there is more scope for a different division of labour in the household. Fathers may become more involved with their kids' schooling and in family life. But the contrast should not be overdrawn. The work demands of setting up a practice can also be heavy (for example honorary work by doctors in hospitals). When professional men are drawn into the organizational side of ruling-class life, holding office in professional associations, being active in Rotary or the Liberal Party, becoming hospital administrators, joining the boards of companies, or taking on a string of consultancies, their schedules too can begin to look like Mr Walker's.

Working-class families are working-class mainly because they stand on the other side of the great divide in class structure, the labour market. Others hire; they are hired. The importance of dependence on a wage can hardly be over-estimated. It immediately bars these families from the suburbs and schools of the rich, for they have no way of accumulating wealth; at best, and after a good many years, they may own the house they live in. In good times, wage-earning families may do nicely, brick will replace fibro and motorboats and caravans will appear in backyards. They still have no way of foreseeing or preventing a recession that leads to retrenchment, an industrial accident that puts the breadwinner out of commission, a change in technology that obliterates jobs and skills. We have seen the effects of all these events in our interviews.

One wage, especially if it is a labourer's or factory worker's wage, is often not enough. For a family with children to bring up, it is likely to mean marginal poverty. So most of the working-class mothers we interviewed have jobs; indeed some are the main earners for the household. There is nothing new about working-class women having jobs. What is new is large numbers of them having jobs while they also have children at school. They are conscious of this being different from what their mothers did, and some worry a good deal about its possible bad effects on the children, especially when they had to work, for instance to buy a block to build a house on, when the kids were still young.

Nevertheless, having their own source of income has generally strengthened their position within the family. Some working-class families, like the business families, are organized around the father (though not around the father's *career*, since careers hardly exist in their jobs). But a good many are not: they are organized around the wife, or as an alliance of equals. Some have ceased to function much as a unit, and people have withdrawn into separate spheres, staying together mainly for two reasons — to complete the children's education, and because suburbs like Rockwell and Greenway have only one kind of house, the family bungalow, and no couple there can afford to buy or rent two of them.

The workplaces where the working-class parents in our sample earn their keep are very diverse: a boatyard, a railway repair shop, a hospital, a heating plant, a local doctor's surgery (as a cleaner), a local school (as a teacher's aide), new building sites (as a tiler), the windows of city office blocks (as a cleaner), and a considerable number of factories. Most of the jobs are not very skilled, or involve skills that have been learned on the job; one of the greatest assets for workers in the labour market is versatility. Even those men who have a trade ticket have often found themselves doing a quite different job — a butcher who wound up as a window-dresser, a railwayman who found himself in a laundry. Others have started with one trade skill and have diversified by building on it — such as Mr McDonough, an immigrant toolmaker who had gone for a year to Germany to extend his skills on the most modern equipment.

The pride that tradespeople take in their skills, and that less qualified workers also take in being on top of a job they have taught themselves, and that all take in their versatility, creates a basis for a view of knowledge that in some respects competes with the school's. In discussions of work and schooling, the importance of learnt-on-the-job, practical knowledge was often stressed as what was *really* useful. Being 'good with the hands' could be valued as much as being 'good with the head'. It would be going too far to suggest this amounts to a distinct ideology of education; but it is at least a different way of looking at knowledge, firmly rooted in their work experience.

However, workplaces aren't just places where a job of work is done. They are also places where there is authority and control. We saw the top end of this with Mr Walker; at the lower levels are foremen and leading hands. A good many of the working-class fathers in our study, and some of the mothers, have held such positions — or knocked them back.

In the structure of control in the workplace, the foreman is, classically, the meat in the sandwich: exposed to pressure from workers and management, transmitting pressure both ways, able to satisfy neither. Some of our parents who had done it found the demands for higher production and lower costs, and the resentment of their workmates, extremely stressful. Others, who had refused promotion, did so because they knew it would drive a wedge between them and their friends. In thinking about authority structures in working-class schools, it is worth remembering that a lot of the kids are aware of tensions about authority in their parents' working lives. And some of them get a pretty clear message that to climb a hierarchy means to break ties and betray loyalties.

In the absence of an aggressive labour movement, the alternative to climbing the hierarchy at work is to accept subordination. Some people can wriggle sideways, as Mr Arlott has done by becoming a sub-contractor in a service industry:

> The subcontract's better, 'cause when you subcontract, you've got no starting time, no finishing time. If you want to sit down for a smoke-oh for twenty minutes there's nobody telling you to get up and go back to work.

But that's a very private solution, and in current economic circumstances many people (including his wife) are glad to get any kind of job. Mrs Arlott was sacked a year ago by the American-owned company where she was a machine operator. She has only just found a new job — as a packer, on lower pay, with the same firm. On our screening questionnaire she ticked the answer that said she thought her present job was a good one. Why?

> It's a job.

And that message, too, feeds into the kids' schooling.

Space and cities

We talked with all the parents in their homes, and perhaps nothing in the study was so immediately striking as the differences between them. Almost all of our working-class families lived in two or three-bedroom bungalows on quarter-acre suburban blocks. Some houses had worn lino on the floors, sparse and threadbare furnishing, peeling paintwork. Others were modestly affluent, with shag-pile carpets, a bar or a TV den with a wall unit. But all were small and basic by comparison with the homes of our ruling-class parents. Here homes ranged from the discreetly comfortable in the more expensive suburbs, to sumptuous establishments in the foothills, on the harbour, or by the ocean.

The spatial arrangement of the city is itself an important form of social organization. How people organize their domestic life and their leisure partly depends on where they live. And where they live, in turn, depends both on the resources they personally command,

and the way the city has been constructed so as to produce class separation.

Some of the working-class families in our study told us how they came to their present suburb:

> We were offered this house and it was the final offer.
>
> Rockwell: where's Rockwell? No-one's ever heard of it! Back of beyond.
>
> You are on a Housing Authority list. When Rockwell was offered it sounded like an improvement. But the reality was unbelievable — like the last frontier or the end of the earth.

The second comment expresses the dilemma of people who held to the Australian dream of owning your own home. It was an improvement on landlords; but the reality on offer has often meant severe sacrifices, both economic and social. Isolation and lack of services in new suburbs have particularly affected the women and children. Mrs Grey looks back:

> When we first came here it was terrible. We've been here twelve and a half years. It was nothing — absolutely nothing. We'd been living with Mum, we had Mark — he was two when we moved here. You get taken out of a house full of people, and you just get stuck here, with nothing: no 'phone, no transport, nothing. And your husband goes off all day and you're just left. It's terrible. Troubles — anyone hurt themselves, you had to sort of ask the milkman and baker, 'would you go for help?' It was shocking.

As this suggests, the arrangement of space organizes gender as well as class. 'Your husband goes off all day and you're just left'. The suburban home is built for a couple and two or three children. It involves the daily separation, not only of generations, but also of men and women, and the women feel it most.

Most of our working-class families lived in suburbs built since the war, and a good many were among the pioneers: as a boy Mr Roberts went rabbit-trapping in the paddocks that are now Rockwell. For many families, these new suburbs represented a real improvement over decaying industrial suburbs in the inner city, and their opinions of their environment are warmer than the ones we have just quoted. But one feature was common — the choices were, and are, painfully limited. Why do they stay here?

> It's the only place we can afford.

There were other costs. When the Greys first moved to Rockwell,

Mr Grey left home at 5.30 each morning to travel, by bus and train, to work. Mrs Siemens currently spends four hours a day travelling to and from her job in a factory. There is enormous pressure, therefore, to go into debt to buy cars, and two-job families really need to be two-car families. The way the postwar suburbs were built made it almost impossible to live a normal life without cars. At the same time, the fact that people had cars made it possible for developers and governments to build suburbs virtually without facilities or the setting for a communal life. For any kind of social life outside the home and garden — to go to clubs, swimming pools, films, or discos — you have to drive out of Rockwell and Greenway.

The energy and creativity with which working-class families have tackled such bleak conditions is one of the most consistent and notable facts to come out of this study. We spoke at the beginning of the chapter about the Joneses and their loving construction of their own house, garden, and rockery. They are not in the least exceptional. We are thinking of gardens which were wonders of plumbing, stonework and horticultural science; of backyard workshops which turn out motor boats, go-karts and even racing cars; of a family who built their own theaterette, complete with electrically-operated curtain, theatre organ, dimming lights, and seats salvaged from an old cinema; of a failed attempt to set up a small farm, and successful construction of a family holiday house (ironically called 'the shack' after ten years' steady work on it).

Nor is this effort confined to the adults and their concerns. Bill Poulos likes surfing but he lives nearly 40 miles from the beach. So he has organized a weekend roster with his mates, to wake each other at 4 a.m., walk several miles to the station, catch the fast 'milk train' to the city, change to a bus, and at last put their boards in the surf. These are just a few of the countless ways in which working people have faced the constraints of their situations and conjured up resources to make a cultural world.

Yet it is dangerous to romanticize these responses; we must recognize the real deprivation on which they are based, and the fact that the situation also leads, at the same time, to abrasive neighbourhood relationships, hostility, and even violence. Mrs Grey, again, puts it very clearly:

> It's — I find it's not the area, it's the people. What happened, when we all came here, we were all very lonely, I think, and we all got very involved with each other. Too involved. A lot of children's fights, and parents then got fighting. We all had problems. Today, there's still

> problems with children. If you correct a child for doing something, you get a mouthful of lip, four-letter words etc. etc. You know damn well it's no use going to the parent, 'cause the parent wouldn't believe you anyway. So you sort of think 'Well, what's the use of correcting the child. Let him wreck the place!' We've had a lot of trouble with vandals, children and kids, and we had break-and-entries. And we had a steel bar thrown through this window the night of the elections — glass right through here, it came with such force it's a wonder it didn't go through the wall. Could've killed someone sitting on the lounge. It's unbelievable. And this is not the first time. We've had eggs thrown, plants ripped out, money taken. We had a cocky in a cage taken.

Some other mothers sharpen the point. They think it is dangerous to go out on their own streets at night because of the local toughs, have been hassled themselves, and won't let their kids — especially their daughters — go out alone after dark.

That isn't a problem where Valerie Grainger, a pupil at St Helen's College, lives. However, she has others. 'I'd rather live at Vaucluse or Hunter's Hill', she lamented, 'because more people live there'. At least she knows the social facts of life. In Sydney the wealthy and the powerful outlay the lifetime earnings of two or three of our working-class families to cluster around the glittering harbour and on the green ridges along the North Shore Line. In Adelaide prosperity has taken up the Hills slopes, and fills pockets around the parklands and along the shore.

The relationship between ruling-class families and the city isn't just a matter of where they cluster, it is also a matter of their ability to *choose* where to go. Unlike the couples who land in Rockwell or Greenway because that literally is all they can afford, these families can take into account proximity to work; kin, friends and leisure interests; trees and gardens; quiet, pollution-free surroundings; and the choice of schools available for their children. The balance between these considerations may change from time to time. The Balfours, to take just one example, had moved three times in the past five years — from a large suburban home near Mr Balfour's professional practice, to a very large establishment (with sauna and tiled pool) in Sydney's Eastern Suburbs, to a smaller but exquisite apartment overlooking the Harbour. Whatever the current preference, the Balfours (and families like them) plainly have a very different relationship to the city from the Joneses, the Pouloses, and the Greys.

When cities segregate people in their 'private' lives, they also segregate their schooling. While the comprehensive school was proposed as a means of social integration through common schooling, it ran up against the fact of cities segregated on class lines through the operation of the private housing market. Almost all state schools have a 'catchment' drawn from a relatively narrow band of the social spectrum; and this has ensured a large degree of class segregation in schooling, even before we take account of the Independent schools.

When the Siemens or the Greys moved to Rockwell, they moved into an Education Department zone and were automatically assigned to a particular school. What is a zone to the Department is an educational life sentence to a working-class child. That school is immovable, intractable, and unavoidable. On their side, teachers routinely talk of 'good' and 'bad' areas in which to teach. Each morning around 8, they set out in thousands in their cars for the working-class suburbs where they and the students work, and then recede like the tide around 4.

The Independent schools tend to be concentrated in the more affluent suburbs, though because a good many of them go back fifty or a hundred years their location may reflect earlier social maps of the city. (Some are embarrassingly located on what is now prime commercial land, or in decayed districts.) But access to them isn't constrained by anything like the zones of the state system. A good number of the Independent school students we interviewed travel five miles or more to school. Again we see the much greater degree of control ruling-class families have over the organization of their lives. Families like the Graingers and the Walkers can move house, if they wish, to give access to the schools — state or private — of their choice. And from any given suburb, they can decide which of a range of private schools they will employ.

Urban space, then, both reflects the degrees of power that different families have, and determines what the families can be and do. It is not often discussed in this light, but is plainly a very important element in the way families are shaped and connected with larger social structures. The same is true of the schools.

Relations between the sexes

At a number of points already we have seen the importance of relations between the sexes: the division of labour in child care, the pattern of employment, the organization of households, the reform of school organization. These points are related, and it will be useful to make them a bit more systematic. Accordingly, we will speak of them as aspects of a system of social relations structured by gender — for short, 'gender relations'.

Three points about this are vital. First, this is a *system*. It is not a question of one gender pattern in a school, and another in a family, and another in a workplace, all independent of each other. They are related: they mesh with each other to make an overall pattern, one of the most general and powerful structures in our society.

Second, the 'system' is one of male power and female subordination. The dimensions of this are as varied as gender relations themselves: male control of governments and companies, the traditional pattern of marriage, the double standard in sexual morality, discrimination in employment, the way media present women as sex objects and men as the people who matter. It is important to recognize that this persists as an overall pattern despite being reversed in particular instances. There are families in our sample, as we have mentioned, where a working mother is the main economic provider and makes the main decisions; yet girls in these households still generally learn the conventional definitions of femininity and boys are likely to learn that they really ought to rule the roost. Nevertheless in such households a tension between local reality and the larger structure is set up, which may be a force for change.

For the structure can change; that is the third point. These relationships are social, not biologically-given. What is socially constructed is subject to historical change. And it does change. Many conventional modern notions — such as the idea that men are breadwinners and women housewives, that motherhood is a vocation for women, that children are a distinct kind of people in need of special protection, and that the family is a realm of privacy shut off from the public world — are actually quite recent, products of the last three centuries or so of western history.

We are living in a period when these patterns are changing, faster perhaps than ever before. The arrival of reliable contraception, the emergence of the new feminism, and the changing pattern of women's employment, are perhaps the most obvious but far from the only signs. This is registered inside many of the families in this study — changing notions about the rights of marriage partners, about the future employment of girls, and so on.

This change is extremely uneven. There are households (though few in this study) where feminism is more-or-less common sense, and where attempts are being made to share power and re-divide labour. There are others (a good many in this study) where conventional definitions of contented motherhood and fathers' right to rule are unchallenged, and where feminism is regarded as a kind of temporary insanity. We did some interviews in households where the position of men and women actually has changed but their ideas about what is proper haven't; and in households which are split, for instance with husbands trying to reclaim an authority their wives or daughters will not concede. In others, perhaps the majority, a vague acceptance that women's place in the world is changing went along with practices that mainly reinforced the status quo.

In thinking about gender relations, then, we must be alert to tensions and contradictions within them as clues to what is presently changing or is likely to. We must also be alert to the ways they interact with other patterns of social relations — most notably class. This interaction, we are convinced, is extremely important in understanding schooling and will be a continuing theme of this book.

For instance, the puzzle raised earlier about the apparent contradiction between business work lives and the content of elite schooling is partly to be answered this way. What is needed for success in Mr Walker's world of high-powered business competition is a particular kind of *masculinity*: motivated to compete, strong in the sense of one's own abilities, able to dominate others and to face down opponents in situations of conflict. The school Mr Walker's son goes to is very effectively organized to produce that kind of character structure, even though it doesn't teach the specific techniques of modern business. We will explore the practices through which it does this in Chapter Three.

At the start of this section we suggested that families are not closed universes but places where larger structures meet and interact; and we hope to have shown at least some of the ways this is so. We do not mean to suggest that families are simply the pawns of outside forces any more than schools are. In both cases, class and gender relations create dilemmas (some insoluble), provide resources (or deny them), and suggest solutions (some of which don't work), to which the family or school must respond in its collective practice. Conversely, the practice we encounter in discussions with family members must be seen as their creative response to situations that larger forces have presented them with. 'Practice' means an active response. And 'collective' is significant too. A family may not be a sealed unit; but it is usually a closely-knit group which has an intense inner life and a reasonably stable organization. Let us now turn to the impact of this inner life on the children's upbringing and schooling.

HOW FAMILIES PRODUCE PEOPLE

In our society, the close kin in the immediate household are central in that still rather astonishing process by which, in only twenty years, innocent infants are transformed into estate agents, football fanatics, Liberal voters, and the unemployed. We do not pretend to offer a theory of the whole process, but our evidence does suggest some points about the ways social structures impinge on the formation of the person.

One of the main organizing principles of the 'nuclear family' is, quite simply, age. Its social relations constitute each member as either adult or child. In recent history this neat little structure has been complicated by the emergence of a third category, 'adolescent', and this is a fruitful source of trouble. For the state of being an adolescent (or a 'teenager') is a constantly dissolving one.

Consider, for instance, Ellen Oldcastle, a 14 year old at Rockwell High, the middle child of immigrant parents who are comfortable in the neighbourhood though a bit socially isolated. She gets on badly with her father whom she regards as an old-fashioned stick-in-the-mud, while he thinks she is cheeky and ignorant; but gets along better with her mother, a rather quiet person who has given up her job to be home for the kids. They don't allow Ellen to go out unchaperoned. However, a year ago they gave her permission to bring boyfriends home, thinking this might encourage her to mix a bit more widely.

She surprised them by finding one and sticking with him. She now sees Roy, who is an apprentice still living with his parents and a couple of years older than her, several times a week. Mr and Mrs Oldcastle think he is 'a good little worker', can't fault the family, and can't take their permission back. It's all very awkward — she's a bit young for this. Mrs Oldcastle wishes to control Ellen's sexuality and is plainly uneasy that the 'dating' rules she has laid down aren't enough. Ellen stokes the fires by publicly declaring that she doesn't believe in marriage — 'just a piece of paper' — and that people should be able just to live together if they love each other; though she keeps to the letter of her parents' laws. Her parents tend to blame

Roy for putting these ideas in her head; to Ellen herself, she has changed simply because she has grown older.

This classic teenager/parent contretemps — which has developed without the intervention of a peer group or 'youth culture' — very learly illustrates the importance, and the ambiguity, of age relationships as a social force. Ellen is not claiming the right to be a *teenager* but the right to be, in some respects, *adult*; and she neatly, almost wittily, seizes upon the opportunity her parents have given her to press this point. They, for their part, are insisting that she is still a *child*; though also, by the force of their anxiety, covertly acknowledging that she is adult, at least to the extent that she could get pregnant.

It further illustrates the amount of work that goes into negotiating age transitions, especially where they interact with gender. In many homes there is a very carefully planned relaxation of parental control over the kids' sexual life, by finely-graded steps over a number of years. Secondary schools officially treat their charges as being sexually children, though of course other students and teachers know that many of them are not. The tensions set up by covert sexuality are a fruitful source of turbulence at school.

Growing up also means going to work; and here there are complexities where age relations intersect with class. For working-class kids, with a few exceptions, the path to adulthood lies out of the school and into the workforce. Once there, the kids have a new standing in their homes, and attempts to control their sexuality rapidly taper off. For ruling-class kids, the path to adulthood lies through advanced training. Parents will tell them that it would be 'childish' to leave school at 15, and indeed few think seriously of doing so.

We often talk of the nuclear-family unit as mother, father and child, but in fact the more common situation is child*ren*. Our interviews have convinced us of the systematic importance of sibling relationships in understanding the upbringing and schooling of the kids. Brothers and sisters face their parents' regime as an interacting group, and are often treated as a unit at school.

Teachers often think about a second or third child in terms of what the older one was like to teach. Parents are well aware of this and may either worry or rejoice about the consequences. Within the family the kids define themselves, and get defined, against each other: this one is the humorist, that one has brains but can't see a joke, the other is the family idiot, etc. Older children may pioneer a relationship with education for younger ones. Thus Joanne

Carpenter got taken from her friends and sent to a private school because her brother, who was proving a behaviour problem, had already been sent to a private school for the discipline, and her parents thought they could do no less for her. We have already discussed the Owens family, where Ruth's change of plan was affecting the relationship with schooling for all the younger kids.

For all this, it is still the relationship between husband and wife that is the basis of the family's organization. We have already spoken of some of the main forms taken by this relationship, and of course there are as many detailed variations as there are marriages. What is common to all of them is that they are in principle an exclusive sexual and domestic relationship between one man and one woman. And they still by and large convey to kids growing up, that model of domestic and emotional life as the natural and proper order of things.

Arguably, this pattern has deeper significance again. For it is the lynch-pin of one of the major arguments about the fundamental question of how social structures affect human motives, and how social forces thus get 'inside' the person.[9] It is easy, on the one hand, to fall into the habit of seeing children as blank sheets on which social pressures stamp their mark; or on the other, to see children, as many parents do, as having their ultimate character virtually from the day they were born.

The account of human growth coming from the work of Freud avoids this dilemma by seizing both its horns. This approach sees social structure, in particular the organization of the family, as giving form and direction to inchoate native impulses which continue to supply the motive power. On this view the course of children's emotional life reflect the crises inevitably produced by the clash between emotional impulse and social control. A person is formed by the way those crises are resolved; and the family form 'reproduces' itself to the extent it succeeds in this lion-tamer act.

It was no part of our research plan to psychoanalyze anybody; but even at the level we were working, that kind of theory does help to make sense of some situations we encountered. One is the business families we have discussed a couple of times already, where there is a powerful, somewhat remote and strongly masculine father, and a mother entrusted with the house and childcare, who functions as the emotional centre of the household. This seems tailor-made to produce classic examples of what Freud called the 'oedipal' crisis, where love for the mother, jealousy and fear of the father, and repression of the forbidden impulses, result in the little boy's identification with the father and the beginnings of a masculinity similar to his.

We weren't observing early childhood directly, but the emotional patterns in a number of these families during the boys' adolescence looked very much like that. It is not surprising, for instance, to find that John Walker's son is strongly identified with his father; chose to go to his present school because it was where his father had gone; shares his father's affectionate but patronizing approach to women, notably his mother; reproduces most of his father's opinions, his pattern of skills at school (strong on maths and sciences) and his career plans. And it is clear that this is not just simple modelling: there are strong emotions and anxieties involved. Among other things, Ian is acutely aware of the imperfect masculinity of his body, resulting from a late onset of puberty, and partly in response to that has become a fiercely-determined footballer.

The idea of a formative clash between native impulse and the demands of social structure is also strongly suggested by the lives of some kids who are openly resisting school, whom we will discuss in the following chapter. Yet there is something missing from this general formula. Why should Ian, for all his father-identification, be slacking in the traces, not competitive enough? Why do some kids come out in open rebellion when others from apparently similar family constellations knuckle under? Especially girls, whom psychoanalytic theory notoriously has difficulty explaining.

Sartre proposed a radical solution: people *choose*, commit themselves to certain paths. Indeed we cannot help it, we are 'condemned to be free'. Formative choices in early life may be inarticulate and ill-understood but they are made nonetheless — and that making is what constructs us as individual persons. Ian is, at some very basic level, choosing not to become quite like John. We can never 'explain' those choices in the sense of predicting them; but we can sometimes understand them and sympathize with them, and we can certainly follow their consequences.

In this research we have tried to see people's lives as projects rather than as predetermined fates and to see people as active constructors of what they have become and are becoming. There is no inconsistency in recognizing that the project may be launched, and the choices made, under terrible constraints. And we have tried to spell some of these out in our discussions of class and gender.

Yet there is a danger in *this* sort of formula that social structures will seem to be inhuman and external forces contrasted with a really human realm of individual choice. Our image of person and society becomes that of a flea freely hopping around inside a cage and, though that may produce fine dramas about fleas, it isn't very helpful if our concern is to do something about the cage. A resolution of the problem, as Sartre among others came to see, can only lie in the direction of a theory of practice: for the 'cage' is composed of what people do. The situations that people like the Joneses and the Greys find themselves in are powerfully affected by the existence of people like the Walkers and the Graingers, and the way they conduct their lives. It is only by examining personal choice and motive in the context of social relations which enter into them at the most basic level, which are constitutive of individual lives, that we will get any kind of grip on the processes at work.

This has been a somewhat abstract discussion, but we thought it useful to set down these points, as we have run up against the issues repeatedly in getting to grips with what a hundred families told us. Our understanding of them has (it is very clear to us) partly depended on the progress or lack of progress we made with theoretical issues, in developing a framework for understanding the relationship between personal life and social structures.

Among other things, it has helped us to get beyond the assumption — which as we have suggested is often in people's interests to make — that family and school are separate spheres containing separate processes. 'The family' does not form a child's character and then deliver it ready-packaged to the doorstep of 'the school'. The family is what its members do, a constantly continuing and changing practice, and, as children go to and through school, that practice is reorganized around their schooling. For its part the organization of the school varies with the kinds of families in its catchment and the nature of their collective practices. It is time to look more closely at those schools.

3
Kids and their schools

WHAT IS A SCHOOL?

The first thing that struck us about the schools in this study is that they look and sound different from each other. There is a lot more noise, movement and mess in the working-class comprehensives. The kids rush, slouch, stroll and huddle around, in a mixture of uniform, part-uniform and anti-uniform clothes. At breaks, the grounds give off a tremendous babble punctuated by yells (some from the teachers), with a general air of undisciplined energy. After breaks, there is likely to be a layer of wrappers, paper bags, leaves and other junk left stirring in the breeze.

By contrast, the impression created by the Independent schools is one of effortless good order. The contrast forces itself on anyone coming from the state school system. The buildings may not be palatial but the grounds are carefully planted and cultivated and punctiliously clean. All the kids wear uniform and all the uniforms are neat. There are rarely raised voices to be heard and (apart from the junior boys) not much running in the playground at breaks. As we will show, the good order is far from 'effortless' and not at all incidental.

One of the facts that underlies this difference is that the two types of schools have a different relation to educational selection. Most of the pupils in the Independent schools move steadily through to Year 12, most of the pupils in the working-class comprehensives leave from Year 9 or Year 10. The principal of one of the latter described his charge aptly, though somewhat sadly, as being basically a junior high with a small matriculation class stuck on top.

It's important that the kids and their parents don't see it exactly this way. Heather Arlott, a very strong and lively 14 year old at Rockwell High and something of a problem for her teachers ('hell to teach' is the staffroom consensus), would actually like to be a teacher herself,

> but the work's too hard now for me.

And in her Dad's view:

> she just finds it a little bit hard to cope with . . . she does all right at school but she's not really brilliant at it.

And in her Mum's:

> She'd go to fourth form, and at the moment she's battling, and she's only in third form . . . If she found she was coping all right, she'd probably go on; but she really battled to just scrape through.

When the Arlotts think that the work gets *harder* in the upper years, what is really happening is that the school is getting *more selective*. It isn't that Heather is incapable of another year's full-time learning on top of what she knows already. It is rather that the school is institutionally presenting her, and the other people in her year, with a narrowing offer of learning resources.

This translation of *a fact about the institution* into beliefs about *the pupils' inability* to proceed beyond a certain level, is a crucial feature of working-class schooling. Schools generate a distorted picture of themselves and their clientele, which is condensed in a particular concept: 'ability'. In its most popular form it is the notion of 'brains'. If you have got 'the brains' ('the ability') you'll get on well at school; and if you haven't, you won't.

Not all working-class schools are the same, of course. Teachers commonly think of schools in terms of their 'areas': they usually like teaching in a 'good area' (prosperous, established suburbs) and avoid schools in 'rough areas'. The state schools in our sample are not generally regarded as good places to teach, and most have had a fairly high turnover of teachers. The staff tend to divide into a cadre of old hands who have settled in the school, and a changing population of young teachers on their first or second appointment, most of whom won't stay any longer than it will take to get a transfer to a 'better' school.

When they do move elsewhere, they are still with the same employer. When teachers in a private school move, they change employers, as each is a separate corporation. For all their shared curricula and teaching methods, the legal situations of the two institutions are very different. The private school is much less secure in its very existence than the state school. When a state school closes there is still a guarantee of education for its clientele and jobs for its staff. When a private school closes, a legal, economic and social entity disappears, and its staff are thrown into unemployment. Smaller private schools do collapse from time to time; and it is possible even for large and well-established ones to get into dire financial trouble and have to contemplate closure. As this may on the face of it seem peculiar for schools we are talking of as connected with a 'ruling class', and which service the wealthiest and most powerful families in the country, we make the point strongly. We will argue that the *vulnerability* of such schools, and the uncoerced nature of attendance there, is crucial for the way they operate and for the role they play in class relations.

And yet, a school is a school. Just as we were sharply aware of the differences between those in our sample, so we were always aware that we were working in the one kind of institution. The most obvious (though easily forgotten) thing about them is that they are massive concentrations of kids. There are, in a sense, two schools in every set of school buildings: the 'informal' school which is the world of the kids themselves, and the 'formal' school, the official structure, often mistakenly taken to be *the* school. The second great distinguishing characteristic of schools is that they are organized around knowledge. Schools institutionalize a distinction between those who know and those who don't.

Schools are not the only institutions which are organized around age (the family is another); nor are they unique in dealing with knowledge (the media do too). But the *combination* of relations organized around age and relations organized around knowledge is what makes a school a school and marks it off from other social institutions. Being a student and being a teacher are very distinct experiences, and schools are peculiar places. In studying them, nevertheless, we will be constantly reminded that the school is no more an island, a closed unit, than is the family. Just as getting to understand the workings of the family required us to look at the complex ways in which it is shaped by class and gender relations, so too with the school.

Our first concern will be with the problem of order and authority already broached, and we will tackle this from two sides: first looking at it from the side of the kids, considering the different kinds of relationship they have with the institution and how these relationships are produced; then looking at it from the side of the official institution. We will conclude by looking at the way in which these patterns are shaped by a central fact of secondary schooling: its organization around a competitive academic curriculum.

HOW KIDS ARE ATTACHED TO SCHOOL

Resistance

There are many ways of being a school pupil, some rather 'invisible' within the school, others very visible indeed. Perhaps the two most visible and familiar are the teachers' delight and the teachers' bane, the 'good student' and the 'troublemaker' — stock figures in the folklore of education as well as in sociologies of schooling.

These patterns certainly came through strongly in our interviews, with teachers readily able to name members of both groups, and parents and kids often making a similar distinction. For instance, Mark Grey, an 'A' stream student at Rockwell High:

> All them hoods I was talking about, you know they're in, I suppose they're in G and E classes, you know dumber, stupid. And don't care about school and that, they just waste their time. Their parents, they must just go up the club every now and then, and the pub, and neglect them a lot. Don't care about what they're going to do when they leave school, so the kids just do what they want.

Mark's spontaneous explanation of the 'hoods' draws heavily on his own family's battle for respectability and sense of being besieged, but the category itself is absolutely standard. In an utterly different context, the same kind of distinction informs the sociology of student types offered by Colleen Rossner, an 'A' stream student at Auburn College:

> . . . they're always wearing make-up and you associate them with, a sort of, rather a down group or something like that, a cheap group. I mean, they go out with Rockers or something like that . . . Also there's another group, kids that — the snobbish group, they always wear make-up. In every year, you always get the sort of snobby groups who just think they're 'It' . . .
> *Which group are you in?*
> I'm in an in-between group!
> *How would you describe that?*
> I think — more intellectual. I mean you get kids who want to work, come to work, and you know, want to work and do well . . . They can

> mix with both groups; you won't usually see the rowdy group mixing that much with the other group.

So these patterns do have some reality on the ground. But what kind of reality?

Let us consider four of the 'troublemakers': Heather Arlott (whom we mentioned in the last section), Bill Poulos, Chris Legrange and Millie Hailey. Heather's mother and father both tell of teachers who have told them that at times they could strangle her. She simply won't be told what to do in the classroom; she answers back, shouts back, and has a well-developed technique for stirring up a class. Bill is much the same way, perhaps a bit less aggressive and a bit more contemptuous of teachers and the experience of schooling. Faced with a teacher (in a subject he likes) screaming at him, he simply walked out of the class and never came back. It was Bill who produced the classic line about job choices:

> I'd never be a teacher. You'd be in school all your life!

He's in with the 'smoking crowd', repeatedly gets caned, and once turned up drunk at a school dance.

Chris Legrange hasn't done that, but he and his mates get drunk at parties they throw at home. His parents too have been told he has fallen in with a bad crowd: he fails exams, fights with the teachers, jeers at school prefects and the school principal; declares that school is boring, pointless, restrictive and stupid; and wants to get out as soon as possible. Millie is agreed on all sides to be 'a problem' and will probably drop out soon. She hangs about with a couple of like-minded mates who poke fun at school authority, and has constructed for herself a reputation as a poor student and a pretty stroppy character who swears, smokes dope, and all the rest of it.

A familiar picture, to anyone familiar with schools. And, one might expect, four ripe cases of the kind of slack, no-hoper family that Mark Grey sketched as the seed-bed of the 'hoods'. It's interesting, then, to know that Chris comes from a wealthy professional family and that his grandfather, father and elder brother have all gone to university. Bill's father, a political activist with a strong sense of social responsibility, is utterly committed to the value of education and is trying to make Bill stay and get his Matriculation, as is his mother who constantly tries to help him with his work. Heather comes from a close-knit, lively family which takes great interest in her and her schooling. Her father takes her to and from discos and school dances, her mother jokes that she knows the work for the last round of exams better than Heather does. And Millie's father and mother own their own company and have supported four children at private schools. The conventional picture of the 'hoods' won't wash at all — for what is nevertheless, in each of these cases, real strife and opposition.

The events in which these people are caught up will only make sense if we abandon the habit of thinking about troublemaking as a kind of irrational, pathological syndrome, that is, as a kind of person, and start thinking of it as a particular relationship, a form of *resistance* to conventional schooling. All of these four teenagers in fact told us, quite clearly and reasonably, what they were up to and why. Each has a case to argue against schooling.

Chris, perhaps the most articulate of them, levels an indictment against Milton College that centres on three main items:
a) Heavy-handed discipline: prefects, teachers and the principal abuse their authority and hand out degrading, sadistic punishments; and the school enforces archaic uniform regulations
b) The moral calibre of staff: most of them are 'gutless', one being an out-and-out hypocrite who caned a boy for swearing though he swears himself; most are humourless, some ill-tempered; they have favourites, suck up to authority, stigmatize and victimize Chris, for instance picking on him when the whole class has been talking
c) Poor teaching: most classes are boring; his own learning problems have been ignored or dismissed when he took them to the teachers, who favour the bright boys; curriculum content is irrelevant; though he's had better experiences in the past, none of the masters now are people whom 'you could have a serious talk with'.

It's a picture of an oppressive, stifling environment, in which the first imperative is to survive with some self-respect, and the second is to get out as soon as possible. Chris' tactic of negativism in school is an economical way of achieving both.

Heather's critique of her schooling at Rockwell High has much in common with this, but stresses rather more her demand to be treated with respect and consistency. A characteristic episode, from her account:

> My English teacher, I was reading my book and he blamed me. And he said to stop reading, and I did. And he goes, 'Now read the proper page', so I started reading that. And then he said, 'You're not supposed to be reading that'. And I said, 'You just told me to'. And then he started blowing me up for *not* reading the book. Then 'cause he started yelling at me, I started yelling at him. And I got sent out. Then

> I wasn't allowed back in English for a week, or so. He knew he was wrong, but I still got kept out for a week.

Reading between the lines of this and other incidents, some more serious, one can see a well-developed technique for irritating adults; exasperated teachers overreacting for fear of losing control of the class; much injured innocence, and Heather and her mates all enjoying the stir as a break in boredom. But one can also see a much more serious claim to civility, to fair and equal treatment from adults. Heather is in fact contesting the connection of age and authority in the school which defines her as less respect-worthy than a teacher. (The key point in the passage just quoted is 'he started yelling at me, I started yelling at him'.) Whatever the course of events really was in that particular episode — we don't have the teacher's side of it — this is the kind of claim repeatedly made by our school resisters.

We would argue that this is a serious and significant critique of the school as an institution, and that elements of it are widespread among school pupils. We have two reasons for thinking this. One is that the same kinds of criticisms — arbitrary authority, poor teaching, inconsistent discipline, favouritism, lack of respect for the kids — were made over and over again by our interviewees, including those who are doing nicely at school and are far from being 'hoods' or resisters. The second is that sustaining a resistance to teachers in the way Heather does, or Bill Poulos does, is pre-eminently a social activity. It can't be done by isolated individuals, but depends on a good deal of support and encouragement by the rest of the class. Hence we get the kind of event that teachers see as 'ringleaders' stirring up a class and the students concerned see as being 'picked on' unfairly when the rest of the class is rabbling also. The idea that resistance to schooling is the preserve of a small group of toughs who lead the good kids astray, though popular among parents, is strictly a myth.

It is still true that outright resistance only becomes the *predominant* mode of attachment to the school for a minority; and here we begin to see some of the social forces that shape resistance over and above the authority structure of the school to which it is an immediate response. There is, for one thing, a great deal more of it at Rockwell and Greenway High Schools than at Milton and St Helen's Colleges. Chris Legrange and Millie Hailey are much more exceptional in their milieux than are Heather Arlott and Bill Poulos in theirs. Is this because the working-class comprehensives are more taut and tense as institutions? There are, of course, some which are — such as the one dubbed 'Port Arthur' by Hills in *The Schools*.[10] But we doubt this is generally true; it is certainly not true of our sample. If anything, the private schools are tauter, as Chris Legrange observed; when he came to compare private with state schools, he voiced the universal opinion among those of our sample who talked about the issue, that the state schools are 'slacker', the teachers more relaxed, the discipline less insistent

Chris also notes the class dimension in this: Milton, as a private school, is 'supposed to be better', and the teachers try to make you live up to it. The boys in effect carry the burden of the school's social reputation. He is particularly sensitized to this kind of issue because there is virtually a miniature class war going on in his own family: his mother is a miner's daughter and a former air hostess, and the impact of a strong-minded working-class woman on a silvertail family has been quite explosive. Chris himself is fighting her with every weapon at his disposal.

A distinctive dynamic is also going on in Millie's family. Mr Hailey is, by the standards of his childhood, downwardly mobile; he has a business which is operating on the fringes, in the interstices left by big capital, and the position is distinctly insecure. One of Millie's brothers was expelled from his elite school. Mrs Hailey comes from a working-class background and went to a technical school. Millie is a shade marginal in terms of the social composition of St Helen's College, and it's not surprising that her critique of the school is informed by a sharp criticism of the snobbishness and pretension of the other girls.

So class tensions help generate resistance even in ruling-class schools. More: they shape the *form* taken by resistance in this milieu. Millie, for instance, often adopts a deliberately proletarian style ('she sometimes uses *vulgarities*', said one shocked teacher) and has rejected the conventional futures of her schoolmates. Chris too is rejecting the educational future his parents have mapped out for him. He wants to leave school and get a job up the country, like a friend he admires who has done just that and is earning good wages — at least good enough to buy guns and a motorbike! Foul speech, rough manners, deliberate disregard of the niceties current in his class, are among the weapons of Chris' revolt.

Yet whatever happens in Millie's and Chris's schooling, their families' wealth will cushion them to some extent. Working-class school resistance is played for higher stakes. When they choose to resist the school, working-class children face unemployment or the rotten jobs all the kids want to avoid. So why is it more common here? One reason is that it expresses a widespread, if inarticulate, class anger. Heather Arlott's experience with teachers, for instance, is exactly of a piece with her parents' experience of being pushed around by a whole procession of authorities, bosses and bureaucrats; and her vigorous and aggressive response is only possible because of the strength her family generates. 'Don't let the bastards get you down' is a phrase from another interview, but exactly expresses her family tradition. And her parents will support her in her fights with the school whenever they think she has been unfairly treated.

Bill Poulos, as we have already noted, is the son of a union militant who has no respect for governments, bosses or experts (least of all educational 'experts'). Nor, for that matter, gutless union bureaucrats. Both Bill's parents object to stuck-up and snobbish people they have met at work or elsewhere. He has plainly absorbed all this, and to his parents' discomfiture, turned it against something they do believe in — the value of schooling.

Our evidence, then, does offer some support to the view that has come out of English research, that school resistance is a consequence, even in some respects a form, of class struggle. But this insight needs to be very carefully phrased. It is all too easy to slip into the idea that this means, simply, struggle between working-class kids and middle-class teachers.

There is certainly a class element in the tense relations between those two groups. If anything, this is more conscious on the part of the teachers, who slip easily into discussion of 'bad homes', 'deprived backgrounds' and 'rough areas'. The kids we spoke to never talked of teachers as better-off, stuck-up, or 'them' (as against 'us'), let alone as agents of the rich and powerful. For the most part, the class forces at play are indirect.

Further, there are other relations at work in school resistance. Consider another side of the Poulos family. Mr Poulos, militant against bosses at work, has a firm belief in the subordination of women, and insists on being boss in his own home. He believes that women should stay at home with their kids and not take jobs from men, is glad he doesn't have a daughter, and so on. He used to belt Bill with a strap, as he had been belted — it 'made a man of me'. His wife has accepted a firmly subordinate place in this world. And young Bill has taken over this gender politics. When he has power, he uses it in a way he would deeply resent if it came from teachers:

> I just got rid of my girl friend a while ago. She complained I was going down the coast all the time.
> *Have you talked about it together?*
> I told her.

Kicking the dog? Or school resistance as the assertion of masculinity, in a situation where working-class boys bolster their self-esteem by oppressing girls? Certainly there's a lot of sexual antagonism at places like Rockwell High, and a lot of male chauvinism among the boys.

Yet, we should remember, school resistance arises among the girls as well; and there it *violates* conventional expectations that girls should be controlled, polite, biddable, and so forth. Swearing, smoking, yelling at adults, wagging it, can only be read as a protest against femininity, not an exaggeration of it. We have a strong impression that in some cases resistance to school is indeed part of a struggle against the walls that close in around working-class women in adolescence; an attempt to avoid the kind of fate they can see any day just by looking up and down the street.

To put these points together, from a slightly different point of view: resistance is a relation to school that is generated on quite a wide scale (though in greatly varying intensity) by the interaction of the authority structure of the school with class and gender dynamics. In some circumstances — possibly those where class strains are more acute than usual — it becomes kids' *main* relation to the school, as the school becomes a focus of struggles with authority, with parents, or against oppressive futures. Among ruling-class kids resistance appears as taking on working-class styles, among girls it means acting like a boy, among boys it is liable to mean hypermasculinity: in each case there is an appeal to something felt to be potent and objectionable.

Compliance

If resistance to schooling changes its meaning and basis from one milieu to another, so too does compliance. We can make an interesting comparison between Auburn College and Rockwell High, where in both cases we have a number of interviews with pupils in the 'A' stream and their teachers, and can thus form some impression of the character of the group and its dynamics.

The 'A' stream at Auburn is, more or less, the 'in-between group' described by Colleen Rossner in the last section: 'kids who want to work and do well'. Indeed they do. The 10A class is a distinctly competitive lot: all are headed for university, and most are in the hunt for high aggregate marks and selection for prestigious courses such as medicine. Colleen herself, the daughter of two university graduates, is conscious that 'I can't be anything unless I do well at school'. She always does her homework and a bit more, always does well on tests. Alison Middleton, headed for medicine or law, works several hours a night and more at weekends. She disapproves of girls who let their social life interfere with their work, because 'the last school years set the pace for the rest of your life'. Teachers record her as being hard-working, enthusiastic, pleasing, consistent; their only complaint is that she talks too much. 'If I really did everything I wanted to do', she says, 'I'd be a student for always'.

A class full of girls like this sounds like a teacher's dream, highly motivated and articulate. 'Compliance' in this milieu is an enthusiastic *engagement* with the school and its project. It can, in fact, be too much of a good thing for the teachers' comfort. These girls very much want what teachers have got and put a lot of pressure on them to get it — the *girls* demand a constant high level of academic performance from their *teachers*. As one Auburn teacher put it:

> The school's run by the kids. I mean, the level at which the teachers work — and they work very hard here — is controlled by the kids, their expectations. If you don't match up, you're out.

He goes on to tell the story of a teacher who was sacked after pressure from parents cued by the kids. Wendy Durrell, another member of this class, sharpens the point:

> *Do you think the teaching is good here*?
> Yeah. They are good. The geography teacher got 100 per cent pass last year in Matric, so that's pretty good. Yeah, they have got good teachers. If they don't get good results . . . [meaningful pause] . . . then Miss Johansen (the principal) I think will look into it very seriously!

Those teachers who do measure up find the pressure stimulating and the milieu professionally satisfying to a high degree.

There is nothing remotely like this pressure put on the teachers of Rockwell High's 'A' stream. There is no principal breathing down their necks for 100 per cent pass rates at Matriculation; who in their right mind would expect anything like that? There is no gang of articulate, self-confident, university-educated parents waiting to descend on the school and demand the removal of a teacher who isn't shaping up. Above all, the kids have a different relation with their teachers; on whom they depend for the possibility of social promotion through education, in a way quite different from the girls at Auburn (whose teachers, if anything, depend on them). The teachers find the 'A' stream stimulating to work with; but when Rockwell teachers feel pressure, it is the pressure to keep control in the lower streams.

The 'A' class itself is uncertain about where it is going, and why. Mark Grey is faintly worried about his relation with the teachers, as we shall see. Carl Siemens, the 'joker' of the class and a remarkably lively and creative person, describes himself as 'bored' and is not putting in much effort at the moment. Elaine Markham, whose mother is strongly supporting her education, who wants to go to university and do a veterinary degree, and who is coming top or near top in most subjects, sometimes comes home from school crying. She sets Rockwell High against golden memories of primary school:

> Up here — it's more *dead* here. You're just here for one thing. But there, you were there to socialize and so, they bring you out socially as well. And here you're just for learning. You just go from one class to another, one test to another, you know.

In a nutshell, Rockwell High, despite having creamed them off, given them the experience of success, and mobilized support for educational advancement from their parents, has not succeeded in getting these kids to commit themselves to the project of competitive academic achievement. Their compliance with the school, and involvement in promotion through it, is much more a way of distinguishing themselves from the 'failure' around them than the positive project of 'success' of the 'A' class at Auburn.

Pragmatism

To most teachers, most kids most of the time are neither stars nor troublemakers but something in between: what they variously call 'normal', 'sensible', 'ordinary' or, most tellingly, 'invisible' kids. They are the kids who require or attract little of their stretched resources of time and energy. What often lies behind these labels is a strategy, the working-out of another form of relationship to school.

Ellen Oldcastle, for example, is just the kind of pupil that Rockwell High teachers depend upon, simply because she demands so little. Ellen's results fluctuate by year and by subject, but she has never failed in any subject. Overall, they are quite good enough to persuade her to have a go at Matric. Neither this, nor her low profile at school, can be taken as anything like compliance with or acceptance of the school's programme, however. Indeed Rockwell's teachers might be less sanguine in their approach to Ellen if they knew what she thinks of them. *A* is bad, teaches 'stupid stuff' rather than the real syllabus, and she is bored; *B* is good, practical; *C*'s classes she is liking more as she gets on top of the subject; *D* is 'really horrible', sour-faced, picks on kids for a couple of weeks at a time, and is currently picking on Ellen; *E* is unfair, not taking account of her work for a good teacher in that subject who left earlier in the year; *F* stinks — literally — and the class gives her hell; the principal is sometimes an idiot who goes mad over trivia in assemblies, though he is actually quite sensible to talk to, as she discovered when she was interviewing him for a class newspaper.

Little or none of this comes out in the classroom. Ellen is as far from resisting the school as she is from accepting it. There is perhaps something to be got out of it. She has toyed with the idea of becoming a teacher, or a secretary, or a nurse, and certainly doesn't want to work in a shop or a factory. She notes that 'better the education you get, the better the job you get', and tells tales of a cousin who couldn't get a bank job with excellent Year 10 results while a neighbour with Year 12 did. So she has a vague positive reason for staying at school, and also a vague negative one: what is the alternative?

In short, Ellen has chosen pragmatism as a form of relationship with her school in particular and with schooling in general. It is a choice which, like resistance and compliance, is made both by boys and girls, and in ruling-class and working-class schools. And, like those relationships, its content and meaning vary from situation to situation. So, for instance, some pupils in ruling-class girls' schools choose to exploit their school's function as an arena of training for and placement in the marriage market. Amongst ruling-class boys, the pragmatic strategy arises out of family attempts to use the school to guarantee entry to the top end of the labour market:

Have you ever thought of not going to university?
Yes. Although you miss a few years of getting money while you're actually at university, you get more when you do, (so) it's not really important.
What is?
Enjoyment of life — as long as you enjoy life. But you need a certain amount of money to enjoy life.

Do you think that most people have got enough money to enjoy life? So it wouldn't matter that much, perhaps, if you didn't go to university?
Yes, but if I went to university, I'd enjoy life afterwards more than if I didn't, I think.
Why?
Because I want jobs that come from a university degree.
Why?
Because I'm interested in those jobs. Vet, or medicine or agricultural science. Something to do with animals. Don't really want to do medicine because my brother did it.
What about being say, a veterinary nurse? You needn't go to university for that.
That's true — I don't know why I want to go. Perhaps because my father wants me to get a degree.
Does he?
Yes.
How do you know?
Because he's told me. He'd like me to get a degree, but he doesn't force me to, but he said he'd like me to.
Why do you think he wants you to?
Because the rest of the family all have one, and he wants his children to be — I don't know — he wants something from his children, but I can't really explain . . . he wants . . .
Try and give me some idea?
He wants them to be — perhaps he wants them to be in the middle-class type of people.

There is nothing sacred about our three categories of relations between kids and their schools — resistance, compliance, and pragmatism. Such a scheme could easily be revised or elaborated. We offer it simply as a help to thinking about the range of relationships in a given school or situation, and how they might be related to each other.

There are, nevertheless, two points we do wish to stress. First, however the varieties of relationship with school are named, each must be seen in its relations with the others. No relationship with school exists in isolation, each is conditioned by the presence of the others. Second, we are speaking of forms of relationship, *not* kinds of individuals. Indeed, most kids employ more than one strategy, at different times, in different subjects, and with different teachers. We saw in the example of Kevin Jones, at the beginning of Chapter Two, a striking case in point. The diversity of teachers' perceptions of Kevin arose out of his experimentation with different ways of relating to school. Most kids do find a way of dealing with school more settled than that, partly because there is in school life a strong tendency to type-cast kids. Not least, along lines of gender.

RELATIONSHIPS WITHIN SCHOOLS

Making girls and making boys

At various points in our discussion of resistance, compliance, and pragmatism we have seen that their form and consequences are different for girls and boys. Schools have always had a regard for the gender of their inmates, of course, most obviously revealed in simple separation and differentiation: boys' schools and girls' schools; boys' yard and girls' yard; woodwork, metalwork, maths and physics for boys, domestic science, needlework, English and biology for girls; cane for boys, detention for girls; and so on. These patterns are historically variable, and we will explore some of their recent changes later. For the moment we wish to argue that the school's relation to gender is not only one of reflecting patterns of separation and association between male and female; the school is also deeply implicated in the production of masculinity and femininity.

Where this is a question of activities quite clearly directed to this end, we can speak of masculinizing and feminizing practices. In ruling-class boys' schools the project of 'making men of them' has historically been quite explicit; and much can be learned from an examination of their most visible masculinizing practice — sport, and especially football. Brian Andrews, for instance, the son of a company manager, is being comprehensively trained as a competitor by his family and his school. There is a fierce push behind his involvement in football. Unfortunately he is still physically small and consequently last year ran into a series of injuries, culminating in concussion — it took an anxious teacher getting on the 'phone to Mr Andrews before Brian, to his chagrin, was put down to a lower grade playing with smaller boys. Asked what he would most like to improve about himself, his answer was 'to grow bigger physically'. He strongly identifies with his father, and his father puts emotional weight on football as a mark of masculinity. 'I hate football', says Mrs Andrews; but Mr Andrews says 'I like them to win', and turns out regularly for Brian's Saturday matches.

Ian Walker is a much better footballer than Brian; indeed, has been picked in representative teams. He has a precise knowledge of his body's capacities and limits at this game, refusing, against severe pressure from his coach and peers, to play on the wing because his skills and weaknesses suited a forward position better. His father backed him up in this and discussed the episode with some pride as a sign of Ian's independence and judgment. In Ian's first year at Milton College he was playing no less than three matches every week-end, one for his school and two with local clubs, though eventually he found he couldn't keep this pressure up.

Anthony Graves has even more push from his parents. Mrs and Mr Graves follow all their boys' matches, yell from the sidelines, praise good play, abuse bad. Dad gives up his Saturday golf to come and Mum is at every sports day: 'Wild horses wouldn't lead me away'. Alluding to the school's sports colour, she says

> the three of them are very much blue men — we are blue men

adding to the point by defining herself out of existence.

A dose of old-fashioned school spirit, rather overdone? We think not; something systematic and important is going on here. Competitive sport, and particularly football, is important as a means for the production of a particular kind of masculinity linked to the class situation these boys are moving towards and the work they will be engaged in.

Why football? It's rarely played by women, therefore unambiguously male; it's rough; it's competitive — a constant test of what both the Walkers and the Andrews senior call 'drive'; it's highly ritualized; and it's confrontative in a way that other competitive sports are not — in the course of play you are constantly running up against someone and have to overcome him in a test of personal superiority. The game is well suited, then, to be the emotional focus of the masculinizing practices of the school. We stress, however, that it is only a focus, and that the whole process is very much broader and more complicated. Some kids, after all, reject football. Ian Walker is going off it a bit, the pace has been too hot. Other sports can and do serve: Anthony Graves is more involved with cricket and athletics, and we can see how athletics became an important affirmation of his masculinity by noting the pain caused when an injury forced him to give up the event at which he was school champion.

Crises such as this give clues both the pressure these boys are under and to the peer group dimension of the process. The boys themselves become the police of masculinity. Two of the boys we have been discussing — neither of them particularly rough or aggressive people — have had fights to prove their masculinity, in schools where fights are not particularly common. Anthony Graves' father told one story, with more than a touch of complacency:

> Socially he is not as mature as his peers; and these days if you're not interested in girls in first and second year, you're 'a queer', automatically. No questions asked; that's the end of that. And he had a bad time in second year because two or three kids in his class kept on and on and on. A couple of them he wouldn't do anything about because they were smaller and he didn't want to hurt them. The third one was as big as he was, and he was biding his time. And he was a friend, and once again he didn't want to stir up trouble. And then he had enough: and beat the daylights out of this kid. And that was the end of that.

Mrs Graves notes that actually both boys got hurt in the fight. Brian Andrews, on arrival at secondary school, was nicknamed 'Squib' on account of his small physique and eventually attacked a boy who kept jeering at him on the theme of this name. Brian lost the fight but saved his self-esteem.

There are some important clues here about the nature of masculinity and its making. First, it is far from being a matter of simple role learning. The beginning of secondary schooling coincides roughly with the onset of puberty; boys often begin it at a time of rupture in their relations with their mother and father, and at a stage when there is much unsettled about the kind of person they are going to be. Great exertions by the boys themselves, and by the school regime, directed at a most vulnerable region of the psyche, suggest not the emergence of a 'natural' pattern of personal formation ('boys will be boys'), but social and psychological responses to diversity and fluidity.

That the Independent boys' schools are generally successful in constructing a dominant pattern of masculinity is easily observed. It is not the case, however, that the outcome is a *uniform* or universal form of masculinity. The process is essentially one of conflict, and in the struggles which involved the three boys we discussed a moment ago, some emerge as winners and some do not. Those who do not must make their own peace with the competitive, physically aggressive, space-occupying form of masculinity which dominates their schools. Some resist through a defiant inversion, and go in for study, debating, theatricals and the like ('the Cyrils' as they were dubbed in one school). Others — Anthony Graves is one — piece together a way of being male which capitalizes on specialized strengths (athletics) and avoids the most threatening areas (locker room bonhomie). He wants to be a vet, an unusual choice for a boy of his class. The school's efforts do not abolish diversity, in short, but place limits upon it and construct a hierarchy of forms of masculinity.

This limiting and ordering, and the practices by which it is achieved, are subject to historical change. Indeed just such a process of change was going on in the Independent girls' schools in our sample.

Until very recently several of these schools took as their main task the production of a femininity which complemented the masculinity dominant in the class milieu. They addressed themselves to producing girls whose character was organized around sociability rather than competition, prepared for subordination in marriage rather than dominance, equipped with the interests and skills that would grace a well-appointed home rather than offer challenges to its master. This still goes on, even in schools with an academic leaning. Jenny Lucas at St Margaret's, for instance, brought up in a totally patriarchal home, has a vision of her future in which having a job is very much on the margin. In detailed focus are marriage, and being at home when the children come from school, in a suitable setting:

> *What kind of house would you like to have?*
> I've always had a fascination with being rich [laughs]. Have a nice big — not big — oh yeah, big sort of mansion; not a *big* mansion, but in the country; not here, in England, somewhere nice, all green, and all free . . . all nice furniture and wallpaper and carpet everywhere and chandeliers and you know, sort of all really nice. So it's all homely like and not — I don't want something that's all neat and tidy and doesn't make you feel at home.

Her father reports that she's even got into detailed discussion with him about the cost of her wedding reception. (There is, we should observe, no particular boy in sight.)

At the same time, and in the same schools, another kind of femininity is being formed, in which personal achievement and mastery of knowledge is much more central. We saw the paradigm of this in the Auburn College 'A' stream a few pages back. Girls of this stamp too are mostly looking forward to marriage, but marriage structured differently from their mothers' — organized to service their careers, as well as their husbands'. There is every prospect that those demands will be incompatible with the boys' masculinity, and a good deal of strife is going to result. Tremors are already detectable. Some of our businessmen fathers have already given thought to their bright daughters following in their footsteps and becoming managers. And the conclusion seems to be that they shouldn't, because the men in these firms just wouldn't stand for it.

Male resistance, then, is likely to exclude women from that sphere where capitalist authority fuses most completely with masculinity, *management*, and therefore deflect career-oriented girls towards the *professions*. It is notable that that is already where the schools are pointing them in their academic programmes, while in their non-academic curricula there is no equivalent of the boy's training in dominance through heavily-stressed confrontation sports and the like. In both the change and its containment we see how the ruling-class school is an active agent in the construction of masculinities and femininities, and the relations between them. The process has a dynamic growing out of diversity and conflict.

This much is also true of the role of working-class schools in the making of girls and boys, but the relationship is here rather more oblique. We have already seen something of the significance of gender in working-class schools in our earlier discussion of compliance, pragmatism and resistance — especially resistance. This connection is a major theme of Willis's *Learning to Labour*, which argues that working-class boys' resistance to the scholastic culture of the school both cuts them off from jobs requiring certificates of school achievement and brings them to associate masculinity with manual labour. This is 'how working-class kids get working-class jobs', and the means by which a fundamental cleavage in the working class — between mental and manual labour — finds an expression and an agent in the school. 'The lads' follow their fathers into the factories, while the 'ear'oles', the compliers, go into offices.

There is some evidence in our material to support this view. We saw in Mark Grey, for example, a school 'achiever' who distances himself from 'the hoods', and in the process, forms a particular kind of masculinity. On the other side Bill Poulos, arch-resister and male chauvinist, seems to be a classic illustration of Willis's thesis. But there are grounds for caution about this argument.

There is no simple relationship between class and masculinity. Indeed, what impresses us most are the tensions and contradictions at play, and the range of outcomes which that interplay generates.

Let us digress briefly to recall some aspects of the situations in which Mark Grey and Bill Poulos find themselves.

Mr Poulos and Mr Grey for example, are husbands, fathers, and skilled workers, but their relationship to their workplace and their families have taken very different courses. The position of working-class men in the work-place is often deeply ambiguous — the celebration of physical strength and skill going intimately with the humiliation of being subject to control by bosses. Mr Grey has been defeated by the latter; Mr Poulos has not. In the Poulos family patriarchy reigns supreme; in the Grey family it is failing.

Mr Grey's failure has been his wife's opportunity — it has given her a strong hold on her son's schooling which she has used to push Mark away from the rough masculinity and class-based resistance of 'the hoods' and toward compliance with the school's programme of academic competition. Bill Poulos, powerfully father-identified, keeps his girlfriends down, resists the teachers, and heads for the factory floor. There are two crucial points here. First, as we saw when discussing the Independent schools, 'masculinity' cannot be grasped as a simple social form; it is *not* the case that Bill is masculine and Mark not. Mark is learning to push his mother around, and is strongly influenced by his rugged scoutmaster. It *is* the case that Bill and Mark are constructing different kinds of masculinity. Bill's is the classic 'macho' mould, Mark's is increasingly (though problematically) centred on competitive achievement. What we see are signs of the struggle between forms of masculinity, and the emergence of hierarchies between them.

Second, one of the most striking things about the relationship between the ruling-class boys' school and the production of masculinity is a sort of synchronization of the activity of home, school, and individual, so that the school is the locus of what is usually a mutually-supporting set of family, school and peer practices. The production of a specific kind of masculinity, and the process of class formation, are virtually one and the same. In the working-class school, on the contrary, the production of the dominant form of masculinity is achieved in and through *resistance* to the school. And at least one subordinate form of masculinity, competitive achievement, requires a break with class practices in its constitution.

A similar pattern of disruption is evident in the relationship between the school and working-class femininity. If anything its dislocations are greater than those of working-class masculinity. As we have seen, Bill Poulos's resistance to school is an affirmation of a particular kind of masculinity, where Heather Arlott's resistance to school breaks with conventional notions of femininity. Where the girls of Auburn are conducting a fruitful insurgency on male prerogatives, and are able to look to a viable (if troubled) long-term strategy of career-and-marriage, Heather's strategy leads directly to greater vulnerability in the labour market, and an economic need for dependence on a man.

Heather is in a minority at Rockwell, of course; also in a minority are the girls who opt for attachment to the school's academic programme and, thus, for a chance of promotion out of their milieu via school success. Yet these girls, too, face very hard choices — between the femininity modelled by their mothers and that of the 'career woman', and between the social practices of their families and an unknown which lies beyond Matriculation and tertiary education. For the majority of girls in these schools, the future looks rather more familiar: early leaving, a job, early marriage, and full-time motherhood.

But even a traditional kind of femininity still has to be produced. Delia Prince, for instance, is growing up in a patriarchal household that revolves around the work and leisure interests of her father Fred, a maintenance worker for a public authority. Her mother Rae is a nearly full-time clerical worker, and a full-time mother. Delia's older brother has an apprenticeship, and her older sister is undertaking secretarial training. Delia would like to be a vet, but if she doesn't get the grades, will get a clerical job. She then expects to marry at twenty and have her children.

It all seems like effortless 'reproduction'. Not so: there's a lot of tension behind this. Delia's Mum didn't stay at home when she had young kids; and now feels guilty about that, and about her job now, and tries to make up for it by being an ideal Mum in every other way. She is running herself into the ground doing this. The dominance of Fred Prince's work and interests didn't fall from the sky. When Fred met Rae, she was hoping to become a nurse, which he didn't like — so she got a job in a bank, and was sacked on marriage in accordance with the bank's policy. Delia's peer relations are carefully supervised — her parents introduced her boyfriend to her! Fred tackled the school about drugs and sex amongst students, was told it did happen but Delia wasn't involved. Rae separated Delia from a group who smoked and got drunk on weekends. Delia's femininity has involved, and still involves, a lot of work on all sides.

The school seems marginal in this process. Delia gets a bit of training in Domestic Science. She doesn't rely on the school for her main peer group. We will later suggest, however, that the school is more closely implicated in changes going on in working-class femininity, which a superficial view of its sexism is likely to overlook.

The construction of teacher-pupil practices

We have concentrated thus far on the activity and circumstances of students in their schools, and have left the central relationship in the shadows. It is a curious fact that the sociology of education has usually taken the student-teacher relationship, the core of schooling, as given. Mainstream sociology has treated it as an expression of underlying values, attitudes and orientations (as in the formula of 'value conflict' between the 'working class family' and the 'middle class school'), while structuralist sociology takes it as mere variation on a fixed pattern. We wish to argue that this, like all other relationships of schooling, exists only as practices; and that practices are always being constructed anew. The particular form of these practices, their circumstances, changes and consequences, are matters for investigation, not assumption.

Let us consider some remarks by Joanne Carpenter, a middle-ranking Year 9 pupil at St Margaret's College;

> *Are there any subjects you didn't do well in?*
> Oh yeah [laughing], most of them! No. I didn't do well in English, and History. And Art History. 'Cause I don't like History. I just can't concentrate on History 'cause it — I suppose it is relevant but it just annoys me. I don't like reading about it. I don't mind Art History so much because I like Art . . .
> *What's the difference between the subjects you do find interesting and the ones that you don't?*
> [Pause; then a laugh.] I don't know.
> *It's a difficult thing to work out.*
> Yeah. Oh, things that don't interest me I can't concentrate on. But if I'm interested in something or I want to learn it, I can sort of concentrate. I can notice myself when I concentrate properly and when I'm not concentrating.

Joanne and the interviewer start out talking a familiar language — subjects she does well and badly in, subjects she likes and doesn't like. This is a language used both by teachers and students, a common-sense reality that is adopted unquestioningly by those educational researchers who use scales measuring aptitudes and attitudes — that is, what people are good at, and what they like.

It is very interesting, then, that when Joanne is asked to explain why she likes or dislikes, she finds it very difficult to answer. So do other students faced with the same question. Eventually she comes out with the rather curious and illuminating suggestion that she finds out whether she is interested in something by noticing whether she is concentrating on it or not.

It is worth following this into the finer detail, as Joanne starts to talk about her experiences in particular subjects.

> *What's the science teacher like?*
> Oh, I don't like Mr Andrews much.
> *What's the trouble?*
> I don't know. He's — boring. He cracks these smart jokes that aren't funny. And then gets annoyed when everyone doesn't laugh. If I didn't like Science I wouldn't — [pause]
> *Enjoy the classes?*
> No. The fact that I do like Science is the only reason that I concentrate in that. We've got a student teacher that comes in. She teaches a lot and I like her better.
> *What does she do that's better?*
> She gets us to work but she doesn't sort of — I don't know — push us that much. He says 'Right you've got to do this'; and she says 'Right we'll do this now, okay?' Everybody just says 'Oh yeah, right-oh' and they do it. But he just says 'Do it now quickly' and you just sit there going 'ooh-er'.
>
> Mrs Brown my Maths teacher, she gets you to work but she doesn't, she forces you but she sort of does it in a nice way, in a way that you don't really mind. And if the class has a joke, well she laughs. But then we sort of get back to our work. But other teachers they don't laugh, and make you get straight back to your work, and that just annoys you, annoys me.
>
> My English teacher Miss Cartwright, she's sort of pretty understanding. And everyone can have their point of view, to a certain extent. And then if she feels she's losing an argument, well [laughter from both], we do something else. But she's just a really good teacher.
>
> I don't like History. I suppose it's partly my fault 'cause I just don't like it, but the teacher is very sarcastic. She makes everything — everything you say more or less is made out to be a joke. And she picks on certain people, a certain group. She sort of picks on most of the class, but a few in particular. And she always has to be right. Like if *you* are, well her theory is put into yours even though it might be the complete opposite. But she's always right. She just sort of says [imitating Miss Denning's voice]: 'Well I'm sorry but that's fact!' Just sort of goes about it in such a way that you can't be bothered listening to her.

In these five vignettes we see a range of 'teaching styles', as the textbooks have it, but we also see something more. These are accounts of interactions, of practices under construction, in which both pupils and teachers are agents. Of course, they are acting within a very definite context — most obviously the age/knowledge structure of schooling, and the school's need to attach its pupils to a particular programme. Apart from rather exceptional groups like the 'A' class at Auburn College, the school cannot assume a consistent desire to learn everything its staff (under a panoply of constraints ranging from school timetables to Matriculation regulations) offer as worth learning. It can get the kids to participate either by persuasion or coercion; 'boredom' is the usual way they experience their participation if the persuasion has failed.

To someone like Joanne, then, who attributes a general legitimacy to the school's programme but who isn't an academic high-flyer, a 'good teacher' is someone who is successful at persuasion, who stimulates participation — like Mrs Brown. Because she feels that there is something to be got out of school, she doesn't like teachers who are completely slack, who just let the class rabble. (This is a view almost universally held by the kids we talked to. Contrary to what is supposed by some critics of progressive methods, teachers cannot buy popularity by abandoning 'discipline'.) But Joanne, like most, also doesn't get on well with teachers who can't persuade, who have to rely on coercion, whether psychological or physical. The kids resist this by the rather limited techniques at their disposal, such as the wandering-attention method used in Miss Denning's classes, or the deathly-silence-at-teacher's-jokes and the go-slow methods used in Mr Andrews'. Hence the unending guerrilla-war aspect of classroom life.

Of course the extent and ferocity of this warfare varies greatly according to its context. The girls at Auburn note how it subsides after Year 10 as everyone settles down for the run to Matric. In working-class schools the techniques of battle are many and skilfully deployed, as one of our teachers ruefully observed:

> *Do you like your job?*
> Yes, I do. (But) I find it a big strain.
> *What is it about it (that is) a strain?*
> I find — the psychological and even physical confrontation with kids constantly. In the first year of teaching, the strain is immense, if you care at all about what you are doing the strain is immense. And I truly felt at one stage at least during my first year that I was really going

> insane — I mean that quite seriously. I was losing my sense of judgment. Tiny little incidents became terrible catastrophes, and I really was beginning to go off the rails mentally and emotionally. I would feel like bursting into tears at the drop of a hat.

It is worth stressing that Lorraine Smart does care about her work, works hard, and teaches in a school, Greenway High, which is far from being one of the roughest. The distinctive experience of teaching in a working-class secondary school is understood by Janet Bagshaw, an Auburn College teacher who like many of her colleagues is a refugee from the state system:

> I *enjoy* the work here, and I feel that as a professional I *enjoy* teaching. I found that in the state schools — *some* of the state schools I was in — I wasn't teaching. I was just trying to discipline apathetic students who didn't want to go, whose parents didn't care, and so I was — I looked after them. I almost baby-sat some classes, some of the lower streams . . . But here the response is *superb* and as a teacher I thoroughly enjoy it.

Many of the older teachers we talked with were of the firm opinion that the problem of 'getting on top', and staying there, had increased considerably during the course of their teaching careers. Their perceptions coincide with those of the parents and with some research evidence. Whatever the case in the past, there can be no doubting that nowadays, from the point of view of the individual teacher in a working-class secondary school, authority is not something given them by virtue of their position, but must be achieved. And this has two very important consequences.

First, teaching is an emotionally-dangerous occupation. To the extent that teachers' authority is something which they construct in isolation and out of their own resources, it is a part and extension of themselves. To the extent that students resist, challenge or subvert their authority, so do they threaten them personally.

Second, most teachers try to protect themselves and reduce their vulnerability by withdrawing themselves as far as possible. A cardinal rule for many is, quite simply, 'keep your distance'. This is the teachers' contribution to the formality, or thinly-veiled hostility, which characterizes so much teacher/student interaction in the working-class milieu. Andrew Gallea, a young, enthusiastic teacher at Greenway High, explodes in frustration:

> But they're good kids. With reservations, because — I think in general

> kids — bloody kids are liars, towards teachers. I think it's terrible. Most kids, in general, have got no hesitation in lying to a teacher. And it really pisses me off, because you can be really honest with a kid, and you could say: 'Look, you ought to do this, you ought to do that' . . . They say 'Mr So-and-so said we could come over here'. Bullshit! He didn't really — I mean, they just tell you that. It really shits me.

Teachers, or most teachers most of the time, find ways of surviving from day to day rather than once and for all. Relations are constantly being negotiated in the flux of daily school life. And this is far more than a matter of how teachers and pupils get on with each other as people. The pupils' relations *with the curriculum* are contained within the joint practices they construct with their teachers. From the vicissitudes of these practices, over periods that may be weeks or years, are precipitated the attitudes and traits that are everybody's shorthand for talking about school life — 'liking' a given subject, 'being good at' a subject, finding it 'boring', being a 'really good teacher', and so on.

It is because these attitudes and qualities are the precipitates of complex practices involving numbers of people that they are very hard to analyze on the spot. This is why most students find it extraordinarily difficult to give a meaningful answer to such apparently simple questions as why you like a particular subject, or what makes so-and-so a good teacher, or what is the difference between topics you find interesting and those you find boring — questions which naive sociology takes as simple building-blocks to an understanding of the school.

Such a view of the pupils' relations with the curriculum doesn't only flow from descriptions of everyday life in the classroom. It also seems to be required to make sense of both parents' and kids' firmly-held view that exam results closely depend on relations with teachers. Stories of being 'brought on' by a particular teacher, or turned off a subject because its teacher was objectionable, abound. And it is, of course, folklore in schools that particular teachers are good value for Matric, while others are best kept away from the academic streams if the school values its pass rate. Some teachers are more skilful than others; some of the 'survival strategies' which they construct are more appropriate, more open, than others.

But the academic search for the attributes of 'the effective teacher' has been fruitless, and is bound to remain so. Being an 'effective teacher' is not a settled trait of a person, like height or hair colour, but the consequence of a complex, multi-person practice. It depends on context. Thus the 'human relations' approach practised by some depended heavily on the fact that it was an *exception* to the rule, an antidote to boredom. More, our evidence shows that the same person can be involved in significantly different practices with different people and groups. The same teacher can be liked and successful with some of our interviewees and quite disliked by others. Similarly the same principal can be regarded as interested and fair by one group of parents who have had dealings with him, callous and careless by another.

It is also clear that 'being a good student' is a constructed fact, not a given. We can show this more clearly than in the case of teachers, for we have in the research design a group of observers who have followed the students' school careers rather closely over nine or ten years — their parents. We have been struck by the number of parents who, in reflecting on the pattern of their child's school career, speak of a distinct change of pace at some point or other. Chris Legrange, for instance, the Menace of Milton College, is coming last in his class (deliberately) and creating endless trouble for his elders. But his parents make a clear distinction between this time of troubles and a time when he was happy at school, in fact coming near the top of his class; and he remembers some of his primary teachers with warmth. Wilma Roberts remembers having been brought on by her fourth class teacher and never looking back, but as we recorded in Chapter One, is now 'browning off' and 'losing interest'. Maureen Bridge, fearful of school and unable to trust relationships outside the protected circle of the home, began to run away from school in Grade 5 and go home; after some years of trauma she began to get herself together, was helped by sympathetic staff when she went to high school, and is now cruising along nicely. We could multiply the examples.

It is clear that the form of attachment to school, and the depth of commitment to its programme, is subject to change over the years, sometimes to radical mutation. It is also clear that experiences with particular teachers can be significant parts of these changes (though our evidence is not usually detailed enough to show very clearly how it happened). In the parents' recollections of their own schooling, particularly working-class parents', we repeatedly heard stories of individual teachers who had meant a great deal to them, who had sponsored them in some way (or tried to), and whose memory often lightened a decidedly bleak landscape.

A crucial implication of this line of thought is that academic success generally depends on the construction of certain kinds of teacher-pupil practices. In understanding the academic failure of working-class schools, then, it is important to understand the difficulties they encounter in constructing these practices. We'll come back to this point in various ways, as the difficulties are multiple. For the moment, let us note that they can be precipitated on either side of the teacher/student relation.

The constant wear and tear of keeping control can lead to demoralization on the part of the teachers, turning classroom work into a routine. What this in turn can mean for the students is very clearly set out by Greg Wilkins, one of the 'A' class at Rockwell High:

> *Are there any teachers you've had a hard time with?*
> Oh, my Science teacher. He mostly just, we're working out of a book. And we're hardly ever doing anything with him, he's just out the front. And we do an objective test and he marks it. Marks our books. And when we did the Science tests in Year 9, our class, we didn't do any work on muscles, and didn't do any work on rocks. The only thing we did was classification and a bit of electricity in the whole test! And most of us got low marks, in 'A', compared to all the other classes.
> *What happened then?*
> All the class was mad at him. We asked him should we learn the work on muscles and that, 'cause they told us what was on the test, and he said 'No' . . . he told us just to learn the stuff on electricity and that.
> *Did any of the parents get annoyed at that?*
> No. I don't think they were told, none of the parents. Kids just kept it to themselves.

In fact Greg's father had heard of the incident; but there is nothing remotely like the pressure on teachers that would be forthcoming at Auburn or St Margaret's if that kind of teaching were to occur.

One of Greg's classmates, Mark Grey, describes another hitch in the construction of a successful academic practice. He wants school success as he hopes to get into a profession, and is strongly supported by his parents who see it as the way for him to escape the demeaning environment of Rockwell. However they can't give him much technical help, as their own schooling was so limited; he is entirely dependent on the teachers. And this dependence can have untoward effects:

> *What about problems with school subjects — who would you talk them over with?*

> Oh, my friends I suppose. Don't like facing the teachers 'cause they put you down . . .
> *Do they?*
> Oh they don't put you down but you know, it might affect your mark at the end of the year. So I just keep it quiet and go through my friends. But then, if I find out my friends don't understand it . . . I've always got to ask the teacher.

Mark, in short, believes he can't afford to be seen to be in trouble with the work, lest a negative 'halo' descend upon him. And this makes him hold back from establishing the very practices with teachers that are probably necessary to lift him into the academic-achiever bracket.

We have noted several times that the ways in which teachers and pupils construct the practices which are the core of school life are bound up with the context in which they occur. We turn now to examine the school as a unit.

Authority and hegemony in schools

This book isn't a de-schooling tract, and we don't want to labour a familiar point, but it is worth registering again that what the trouble-makers say about schools does not come out of an isolated or marginal experience — it is based on common experience, reported by students who are succeeding as well as those who aren't, by students in private as well as in state schools. The school is an institution that is, among other things, a power structure, and is felt as such by its students. It is capable of intimidating and grinding people down, and it often generates resentment and resistance. Depending on circumstances, this can develop into severe problems of authority, whose effects generalize through a school's work.

The importance of the issue is clearly stated for us both by parents and by students — though in different language. When parents formulated their views of schooling, the commonest criticism was on the theme of what they called 'discipline'; more particularly, the failure of schools to maintain it. Some of them pushed the point further and argued that discipline was not only a problem in school; the failure there was making waves within the home. Mrs Grey, for instance, recalls a 'more modern' headmaster at the local primary school introducing a suggestion box for the kids:

> And they were allowed to sort of tell the teacher how to do things. Well, we had Mark coming home telling *us* how to do things. And this

> is where we started having little arguments which have developed over the years [laughing]. Because they still want to tell you 'Sir said, I can do this', 'Sir said'. Bill always says, 'Well, I don't care what Sir says; you're *here* now'.

Many other working-class parents also contrast the slackness of the present day with the firm discipline, and enforced respect for adults, they experienced as children themselves. Ruling-class parents often raised the issue of discipline as a key reason for their preference for private schools.

Most of the kids don't argue for more controls over themselves, but they raise the issue of authority in another way: their powerful resentment of *unfair* treatment by teachers. We found that the arbitrary use of authority is the most deeply felt, as well as the most widespread, criticism of school made by the students we talked to.

Where the radical critique of the authoritarianism of schools as institutions went wrong was not in saying this, but in not going beyond it. Schools do a lot of things besides maintaining social control, and some of those things are very valuable. Further, problems of oppression, resistance and authority in education arise from causes beyond the structure of schools as institutions. We see this as soon as we begin to examine the different problems of authority that different schools have: in particular, who holds a hegemonic position among the students, and how far teachers hold a hegemonic position in the school as a whole.

In Auburn College, for instance, there is a clear correspondence between the two. Going back to Colleen Rossner's ethnography of student types — 'cheap', 'snobbish', and 'intellectual' — it is clear that the third group actually does have the dominant place in student life at Auburn. The academic high-flyers of the 'A' stream have prestige among their peers, and give what old-fashioned pedagogues would have called the predominant 'tone' to the school, especially in the senior years. Similarly, the staff's definitions of the purposes of schooling generally prevail among the kids. Their authority is, by and large, felt to be legitimate; what they have to offer is valued by the kids and their parents. The whole pattern of hegemonic relationships thus contributes to making Auburn College the taut, efficient academic machine it is.

At Rockwell and Greenway Highs, the official definition of the purposes of schooling, as competitive appropriation of an academic curriculum, prevails only among a minority of the kids. It is not that there is a counter-hegemony, in the sense of an anti-academic group who have established leadership among the kids. It is just that the academic group don't have very much prestige, and there are a good many other equally potent sources of it: sport, sexual maturity, social skills in peer life, jobs and money.

The way teachers respond to this can itself be an obstacle to the establishment of hegemony. We noted a page or two ago that teachers in working-class schools are pressed to find their own way of exerting authority over the kids. They evolve their own survival strategies, which, for the majority, involve 'keeping your distance', not getting too caught up in the problems of the school.

But there are other strategies. Some teachers, like Simon Gallea at Greenway or Sheila Goffman at Rockwell, put in long hours in preparation, in getting to the kids, and in trying to construct more relaxed and productive relations with them. Still others, like Lorraine Smart, opt for the *persona* of 'big sister'.

The upshot is that each of these strategies confronts teachers practising others as a contradiction of their own ways of maintaining authority. As another Greenway teacher put it:

> I'd like to see the staff be more consistent with the things they do. I'd like to see the staff — kids get away with some things in one class but they don't in another. That just depends on the teacher they've got at the time . . . There's a multitude of standards that the kids are expected to meet.

Most of the teachers at Greenway High were aware that the conflict among teachers' policies was a prime source of the 'discipline problem'. Some also looked further, to the school's catchment, and to changes in it which had followed from the establishment of new schools in the district and Departmental policies of comprehensivization and co-education. Doris Willoughby, a social science teacher at Greenway:

> Well, it is basically an industrial area, I suppose. When I first came here there were over 1500 and that was before Southwold High opened and of course we got a lot of kids from up the hill. We are also dragging from Mortendon, well, we lost more of our — what you might call our bad kids never got here because they went to the Tech . . . and the worst girls went to Pallisades Girls High. Then of course Southwold opened and it cut up some of the hill. But even so I don't think Greenway can have any worse problems than some of the other schools, especially those further west, Mortendon and Pallisades West. And it must — I can't see that it doesn't go back to the attitudes of the parents.

This is a nice example of teachers' understanding of the wider sources of their difficulties. At first blush it might seem that our evidence, showing as it does the striking difference in the pattern of hegemony characteristic of ruling-class schools, might confirm the idea that the catchment, and the kinds of parents in it, straightforwardly determine the school's difficulties. There are, however, two problems for such a view of things. First, what Doris Willoughby grasps as a problem *in* a particular social group ('the attitudes of the parents') is, in fact, *a particular relation* between schools and social groups. It is emphatically not the case that some groups are less educable than others. Second, the school as an institution has a history, and each school has its own history, in the course of which hegemony is constructed, contested, dismantled, re-ordered.

Five years before, the picture of Auburn College we drew a page or two back would not have been true. Discipline had become a problem felt by teachers, students and parents, and this was the most visible sign of the breaking-up of a long-standing pattern of organization and practices within the school. That the hegemony of the 'official' school was reconstructed along new lines, and was associated with a shift in prestige amongst the girls in favour of the 'academics' — that was the product of a very definite strategy carried through by a new principal.

We can see some more history-in-the-making at Greenway High in Doris Willoughby's account. The retirement of two or three key staff had, in the context of the developments she sketched, resulted in a marked weakening in the staff's ability to control the pupils, and in the acceptance of the school's academic programme. Reactions to that weakening surfaced in staff meetings and lunch-hour conversation, in a special staff conference, and in our interviews. Differences in teachers' age, sex, status, subject specialization and teaching methods, led to widely divergent opinions about the causes and proposals for action — ranging from suggestions that the school rules should be redrafted, to revamping teaching methods, to reconsidering the content and organization of the syllabus. The argument even touched on the holy of school holies, the Timetable. The hitherto unchallenged dominance of the principal and a few close senior advisors was being challenged as new strategic options were developed, canvassed, and pressed. The outcome was still far from settled when we left the school, and the key point is that it *could* not be known in advance, by us or by any of the participants to its making.

The 'official' school is, then, an active agent in forming the kids' relationships with itself. And this is true not only of convulsions of the entire apparatus such as occurred at Greenway High and Auburn College (not the only cases in our dozen schools, by the way). It is also true of day-to-day practice. Again and again, in parents' discussions of their children's schooling, we were told of changes in orientation that followed from changed treatment by teachers or changes in school milieu. Over a large number of particular actions and decisions a principal or a teacher establishes a strategy; by the interaction of those strategies, in the context of the hierarchy and division of labour among the staff, the school establishes its characteristic ways of handling its students and their parents.

Of course the kids and their parents are hardly passive in the face of the school's strategies. They respond and they initiate, and their actions are by no means independent of the social relations they are involved in outside the school. We have explored some aspects of this in the case of practices of resistance. And if it is correct that there is a strong component of class tension and class resentment in school resistance, it is not surprising that schools which draw substantially from the most marginalized and exploited parts of the working class face the hardest problems in imposing their authority.

THE SOCIAL ORGANIZATION OF SCHOOL PRACTICES

All of the school processes we have discussed so far — the different relationships kids have with their schools, the ways teachers and pupils construct the practices which constitute the curriculum, the schools' role in the production of masculinity and femininity, the ebb and flow of struggles for hegemony amongst the kids, and between the 'official' school and the kids — take place within a context organized in quite particular ways. The school's basis of organization is the segregation of a particular age group, combining them with relatively small numbers of people drawn from another age group; and the interaction of those who are presumed to know, with those who are officially designated as not knowing. We have also observed that the organization of schooling takes note of gender as well. The working-out of these relations of age, gender, and knowledge, and the way they intersect to create the social form of the contemporary secondary school, is the subject of this section.

Gender and the organization of schools

For the past thirty years or more the weight of opinion among professional educators has been against class and gender segregation in schooling, and for comprehensives and coeducation. Most Australian state schools have been reorganized along these lines, and over the past decade or so a significant number of Independent schools have abandoned sex segregation, in what was usually regarded as a progressive step, often contested by conservatives. It is interesting, then, that there are now some progressive educators who ask whether coeducation is such a good idea after all. We have already presented some evidence from this study which on the face of it encourages this questioning. The Independent girls' schools are producing a number of women who are contesting the usually-accepted position of women and are changing the notions of femininity that prevailed in their milieu.

It seems clear that the organization of those schools as single-sex institutions is crucial in this development. That is a condition, first, of bringing together a staff mainly composed of women and managed by women. More, they are a particular kind of women: academically successful, usually career-oriented, economically independent or with a basis for it, and enjoying working in an institution in which their status as women is the occasion for the development of their professional competence, not a barrier to it. In the same way the school brings together a number of girls who have a good deal of pressure from home to do well academically, even *because* they are women. Mrs Somerset explains:

> We've tried to bring them up with the idea that — they could probably live at home for the rest of their lives, and we could keep them — and this is an absolute waste of a life. I've always wanted them to do something. I don't care what it is. Something. So that if anything happens to us, to a husband, or there is a disaster, they can go out and earn a good living and be able to keep themselves. And I've always insisted that this is something they *must* aim at.

Finally, the school puts those two groups together, and the combination opens up unprecedented possibilities. When asked about the position of the maths and sciences at St Margaret's, for example, the senior science mistress noted deficiencies, but insisted that

> The science and mathematics teaching is improving all the time, and I'm quite satisfied that we're going to make this an absolutely first class science school. We've got a very good team of teachers, and

> everybody's very keen, and I don't see why we shouldn't be . . . So many of our children are ambitious to do things like veterinary science or agricultural science, and it disadvantages them, I think, not to have the emphasis on the scientific side of teaching.

There are two important things to be learned here. First, there is nothing in segregation, or coeducation, which *by itself* will produce a given result. Historically the educational segregation of ruling-class women has been the means of marginalizing them and preparing them for subordination to men. Precisely that segregation is now helping to erode that subordination. Second, one of the major determinants of the impact of a given organization of gender in schools is the class context in which it occurs. The effects of segregation in Independent girls' schools are closely bound up with their class milieu; in particular, its stress on competition and achievement, and the recently-changed relations between ruling-class women and the top end of the labour market.

It seems to us unlikely that coeducation has done much to advance the interests of working-class women. 'The girls are all loud-mouthed disco-maniacs, and the boys are all Ocker De Luxes', says Arlette Anderson of the sexism rampant at Rockwell High. She tells the boys that she can see them all in ten years' time — beer-bellied, down at the RSL club boozing, totally lacking respect for women. They laugh. She organized a debate in a Year 8 class about the role of women; universal opinion among the boys was that women should stay at home and have babies. They shy off anything like Domestic Science:

> I'm not doing that, my Dad says sewing's sissy

and rubbish unmercifully the few boys who continue with it after it ceases to be compulsory. (Just one boy in her school is going to do it for the Year 10 examinations — 'truly an individual'.) The girls, meanwhile, have learned by the end of Year 7 that having a boyfriend is a matter of status, and jeer at those who have missed out — 'they don't seem to have any idea of sisterhood at all'. And they agree that the proper place of a woman is to be a mother. Arlette has pleaded with them, aren't they interested even in a small career?

> Oh no. I want to be a mother.

The bright ones are different, she says, but they are few.

Thus the mordant picture of sexism, alive and well in a coeducational school, drawn by a disillusioned-but-still-kicking teacher. We don't take this portrait quite at face value; Arlette misses some significant changes that are going on in working-class femininity. It is obvious that a change in the conception of motherhood has happened, given the massive entry of working-class married women into the paid workforce. Yet her picture of the sexist atmosphere at the school, we would suggest, is broadly correct. Almost all the girls do assume that from school they will leave, work, marry, get pregnant, and leave work to have the kids — that they will become dependent on a husband. Many of the boys do have a predatory attitude to the girls: Bill Poulos, throwing over his girlfriend when she was no longer convenient, could count on support and understanding from his mates. The definition of masculinity as 'machismo', a combination of toughness and dominance in sexual relations, is certainly current among the boys; and with it go the classic tastes — motorbikes, cars, football . . .

Though there are a number of pressures operating against this in the coeducational school, they are far from being overwhelming. The most obvious, the fact that academic success is open equally to boys and girls, and that girls are seen to do as well as or better than boys, is undercut by the lack of hegemony that would make such success important to many of the kids. Yet the presence of women teachers in nearly equal numbers provides a model for something different. And a significant number of those teachers, during the past decade, have personally gone through the changes to which schools like Auburn and St Margaret's have been responding. Some, like Arlette, are conscious of themselves as feminists, at least to the extent of questioning sex-role conventions and fighting put-downs by men. Others, like Sheila Goffman, are not, but still provide examples to working-class girls of career-conscious, sexually emancipated, and personally confident women.

We would suggest that such changes among teachers do have an impact, but a selective one, and one very much bound up with a class dynamic. It is, to be specific, on the academically-successful girls who are involved in a project of social mobility: the bright and co-operative students who can be got out of their present milieu by educational promotion. Arlette Anderson is very much aware of this class dimension. She sees the girls of the bright group she has hopes for as not only closer to her in cultural terms but also closer to her model of femininity. Sheila Goffman doesn't, as yet — she simply can't understand why girls would risk getting pregnant rather than go on the pill, for instance — but she is much more popular with the kids and is probably having a bigger impact in the same direction.

If these clues are sound, we may argue that an effect of a young teaching workforce is to induce a split in models of femininity among working-class girls, which is closely connected with mobility in class terms. Having women teachers in nearly equal numbers is undercut by the fact that principals, deputies and subject heads are mostly men. And the presence of women in schools is handled by the boys (in Arlette Anderson's opinion) by concluding that there is something wrong with them as women, since they have gone beyond their real role in life. 'Careers advising' may stress equal opportunity but has little impact since most of the kids think careers advising is a load of rubbish. They normally get jobs — if they can get them at all — via friends, neighbours, and parents.

In various ways, then, a subtle and extensive system of sexual segregation has been maintained within the framework of formal coeducation (we have yet to hear of a school which has included girls in its football teams) which has limited the actual existence of coeducation and frustrated the hopes of many of its proponents. Yet there is at least one very important part of school life which has undoubtedly been transformed by coeducation, and that is the part owned by the kids themselves, the 'unofficial' school, their own informal social life. We will discuss this in Chapter Four.

Streaming and creaming

All of the schools in our study had ways of putting kids into groups according to their 'ability'. This often occurred within classes or subjects ('setting'). In all twelve schools it also occurred, by one means or another, in the organization of year groups or cohorts. In a few cases this was achieved via the somewhat apologetic device of advising kids to take different combinations of subjects ('tracks'). In most, 'streaming' was direct and unabashed, and the interviews give abundant evidence of its impact. Its forms ranged from the intricate Independent school regime described by Mrs Chenoweth:

> It's a very very structured school, Wellington College, fiercely competitive . . . 65 to 70 boys formed the Grade 5 level at Wellington, and they were divided into three forms, and they're graded according to their ability, and this is done on a test in the first few days . . . As far as we know, but it hasn't actually been spelled out to us, that he is in the lower of the 'B' form. And they go so far as to put a child 1, 2, 3, 4, 5, 6, 7, 8, 9, 10, 11, and 12 and so on right through the class — it's absolutely incredible! So a child knows whether they come lst or 22nd.

to the rougher sorting in the state system described by Mrs McArthur:

> *How did she react when she went to high school?*
> She went to high school, we thought she would have gone into a better grade than what she did. I think she went into 7E, F, G. Very low. But we had heard, Carrum Primary don't give you a very good grade. Evidently, they give you an estimate to go to high school. The high school grades you also, the good from the bad. Put her into 7H and said if she works, and really works at it, you know, she could get put up into a higher grade. Whilst she was at primary school, Kate was always hard to teach. She's obstinate, she's stubborn, she's set in her ways; you're trying to teach her something, if she doesn't want to learn, you just give up. You get frustrated, you know, you throw the books up in the air, in temper. There's no sense in trying, because she's not interested. And the headmistress said one day, 'Look, the world is made up of two people, there are leaders and there are plodders. Kate is a plodder'. And she said, 'The sooner you accept that, the better. Stop trying to make her a leader'. She said, 'Just let her go, she'll go through life happier than anybody, doing what she wants to do'. She said, 'If you're trying to make something out of her that isn't in her to do, you're going to end up with a mixed-up child, and you'll only end up frustrated'. So we let her go. You just can't make her do anything with her education. And she's got this attitude that she wants to be 15, and leave school, and go on the dole. Heaven, it's a great ambition for a child! It's really great! You wonder where do they get these thoughts from.

And at another point in the interview Mrs McArthur carried on this line of thought:

> It's not an ambition that she's inherited from any of us. That's not an ambition that any of us have nursed. I do think a lot of her thoughts come from the element of the children of the class she's in. She's in a low grade; and talking to one of the teachers over there, he explained it. He said, unfortunately, if Kate's education had been better when she was in primary school, if she had come to high school in a higher grade, she'd have been mixing with a grade of children with a higher intelligence, that basically all want to do something. Unfortunately, she's in a lower grade. She's in with children that don't want to be taught; that are forced to go to school until they are 15, their parents couldn't care less. They're leaving school, dropping off like flies when they turn 15. Every day when she comes home, someone's leaving because they're 15. He said naturally that's going to rub off. She thinks she's one of them, the same as them. Instead of setting herself

up higher. But you know, you can't go back to primary school now and do it all again. You've just got to work on what you've got.

We have quoted this important passage at some length because Mrs McArthur has here set out with striking clarity the connections between the organization of the school, teacher ideology, parental knowledge, the labelling of pupils, and the kids' own practices, that are crucial in understanding the social sorting that goes on in schools.

Streaming serves to 'label' pupils as bright, mediocre, dull — this has been a main theme of criticisms of streaming as a policy. It's clear why it has this effect for teachers in high schools. Most teachers don't know much about the kids' learning styles before they meet them in the classroom, and as we saw in Chapter Two, most know very little indeed about their home backgrounds. The one big, indisputable fact they do know about them, and which naturally serves as an anchor for their thinking about them, is which school class they are in. (Indeed we have some reason to think that when teachers in working-class schools do reflect on home backgrounds, they tend to see them *through* the streaming system; for instance constructing images of the 'good', 'concerned', or as academics have it, 'educationally supportive' families for the 'A' stream students, and of 'no-hoper' families for the 'G's and 'H's.)

Streaming also serves as a very clear signal to the kids, and their parents, about what the school makes of them as learners. Kate McArthur was 'shocked' at being put in the bottom stream. Greg Wilkins uses the same term to describe his reaction to the stream he was put in — 'I got a shock' — though in his case it was the kind you can do with more of, as he went into the 'A' stream.

But streaming is not just a once-for-all labelling of the kids. It is a continuing practice by which work and social life are organized. When Mrs McArthur observes that Kate in 9H is 'in with children that don't want to be taught' rather than 'mixing with a grade of children with a higher intelligence', this is the point she is making. The stream becomes a social unit, not just an educational category. A number of the kids talked about this. One force in the moulding is the teachers' opinions and responses, as Delia Prince noted when she talked of her class (9C) having got a reputation for mucking up in its first year. Yvonne Crisp (9A) talks of another force, solidarity: most of her friends are in 9A, and given the congenial relations that class has been able to establish with its teachers and the looser discipline and freer interaction that results, it's a pleasant place to be. There is force in the 'influence' arguments, though what implications should be drawn for the schools' policy is not easy to say.

The implications for particular kids and their families, however, are plain; and in consequence the streaming system becomes an object of strategy on all sides. Mrs McArthur, acutely aware of the mechanisms at work, saw both Kate and her brother sorted into the lower streams at Rockwell High. She suspected that the teachers had stigmatized the family, and fought a battle to prevent her third child being put in a low stream — which she won. Mr and Mrs Tait, doctor and physiotherapist respectively, are acutely conscious of the benefits of elite education, and consider that the best teaching happens in the top streams of the best private schools. So they have sent their son Steven to Churchill College. When he fell in with a bad lot, began to get worse marks, behaved rudely, and finally was discovered smoking, one of their main anxieties was that he would slip out of the top streams. They came down on him like a ton of bricks, forced him to separate from that group of friends, and rallied the school authorities in putting pressure on him to reform, which he did. His submission and embracing of the new path was finally crowned by getting into the 'A' stream.

Most important, streaming becomes a consideration in the strategies of teachers and pupils in constructing their joint practices. This becomes especially clear when what is in question is one of those key moments in an educational career, a promotion or demotion between ability groups.

Recall the situation of Joanne Carpenter at St Margaret's College, which we discussed in some detail as an example of the construction of teacher-pupil practices. On the strength of just-middling marks, Joanne was in the upper class for Social Studies. This year they got a teacher the class didn't like and began to give her a hard time. Joanne got fingered as the 'ringleader' in the disruption. She acknowledges this may have been half true but, 'the others would laugh whatever I said, and then go all stupid' — whether she meant to be silly or not. It's the pattern of escalating peer support for small-scale resistance that we noted earlier in the chapter. Anyway, it got to the point where the school took action. Joanne was put down into the lower class.

She is pretty sore about it. The kids there talk all the time (discipline is far from total, even at St Margaret's), and she can't concentrate on her work. So she is thinking of giving the subject up — though she can't at the moment, because of timetable problems. She hasn't approached the teachers to have her demotion reconsidered, because she is afraid that if she did and got knocked back, she would find herself in a worse situation than before. The only way she can think of to mitigate the risk is to phrase the request as if it were half a joke.

Joanne's dilemma feels rather like Mark Grey's, which we discussed in the section on teacher-pupil practices. The incident is, doubtless, less vital than his difficulty in approaching teachers. It is still a useful illustration of the way practices interact, structured by the system of ability grouping and adult-child power relations, to produce educational 'choices' such as doing or dropping a subject.

Ability grouping is done for quite a range of reasons. It is believed to make teaching easier and more efficient; it allows the school to cream off talent and put the bright kids through accelerated or more intensive instruction; it is a means of social control of the kids, as we have just seen with Joanne Carpenter, and (if staffroom gossip is to be believed) of the teachers too, allowing school authorities to reward and punish. On these counts ability grouping in different schools appears to have much the same logic.

But the overall meaning of the system is radically different in working-class and ruling-class schools. Creaming in the working-class school, the formation of an 'A' stream, is a means of saving a few supposedly talented kids from the common fate of the milieu. It is a means of separating them from what most of their teachers see as failure, rather than attaching them to success. Creaming in the elite private school is about success and nothing else. It is about creating a highly competitive, pressure-cooker situation which will launch the best students into the best faculties at university and gain academic standing for the school as a whole. For this reason some private schools not only stream throughout, but also narrow the 'A' stream about fourth year, so that those who aren't quite in the top bracket won't hinder those who really are in the fight for top places at Matric. (Ian Walker is one who is likely to be creamed down by this arrangement.)

Beyond the top stream, there are still marked differences. Ability grouping in ruling-class schools is designed to create pressure for achievement through all the streams — hence the 'incredible' system of differentiation noted by Mrs Chenoweth at Wellington College. And in a school where the official programme has hegemony, there is no doubt that pressure is created. (It is only in such a context that Chris Legrange can make his protest by coming last in his class.) In the working-class comprehensive it creates no pressure beyond the top couple of groups. Kate McArthur is a good illustration of what happens. She was put into 7H and told that if she 'really works at it' she could get put up into a higher grade. What she did instead was treat it as an insult, give the finger to the whole system, and devote herself to making life as hard for the teachers as she conveniently could.

The hegemonic curriculum

The rationale of the streaming system is differential ability, and that in turn is defined in relation to a particular kind of learning. Any school is the scene of a number of different kinds of learning, and sometimes substantially different curricula; but all the schools we studied are organized around a particular organization of learning and content which we will call the 'hegemonic curriculum'. The crucial features of this curriculum are hierarchically-organized bodies of academic knowledge appropriated in individual competition. The formal examinations that traditionally have gone with it, and have been the subject of a long debate, are less central than the organization of content and learning. These have massive effects even for kids who will never face a certifying exam.

The first of these effects is that organizing the school around the appropriation of academic knowledge has the effect of marginalizing other kinds of knowledge. It's important to recognize that this marginalizing is done by kids and parents as well as by teachers. Unstead High, for instance, has introduced an innovative music programme in which the kids invent their own instruments, listen to music from Asia, and so forth; and the school authorities have made it part of the Year 9 'core', that is, have made it compulsory. The response has been almost entirely negative, and much of the criticism comes from 'good' students who regard it as a waste of time.

> Then you have subjects like Music. That should be an elective, 'cause Music's not going to help me get a job for a dentist, is it?

Neither, as it happens, is English or Social Studies or French or Geography — except so far as the school and certification system make these necessary steps to becoming a dentist eventually. A familiar consequence of this is that skills, interests and impulses that don't fit in the academic mould are pushed to the side. Carl Siemens, whom we have mentioned briefly before, is an excellent humorist, highly imaginative and quick-witted in conversation, an inventor, and a very fair artist. About the only thing the school has been able to do with this wide-ranging creativity is put him to work on the school magazine. So far as the 'serious' work of 9A goes, Carl functions as a disruption, bored himself, and disturbing to the good order of the class.

The school may still succeed in attaching Carl to academic work, or finding further outlets for his artistry. A more serious marginalization is the kind of thing that has happened to Bill Poulos, whom we have discussed as a 'resister'. From the point of view of academic learning, he is by now a dead loss; his teachers say he is 'not trying'. His antagonistic relation with the school carried over (as it usually does) to our interview. Bill was at first sullen, head bowed, monosyllabic. He only gradually unwound as he found a sympathetic listener to his catalogue of criticisms of the school. Once he had unwound, the interviewer found a person who wants to learn (and had a tremendous respect for the only teacher who had taken trouble with him and coached him outside the formal framework); an excellent organizer, as our description of his surfing roster in Chapter Two illustrated; a musician, who is picking up the electric guitar and plays with a local band; and a practical social scientist who is a better judge of the local labour market than his parents and most of his teachers. Here is an array of skills and enthusiasms, and a supply of energy, that simply cannot be integrated into his school's formal organization of knowledge and learning.

The effect of this, in working-class comprehensives where there are a good number of kids like Bill, and where the teachers do keep trying (and don't lapse into what Arlette Anderson calls 'glorified babysitting'), is a splitting of the curriculum — in short, the creation of a multilateral school. The academic programme remains hegemonic, in the sense that it still defines the staff's conscious purposes, and is followed by the top stream who are generally recognized as the best students. Teachers faced with the problem of 'doing something' with the rest of the kids construct alternative syllabuses. Patterns vary, but usually include fragments of the 'real' curriculum in combination with 'practical' subjects (woodwork, metalwork, domestic science, typing, and the newer subjects like technics, electronics, ceramics). Often there is an attempt by enthusiastic and imaginative teachers to deal with topics that are 'relevant and meaningful' to the kids and their lives: early leaving, early employment or unemployment, early pregnancy and marriage, how to get a job, how to relate to employers, what's the state of the labour market, how to relate to bureaucracies, how to relate to each other, contraception, hire purchase, 'consumer education', driving, and so on.

And yet the results are quite often different from what is hoped for. Teachers work under massive constraints of time, resources, experience in curriculum construction, and the dominance of the academic curriculum as the definition of what is really worth learning and doing. In consequence the 'alternative' curriculum is usually in fact a *subordinate* curriculum. It therefore serves to compound the divisions introduced into the school by the academic curriculum: practical *vs* theoretical, abstract *vs* applied, 'bright' *vs* 'dumb'. Here we see the grass-roots version of just those dilemmas which we noted in Chapter One as facing the planners of mass secondary education, from Wyndham to Karmel.

The working-class comprehensive school is decisively distinguished from the old technical schools, or the English 'secondary moderns', by the presence of the hegemonic curriculum. These schools try to attach, and in some measure succeed in attaching, part of their clientele to an academic programme. Here the fact that the curriculum is organized as competitive individual appropriation of knowledge — what schools, universities and testers call 'academic achievement' — becomes important. For this is not the characteristic way knowledge or personal interactions are organized in working-class life. This point is difficult to document in a simple and clear-cut way, but we think it is important. Repeatedly, in studying the interviews of working-class kids and their parents, we have come across a contradiction between the family's practices of cooperative coping and the school curriculum's demand for individual achievement.

It would be silly to exaggerate this into an absolute gap between 'working-class culture' and the 'middle-class culture' of the school. We do suggest, nevertheless, that there is a contradiction between two kinds of practice that the kids are involved in; and that this can disrupt the family, or prevent the school attaching the student to its system of achievement, or both. The experience of the Greys is a fair example of the first of these effects, the experience of the Joneses is a fair example of the second, and both show the degree of hurt that is involved. Carl Siemens, among his other problems, is facing the same kind of dilemma. Security is desperately important to both his mother (who struggled on a deserted wife's pension for most of his childhood) and his stepfather (who was also brought up by a single mother). And Carl is tied into this by very strong bonds of identification and affection with his mother. Though she strongly supports his schooling and wants him to go on as far as possible, he would have to break with his major patterns of relationship, and isolate himself from the interactions which build solidarity among family and friends, to become an academic achiever.

In Steven Tait's life this contradiction is completely lacking. Though he has had his troubles with Churchill College and with his family, notably the 'smoking' incident discussed in the last section, it isn't because of any incompatibility between school-based and home-based practices. On the contrary, the requirements for success in both are exactly the same. His parents are both professionals whose working lives have been built on the appropriation of knowledge in exactly the form he meets it in the school. Careers constructed by individual competition have been central in the family's history for generations past: one of Steven's grandfathers was a company manager and other male relatives have been professionals; and the lives of the womenfolk have been subordinated to their husbands' careers and organized to support them. Mr Tait is hoping to start Steven in his own profession, and has already given some thought to the network of contacts that can be activated to help him. Steven's submission to his parents' plans, his participation in the Tait family's ongoing collective practice, is of a piece with his compliance with the school. The 'solution' to his rather tentative rebellion last year was a solution that worked in both spheres.

The sociology of education has pointed to the importance of the form of educational knowledge; we would wish to stress equally the form of its appropriation. The organization of learning as individual competition is a vital feature of the hegemonic curriculum and its connection with class relations. While pure free-market competition between many small producers is not the basis of economic organization in the present age of giant corporations, big bureaucracies, tightly-organized professions, international monopolies and cartels, competition is still important: both between big organizations and among entrepreneurs for control of them. Formal qualifications are important in this context. In the professions they are an absolute prerequisite to entry and are tied to subsequent advancement. In management, qualifications are not important in the struggle to get on (hence the rather modest correlation that research has found between level of education and lifetime earnings), but they have become nearly essential to entering the contest. Mr Andrews, a senior executive of a major manufacturing company, observed to us that when he went into business it was enough to have gone to the right school, as he did. Now, his firm wouldn't look at a management recruit who didn't have a degree.

Given this, the fine competitive grading at places like Wellington College doesn't appear anything like as 'incredible' as Mrs Chenoweth makes out. It is not only a matter of keeping pressure on the kids, it is also a matter of giving parents information they need. Here, for instance, is Mrs Walker on the same point:

> I think the reports from Milton College are very good . . . We know exactly where Ian stands, because he's given the place in class, then he's given whether he's A, B, C, D standard in the year. Right, so he might come thirtieth in the class, but he still gets an A for that subject within the whole year, so we know *exactly* where he stands; and then they make a comment. I think his reports are excellent. Whereas at the local state school you just get 'outstanding', 'satisfactory', 'improving', or whatever; and you don't know where you are, you haven't a clue.

The information the Walkers need, as this makes very clear, is their child's exact *competitive* standing, which his school duly provides.

A lot of what goes on in and around ruling-class schools has to do with learning the survival techniques for an arena of competition. Brian Andrews, who is being pointed towards the same kind of career as his father but who has to go through university to get into it, is being carefully trained as a competitor, as we noted when discussing football. He was selected for advanced classes at primary school, and placed in the 'A' stream on arrival at Milton College. Last year he slipped, getting his 'worst report ever' according to Mrs Andrews, coming eighteenth in Maths, normally his best subject. Again according to his mother, it was a severe blow to his self-esteem. He has pulled himself back together, 'worked day and night', and is back in the top two or three in that subject. His sister, a year older, is doing likewise. According to her school, she is an 'over-achiever' — that is, by dint of hard work, she is doing better in competition with her peers than the IQ tests say she should. Their mother notes she never has to tell them to do their homework, they organize themselves.

This is the context of the academic pressure such kids place on their teachers, which we noted in discussing the 'A' stream at Auburn College. Brian similarly criticizes his current Maths teacher for being slack, for not checking his homework and for having 'not enough strictness' in his classes. Brian also turns some of the criticism inwards. He says he's having trouble with languages because he can't handle the oral work as well as the written, and with English because he has no ability in creative writing. In fact this is exaggerated self-doubt; but our point here is not Brian's actual skills — it is the *way* he is appraising them. He is developing an unflattering estimation of his own strengths and weaknesses in the world of learning, conceived simply and unashamedly as an arena of individual competition. He has carefully developed the techniques of battle, notably exam technique. (He notes, for instance, the importance of keeping your wits about you in the exam-room, and can spell out the traps of multiple-choice tests.) His mother suggests that he positively *enjoys* exams, as 'one more competition'; this is possible, though it may also be flavoured by the opinions Brian chooses to pass for family consumption. At all events he is a self-conscious competitor, and obviously an efficient one.

It would be difficult for him not to have this view of education, as he has grown up in a family whose whole world is organized by notions of competition and hierarchy. The family's history has centred on Mr Andrews' rise within his company, a career that, as it happened, started with winning a scholarship to the private school that placed him with this firm. His view of education is entirely about 'getting ahead', and both parents carefully monitor school events to this end. Mr Andrews makes knowledgeable remarks on the Matric aggregates needed for this and that faculty at university and about where exactly his boys fit in the pecking order: he observed of his elder son Allen that the teachers at Milton got as much out of him as possible given that 'he wasn't a straight-A man'. He structures the whole world for his boys in hierarchical, competitive terms. Thus he agrees with suggestions made by his friends that Allen, who wants to be a teacher, should aim not to be a teacher but to be a Headmaster: one should always try to reach 'the top of one's field', whatever it is. Even if one were a truckdriver, Mr Andrews suggests, one could get satisfaction if one construed it as a 'challenge' — for instance, striving to get the best safety record of all drivers in the firm.

The total incomprehension of how working-class men actually experience their jobs that is betrayed in Mr Andrews' remarks on truck-driving is a clear signal of the social basis of this way of thinking about the world and about education. It reflects a specific class experience and promotes specific class interests. Learning organized as individual competition is a practice that likewise has a specific social origin, and promotes one set of class interests over another. This is most clearly registered in the class-patterning of school success — the facts recorded by the statistics of the inequality research. But it is a much wider issue than that. The post-war expansion of secondary schooling and its reorganization along comprehensive lines has meant that all working-class kids are exposed at crucial moments of their lives to the practices of competition, to academic knowledge, and to the ideology of ability. More, their experience of these practices and ideas, and their reactions to them, are crucial in shaping the rest of their lives. Just as selection by formal academic qualifications has become more important in the fate of individuals in the ruling class, so have working-class people increasingly had to reckon with schooling when they are doing their calculations about their chances in the labour market.

In the first instance the impact of this has been to spread amongst working-class people the practice and theory of individual competition, the idea that what you get is what you deserve. More fundamentally, the effect of mass participation in the hegemonic curriculum, its surrogates and spin-offs, is to deepen profound uncertainties and conflicts in working-class life. There are few working-class people who swallow the ideology of 'brains' holus-bolus, yet there are fewer still who reject it completely. Under the resister's rejection of school is a deep hurt and sense of injury, which grows out of accepting, at least in part, the school's argument that the individual has failed. The protests of working-class parents against the abstractness and uselessness of much of the school's knowledge are accompanied by embarrassment, even shame, at being 'uneducated', at not having what the school has. Mr Poulos, whose trade unionism is an expression of the working-class value of solidarity, is also humiliated by being a subordinate in the world of work, at having failed to 'get on'.

The effect of the hegemony of the academic curriculum within mass secondary education, then, is not to *obliterate* ideas and practices which grow out of working-class needs and experience. It is to disorganize and fragment them; and at the same time it produces resistance to the imposition of academic curriculum. In so doing it is both part and paradigm of the operation of class hegemony in Australian life. We are now in a position to examine the relations between schools and their classes, and the class system as a whole.

4

Schools and the organisation of social life

'SCHOOL EFFECTS' AND WHERE TO FIND THEM

What do schools do? What difference do they make? Most people answer these questions by looking at the impact of schools on individuals. What they see varies, of course, according to where and how they look. Most research on 'school effects' has looked at a few 'variables' — mainly examination results, and sometimes the social and economic futures which lie beyond them. Even those taking a broader view of what might be measured and counted about schools are usually content just to measure and count.

We have already advanced objections to this way of understanding what schools do. The impact of schooling on people is deeper, more complex, and more enduring than such an approach can possibly grasp. That part of our case has been presented, and we turn now to a further and, in a sense, more fundamental argument. Schooling is not only a matter of doing things to individual lives but is also a way of organizing those lives. Schools help to shape the way society is arranged, from the most immediate and obvious level of friendships and relationships to the most general and extended relations or 'structures'.

This view of what schools do has been implicit in much of our argument to this point. It is time to draw those threads together and elaborate our case. We will begin with the direct relations set up by schools, especially those between teachers and parents; then consider how schools shape and are shaped by class, and then gender; and conclude with an argument about the way schools work in the social order as a whole — their role, that is, in the production of relations between classes and sexes.

SCHOOLS AND THE CLASS SYSTEM

Teachers and parents

Our evidence suggests that in some important respects the relation between teachers and parents has to be understood as itself a class relation; that is, one structured by their respective class situations. Let us consider the situation in our two main groups of schools.

The ruling-class parents characteristically see teachers as their paid agents: skilled and expert, agents nevertheless. 'We hire teachers and preachers', Mr Carpenter remarks, 'and then often waste our money by not listening to them'. To Mr Walker even the principal is a hired gun:

> The high school is very much determined really on what the headmaster is like. And that's true of a private school too, but I think because a private school headmaster reports to a trustee or board, there's more pressure on him to perform than the headmaster of a high school who reports to an education department. The private school on the average will produce better headmasters because if they don't perform they'll be kicked out of school or the school goes downhill very quickly.

The teachers register the same point when they speak of parental interventions resulting in a teacher being sacked, or new curriculum proposals not happening because the parents wouldn't wear it.

This doesn't mean that these parents have fingertip control over classrooms. Far from it. Teacher professionalism resists this, and many of the parents recognize the teachers as professionals. A strong principal, too, will give her teachers protection from interference: we know of instances where parents have been sent away quite brusquely after coming to complain to the Head. Yet the fact that the parents are mostly richer, more powerful, and often better educated than the teachers, and that they are (even if indirectly) the teachers' employers, gives them a marked confidence in these transactions and a strong sense that they have rights to exercize.

The details of this vary with class situation; not all parents 'own' the school in the way that Mr Walker feels he does. With the Ellises, for instance, it was basically Annie's own decision to go to a private school after she had failed to get into a selective state school, and wanted a means of escaping from the working-class girls who were giving her a hard time (for snobbery) at her local comprehensive high. Though her father had risen via his trade into middle management in an expanding firm, he doesn't feel very comfortable as a manager or exercizing authority over workers. And her mother, who had to work an extra day a week to help pay the school fees, is a secretary who went to an inner-city Tech. These parents certainly don't feel they have authority in relation to the school.

Nor for that matter do the Carpenters, who have neither university degrees nor social style, though they do have a lot of money. They are more than a little sceptical of over-theoretical knowledge and social pretension; and therefore in some ways contest the school's programme, especially its implicit programme of cultivating an elite. So when he says 'we hire' teachers, Mr Carpenter is stressing his own economic superiority as well as alluding to a sense of cultural exclusion.

In striking contrast with Mr Walker's view of headmasters is this experience of Mrs Arlott's at Rockwell High. After being criticized by her parents for a bad Year 7 report, Heather Arlott in Year 8 had been telling them that she was doing well and that the teachers had said so. When the next report came home, 'it was terrible'.

> So I rang the High School up, I rang the principal; and he said that she must have been a liar. And I said, 'Do you know the child?' And he said, 'No'. I said, 'Well how do you know she's a liar?' He said, 'I'll talk to the girl'. And he never rang me back, he never done anything. So, I just didn't bother after that. He called Heather in and asked her why she thought she was doing so well; and that was it. He just dropped it, he never rang back to say . . . he'd spoke to her, and she is a liar or she's not, or anything. So I haven't got much faith in him.

There are two notable things about the background to this incident. First, it was the only time Mrs Arlott had approached the school for something, as against being summoned when Heather was in trouble. Second, the principal involved is not unusually bureaucratic, he is well respected by many parents, and is regarded by some of his teachers as too soft and easily pushed around by parents and kids.

So what is in play here is not an unusually demanding parent or unapproachable principal; it is in fact a very typical transaction between working-class parent and state school, throwing into relief the class positions from which it is conducted. The teacher concerned is better educated and better off than the parent, as well as being the possessor of authority in the school, and had no hesitation in passing judgment on the child. Mrs Arlott, a factory worker whose earliest memory of her own schooling is of humiliation, feels this judgment as an insult and demands a better answer; but, when it isn't forthcoming, she has no redress.

In Chapter Two we explored transactions between parents and schools, and it is clear that there are a number of ways in which working-class parents are excluded by the school system. Again, we want to stress, this is not usually because of anti-parent attitudes on the part of the teachers. Most teachers positively approve of parent involvement with the schools, and feel professionally supported when there are signs that their work is noticed and valued.

At the same time their professional ideology draws a boundary around what they are the experts on, a boundary which is naturally much sharper in a school where most of the parents have less education, as well as lower incomes, than the teachers have. Bearing in mind that the conditions of the teachers' work normally prevent them from knowing much about the families their pupils come from, there is likely to be a real social distance between teachers and parents. It is well illustrated by failure of the main form of regular contact that they have, parent/teacher nights.

Where there is a precipitating event, this social distance can result in stark mutual incomprehension and mistrust. The Greys provide a notable example. Mark is very fond of his English teacher, a young live-wire who is highly popular with the whole class.

> Some teachers are really strict . . . Then you get our English teacher Miss Goffman, she'll let you have a joke and that, long as you do your work. And you feel really good in that class.

His mother, however, has a different view:

> I don't know how they teach them anything at times. Mark's come home with some choice jokes from his English teacher. I think — she's a lady — she's been to the club the night before. Cause some of the jokes aren't the best! And I think, 'Well, I'm not sending you up there for that!' He doesn't like me to say that, cause everyone else thinks it's beaut. I don't. I'm old-fashioned.

Mr Grey also is very critical of the English teaching. He considers that it doesn't instruct the kids in skills they will need in jobs — that is, how to spell properly and write well — and late last year he went up to the school and gave Miss Goffman a piece of his mind.

We have Miss Goffman's account of this visit, too, and the difference is striking. She remembers the episode vividly as a case of an 'overbearing' father trying to lay down the law about what his son should be learning, and demanding to know why he wasn't. Miss Goffman is a tolerant and friendly person in general, but in recalling this episode there was a real touch of hostility. She even suspected that Mr Grey had been drinking before he came. In fact, he was ill.

We have spelt this out, not to take sides in a dispute now over and done with, but to illustrate a very important process. It is striking how this kind of transaction confirms working-class parents' exclusion from the school: by transforming a *disagreement over pedagogy*, which is how it started on the Greys' side, into a sign of the *parents' educational incompetence*, which is how Ms Goffman sees it. 'They don't understand it', she laments repeatedly in discussing parents' views of the school's work. She is pleased for them to participate — but on the school's terms, not theirs. She would like parents, for instance, to come and help paint the new Resources Centre.

The relation between teachers and parents in schools like Rockwell High, then, is also a class relation, though one structured in a very different way from that in the ruling-class schools. To say that, implies something that doesn't often come into focus in discussions of educational inequality, except in rather vague suggestions that schools have a middle-class culture. If the parents have a class situation, so do the teachers.

Not that teachers' class situations are simple, or teaching an easily-classified job. In some ways it is like a profession, for instance in its training requirements; and professionalism as the model of teaching has been influentially promoted (notably by the Australian College of Education, a body set up partly for that purpose in 1959). It is also like a skilled trade, in terms of its level of unionization, and a little above trades in average wages. In the past, like trades, teaching has provided an important track along which workers' children could better themselves and gain economic security. Teaching, at least in the state system, is like a bureaucracy in terms of its career structure and tenure; but very unlike one in the nature of the daily work, as teachers work most of the time entirely unsupervised. And with the expansion of the education system since the war, teaching has taken on something of the character of a mass occupation: there are now more than 170,000 teachers in the country. Like other mass occupations, teaching has felt the impact of the economic downturn in the 1970s, with the arrival, for the first time in a generation, of chronic teacher unemployment.

This is hardly the beginning of an analysis of teachers' class situations; but even so, it is clear that they are under pressures that are both strong and contradictory. Like their pupils, teachers can be injured by the class relations they find themselves in; and they too have to evolve responses which are often inconsistent. The ideology of professionalism has plainly been more acceptable to teachers in private schools than a response based on their situation as employees, the definition Mr Carpenter and Mr Walker gave them. Accordingly, these teachers identify themselves with the ideas and interests of their employers much more thoroughly than state school teachers, and have set up separate associations. But with the economic pressure of the last few years these associations too have begun to look more and more like unions, engaged in much more determined economic bargaining than ever before.

State school teachers, for their part, have faced the problem of defining their relationship with a mainly working-class clientele, with whom they share some important experiences: among them common background in many cases, and the experience of working for an impersonal and often insensitive employer. Since the 1960s teacher unions have been taking strike action on occasion; and the downward pressure on wages and conditions that has accompanied teacher unemployment has led to worsening industrial relations, culminating in 1981 with the NSW Teachers' Federation going on strike on the first day of school, and the South Australian Institute of Teachers having its first strike ever.

Yet there are many things holding teachers back from an identification with the working class, including their training, their professional ideology, and their mobility. Economic pressure can sharpen the sense of difference as easily as reduce it. In handling the contradictions of their situation, the main response by teachers so far has been to stress difference, defining themselves as separate from, and often culturally superior to, the working-class families they have to deal with. This is the background to the sharply-felt put-downs of parents we have spoken of. It is only exceptional teachers, at the moment, who can turn these abrasive class relations to positive purposes.

Yet these teachers exist, and are recognized. Parents' narratives of their own schooling often told warmly of particular teachers who had been important in reaching across barriers which they too found hard to understand. Looking at teachers now, they make similar distinctions between those who are 'just in it for the money' and those who 'really care' about their kids — and the second kind matter a lot to working-class parents. There is ground, then, on which a different kind of relationship could be built; and the very contradictoriness of state school teachers' situations means there are potentials for different kinds of practice.

Market and bureaucracy

The relation between schools and the class structure is most immediate in the transactions between teachers and parents or teachers and students. But what happens face-to-face doesn't make much sense unless we see the larger pattern from which it emerges — and which accounts for the way people experience those immediate relationships as intractable. The schools are also related to class processes as institutions, and we need to explore that more general connection.

Our basic argument is that there is a fundamental difference here between working-class and ruling-class education. We summarize it in this formula: the ruling class and its schools are articulated mainly *through a market*, while the working class and its schools are articulated mainly *through a bureaucracy* (or, to put it very strictly, through the state via a bureaucracy). Much of the evidence for this contention has already been given; this section will try to summarize it, propose some qualifications to our main thesis, and spell out some of its implications.

We have already indicated that the Independent schools as a group operate as a kind of market. Parents see themselves from the start as making some kind of choice as to where they will send little Jean or John. Their teachers are aware of this: 'the parents shop around', as one remarked to us. When parents come to the school with suggestions or complaints, it is always with the implication in the background that if not satisfied they may take their custom elsewhere. More than one family in our sample has done just this. Chris Legrange, for instance, was taken away from his prep school when his mother became angry at a 'pig-headed' decision by the principal that excluded him from the school sports. Louisa Doker, who now attends St Margaret's College, was taken away from a more expensive and glamorous school because her parents decided it was over-concerned with social pretension, promoted snobbery, and was neglecting the proper academic concerns of schooling.

In this market, parents literally buy an educational service from one of a number of organizations that are in business to provide it. Many of them put the matter in just these terms, and are very much concerned to see that their money has been well spent. The school's council formally, the school's principal actually, are entrepreneurs in this market, who must in some fundamental ways treat the parents as customers.

This is certainly not a pure 'free market', and there are a number of things that restrain the parents' shopping around. Family tradition is one. Anthony Graves is going to Churchill College, his brothers are going to Churchill College, his cousins went to Churchill College, his father went to Churchill College, his uncles went to Churchill College and his grandfather went to Churchill College. Here is a tightly-organized collective practice that would hardly admit a consumer choice to send Anthony to the rival Wellington College, let alone the local high.

That is, of course, an extreme case but some degree of family loyalty to a particular school is common enough. Sometimes it is the child who insists on family tradition. Ian Walker was certainly destined for a private school, but his parents were hesitating among several; according to both Ian and his mother, it was Ian who chose:

> When I was small, Mum and Dad booked me into Scotch, Loyola, a couple of other schools. And they sort of said, 'Okay, what school do you want to go to?' And I said, 'Milton' because that's where Dad went.

The family's religion may also constrain choice. Most of the elite private schools are formally associated with one or other of the four old-established churches in Australia. Geography also. Each school typically draws from a distinct sector of the city; and one of the schools in our sample was founded explicitly because there was no church school in its quarter of the city at the time. Parents repeatedly observed to us that they didn't want their kids to have to travel too far. Geography is one of the most often-stated reasons for picking a particular school.

These influences, then, complicate the market, segmenting it in different ways. It is still impressive how powerfully market criteria operate across them. Family loyalty, for instance, may be satisfied with having one boy go to Dad's old school, while a brother with higher academic hopes is sent to a school with a stronger academic reputation. And we have some reasons to think that the market has become more generalized, and more competitive, in the last twenty years or so. The schools are less exclusive in terms of religion: even those with a clear church affiliation now make a point of providing for other denominations, and even non-Christian religions, as more than one principal stressed to us. Car-based transport has made geography less of a restriction. One of the basic forms of market segmentation in the past, gender, no longer totally segregates: in the past decade a number of the Independent schools have gone coeducational.

Finally, the continued expansion of state high schools has reshaped the ruling-class education market. The high schools in upper-crust suburbs, and the old selective highs where they survive, compete on even terms with elite private schools for honours in the matriculation race. This makes them a serious alternative in the eyes of those ruling-class parents who are more concerned with academic performance than anything else. We have no statistics to show how many have been drained away from the private schools like this, but we can certainly say that a good number of our parents, who did choose private schools, are aware of this as a serious alternative. Megan Ryder was sent to St Margaret's, for instance, for reasons she doesn't entirely understand as there is a state school with an excellent reputation nearby. Her father's account of the decision revealed a remarkably sophisticated analysis of the merits and recent histories of the two schools, in which the decision finally went for the private school because he felt the push for egalitarianism in the state system resulted in less of a commitment to the very brightest students.

We have laid stress on the market, partly to counter the popular but anachronistic image of these schools as havens of mindless loyalty to the Old School Tie, but more because the *effects* of a market in educational services are profound. The attitude of calculative appraisal, which a market demands, penetrates every aspect of these families' relationships with their schools. Mr James, an insurance broker, was sufficiently committed to St Helen's College to put in a lot of time and effort in helping it get over a recent financial crisis; but that loyalty didn't stop him, on the morning he first got inside information about trouble brewing, ringing up two other private schools to see if he could get his daughter in there. The daughter in question, reviewing the state of teaching at the school, passed judgement on several teachers and eventually came to the Physical Education teacher, who is getting old and fat and not too energetic:

> The sooner we get rid of her, the better.

And she's only 14 years old.

Of course she is right; it *is* better for her if an ageing and inefficient teacher is 'got rid of'. And the point is much sharper when it is a question of academic subjects. The market structure thus creates a distinct milieu for teachers, subjecting their performance to constant appraisal in terms of the commodity the school is placing on the market.

That commodity is not fixed, which brings us to another crucial effect of the market: it provides the central mechanism of change in ruling-class education. For each school, individually, is vulnerable. It may be that the oldest and most famous would never be allowed to collapse completely; but others have, and even top-flight schools have got into serious financial difficulty at times. Without necessarily going out of business, a school is still sanctioned if it slips in the market. Its income from fees stagnates or contracts, the best teachers are harder to hold, more of the energy of the school administration goes into just keeping afloat, and so on. These pressures can be severe, and they promote change in two ways.

One is that poor market performance can lead to a change of regime: a new principal, a heavy turnover of staff, a renovated curriculum. Something of this sort had happened in a number of the schools we studied, and teachers were familiar with similar events in others. A change of regime doesn't always work, as in the case of the too-progressive headmaster who set about refurbishing a somewhat stuffy establishment school with student-centred pedagogy, socially-relevant curricula, coeducation, and a relaxation of discipline on points like uniforms and allowing senior students to smoke on the school grounds. The parents soon decided that he was going too far, the market mechanism operated against him, and the Council eventually brought in a more traditionally-minded principal to get the school back on the rails. But in other cases, schools which had grown slack under ageing or unimaginative principals have been restored dramatically by this kind of process.

There is also incremental change within an existing regime. The pressure of the market requires these schools to keep a close watch on each other. The progress of innovations in one, such as coeducation or relaxation of discipline, is monitored and debated in others. Dissatisfied teachers may well go to another school where their professionalism is better recognized — an important constraint on the power of the principal. Parents at one of our schools repeatedly criticized the principal as too autocratic and hence unable to hold the best staff. This school had indeed slipped in the academic ratings.

The point of our examples is this: the market provides a mechanism by which schools can change in response to changes in the ruling class. There is nothing automatic or simply functional about this. For one thing the pressures from the market are diverse and sometimes contradictory (when, for example, girls' schools are expected to produce both marriageable femininity and high-powered academic competitors). For another, market pressures must be transformed into a viable educational practice. What the market mechanism provides is the space within which this can be done.

By contrast, the working class is related to its schools through a bureaucracy. The state lays down — as it has for a hundred years — that all children shall go to school between particular ages. It provides schools so that this can occur and a department to administer them. As we have seen, the schools are organized regionally and the department defines and polices their boundaries (and determines whether there shall be exceptions, such as special purpose schools, or selective schools). The education department is also the employer for the staff, including non-teaching staff, of these schools, and the body with which teacher unions negotiate.[11] It posts teachers to particular schools, determines promotion, and undertakes their inservice training. It lays down, in general terms, the powers of school principals (which do *not* include the power to sack teachers) and deputies, and determines the funds they have to run their schools with. It influences the division of labour among the teaching staff, lays down in broad terms the rights and responsibilities of classroom teachers, and the kinds of curricula they are to pursue.

The Department (the capital seems appropriate) is thus the means by which most working-class education is organized. (We say 'most' because a minority of Australian working-class children go to Catholic systemic schools, an aspect of the diversity of both schooling and the working class which we consider again below.) Where parents in our study had direct contact with the Department, it was usually over the rules allocating children to particular schools, as we saw in Chapter Two. There is some contact over issues of attendance, although the selection of our sample virtually guaranteed that it would not include hard-core truants. Several of our parents, however, have vivid memories of truanting when they were kids, and of the apparatus of enforcement, including for one mother a stint of two weeks' imprisonment in a home for delinquent girls — as a result of being frightened to go to a new high school.

Direct contact, then, is likely to be abrasive; but direct contact is uncommon. For the great majority of working-class families the only significant contact with the Department is in and through the local schools, and especially through their principals. The Department is usually a distant and unknown quantity, and there may be good reason for a parent not to approach it. Mrs Midland, for example, described an occasion when she decided not to take a complaint 'higher' than the principal for fear of disadvantaging her child. On the other side, most principals try to channel parent/school contact through their own offices, or strictly regulate access to teachers. The state school principal is, like the principal of a private school, the focus of school-home relations. But here the resemblance ends.

Rather than marketing a service which parents can readily buy elsewhere, he (most are male) administers a service they are legally obliged to accept. Rather than being employer of the school's staff, he is a supervisor of workers employed by his employer, and whose careers have intersected with his more or less by chance. Rather than being the parents' agent, philosopher and friend, he is a figure who normally has no informal social contact with the parents; from their point of view, a face that appears out of the mists, acts as a law unto himself, and at the end of the day departs they know not where. Some principals do make a real attempt to get known in the neighbourhood, but it requires a special effort. When teachers in state schools talk together, the principal is usually called 'The Boss' — sometimes with affection, sometimes with hostility. He isn't an employer, but he is a power in the land; and in many places is the most senior representative of the state in the district.

The teachers too are functionaries of the state, not just its employees; they bear certain powers over the kids which are not delegated to them by the parents. Thus they stand in a significantly more authoritative relation to working-class families than the teachers in private schools do to ruling-class families, where the only claim to authority lies in their professional expertise. This is one cause of the higher levels of tension and conflict between teachers and pupils in the working-class schools. The teacher-pupil relation here is the carrier of a relation between state and subject, a coercive relation of a kind which always produces resistance, however muted.

Not that classroom teachers personally are likely to feel in a position of power; indeed teachers in working-class schools are more likely to feel like cogs in a machine, even under threat. The bureaucratic organization of teaching as an occupation has important consequences for teachers' relations with working-class communities. Teachers facing the problems of a tough school can always think of solving them by escaping through transfer to a 'better' school (though this is getting harder), or ignoring them by relying on security of employment and 'working to rule'. Further, career advancement in the state system usually means movement from one school to another. Given this, it may disrupt a teacher's career to form too close an attachment to the district she is currently teaching in, and to its people.

Like the market, bureaucracy is a means of change. This should be stressed, as 'bureaucracy' is often supposed to be inert, or even hostile to change. The state systems have been the scene of a great deal of the innovation in Australian education in the last generation. It is, however, innovation that stems mainly from ideas circulating among professional educators. With the sole exception of the diffuse demand for *more* education, it is difficult to think of any major change in state schools postwar that has actually stemmed from demands articulated by their working-class clientele. Changes have been imposed upon the working class; and a close examination of parents' comments on the differences between their own education and their children's shows that the changes are felt that way. Whether liked or not, they are things that have *happened to* these families, rather than things that they and their friends and relations and acquaintances and people like them have caused to happen. The contrast with the ruling class is marked.

Education and 'social mobility'

People's circumstances change, for better and for worse. In the 1920s the term 'social mobility' came into use among sociologists as a way of referring to such changes, and it has remained in common academic usage. The 'mobility' literature is extraordinarily confused, fundamentally because 'mobility' is not so much a theoretical concept as a metaphor, which requires us to think of social structures as ladders or pyramids, and social situations as their steps and ledges. Perhaps the most important confusion that needs to be put straight is the way 'mobility' is related to class.

Academic and other defenders of the established order like to claim that Australia has high rates of mobility, or to exaggerate the 'social mix' of independent schools, or to point to plebeian recruits to top business or political leadership; and then conclude that Australia is an 'egalitarian' or even 'classless' society. Schooling is often seen as the engine of this destruction of the class order, especially as it has expanded and been organized along meritocratic lines in the postwar period.

On the other side, critics who are convinced that capitalist societies like Australia *are* class societies often fall into the trap of minimizing mobility rates, sniffing out 'privilege' in all its forms, and mapping Old-School-Tie connections — as if that proved their point. The crucial confusion on both sides is in thinking that 'class' and 'mobility' are *opposed* terms.

There is a further radical position which insists, on the contrary, that 'class' and 'mobility' are entirely independent. Much of the reproduction theory which we examined in Chapter One, for example, argues that social places or positions exist as a result of the general structure of society, regardless of who occupies them or how they got there. This won't do either; if only because social struggles do often arise around the questions of access, of who gets where. Indeed, much of the school system and its organization must be understood as outcomes of such struggles.

We would argue that 'mobility' — or, more exactly, the events and processes to which the term refers — is both constituted by and helps to constitute class relations. Class practices are organized around this possibility, class relations are structured by it, and class struggles are fought over it.

To make sense of the issue and of the role schools have in it, it is vital to remember two things. First, that capitalist society is dynamic. This is one reason why the idea of 'mobility' is not a very helpful tool for grasping change. The 'scales' of occupational prestige and the like won't stand still, and it is impossible to get straightforward comparisons from one time to another or even one place to another. Changes in circumstances are common. No-one's position is fixed or guaranteed. In particular, no-one can guarantee the social position of their children. Second, 'downward' mobility occurs as well as 'upward'. Which of the two comes out as more frequent depends on how you set up the statistics; but there can be no doubt that the *possibility* of being worse off, or one's children being worse off, is a lively one for very large numbers of people, and has profound social consequences.

Take, for instance, the issue of when to leave school. A number of our working-class parents, looking back over their own lives, had a strong sense of having come out of poverty and deprivation into a kind of prosperity — a sense particularly sharp among those who grew up during the Depression. Some think, like sociologists, that it is a move up the ladder, but most see themselves as having come out of darkness into light. And they keenly wish to protect their children from slipping back into poverty in the future. Having learned that educational qualifications were a ticket to a better kind of job — usually by not having them — this made them strongly support their kids' staying at school as long as possible. The parents, in short, saw the school as a way of putting a *floor* beneath their kids' future economic circumstances. Though the kids usually had a cooler view of the labour market, and had other motives for leaving school anyway, a lot of them shared their parents' views at least to the extent of seeing a greater-than-minimum schooling as a way of escaping the *worst* jobs (which they talked of as 'factory' jobs).

The same kind of reasoning underlies some ruling-class parents' thoughts about the private schools: though here it is not descent into absolute poverty that is feared. In most cases the issue is thought about in an individual way: a matter of fitting out one's boy or girl with the set of technical or social qualifications needed to get the right job, make the right marriage, keep the right friends. At this level, the prevention of 'downward mobility' of the individual family becomes the motive for the process that at the larger level we can see as the formation of the class.

In some of our interviews, however, there is something even more interesting: an appreciation of this issue at the collective level — an element, in short, of class fear. When one of our ruling-class mothers justifies her daughter's private schooling by saying

> If you've given them an education that's the one thing nobody can take away from you

she has plainly got the idea that the other things the family possesses *might* be taken away. And she wants to make sure her daughter will still have some claim to preference.

We have stressed the theme of the *prevention* of 'mobility', as we think this bulks much larger in the class organization of schooling than the literature would suggest. It is, of course, still true that the school can be used to organize, or at least attempt, actual social promotion. Let us consider briefly an example. Amy and Jerry Wootton emigrated from Britain some years after they were married, and after a rather unsettled and unsatisfactory work experience; since then, they haven't looked back. He's a technician, she's a full-time secretary. In the fifteen years since they came to Australia they have acquired a house of their own, a car, a camper van, a boat, and in a few years they hope Amy can give up her job. They also have four kids, have put a lot of energy into the family, and look to the kids to keep up the momentum. As Amy sees it:

> We put our children one step higher up the ladder than we have, in education, their standards, their outlook in life, we have done a good job. But if we keep them on the same level as us, we haven't benefitted and neither have they.

The trouble is that much of the prosperity they read as the result of their own efforts was the result of emigrating into a boom — which has now ended. Getting their sons and daughters to stay at school for extra years is a matter of running harder to stay in the same place. And even where there is a clear goal, as with their daughter Pauline's wish to become a physiotherapist, the means are not automatically to hand. In Chapter Three we explored some of the problems working-class kids have in constructing the necessary teacher-pupil practices. Pauline Wootton is running into these problems in full measure. In fact she is engaging in a kind of low-profile resistance, including mentally abstracting herself from the lessons, turning up late for classes, ignoring teachers' authority in the classroom, not handing in assignments, and occasionally not turning up at all. To her parents, Pauline is a lively, affectionate, determined, independent-minded person with a clear goal. To her teachers, she is 'untidy', 'slow', 'cooperative', 'fairly responsible', 'lacklustre', 'moody', 'very thick at times', 'a fairly hard case without being a real bad one'. Very plainly, the school isn't serving her as the tool for advancement that her parents think it is. Though there is a will, this is not working as a way.

In the 'A' streams of schools like Greenway High and Rockwell High there are kids for whom it is working rather better; but a serious problem arises there in the relation with their families. As we observed in Chapter Three, the collective practices of working-class families typically work on principles of collective support and coping, rather than on a principle of individual competition. For the child of such a family to 'succeed' by 'academic achievement' requires practices in rupture with that. This tension can be worked out in a wide variety of ways — about the *least* common of which is overt opposition to more schooling. Mr Grey, for instance, firmly supports Mark's project of advancement through schooling into a profession. But it still involves Mark in a rejection of his father's 'On-The-Job' philosophy and self-image as a practical man, and, to an important extent, of his father personally, and the family and world which have formed him. It plainly hurts and puzzles both of them.

Private schools also are used as means of social promotion. The kind of trouble Pauline and Mark have run into is much less likely to happen in a family which is already organized, ideologically and practically, around the career of the husband/father and where the techniques of individual competition are bread-and-butter matters. We should note, however, a significant difference within the clientele of such schools. Professional families are dependent on the school in a way that capitalists (owners of family firms or corporate managers) are not. There is a crucial connection of professions with academic knowledge and academic competition. The refurbishing of ruling-class schools, of which we spoke in the last section, is thus more important to the professionals; conversely, the school has more leverage on them.

We'll return to the theme of 'mobility' several times in what follows but it may be useful to draw a few threads together here. Both as fact and as possibility, change of circumstance is an essential part of the class structure and of the class/education complex. Contrary to various shades of popular and scholarly opinion, it is a fundamental feature of schooling that it routinely produces 'upward' mobility, 'downward' mobility, and no mobility at all. The collective practices of families acknowledge this fact. They are organized both by the fear of becoming worse off and by the possibility of promotion. Social promotion through the education system is not an easy proposition where family practices have been oriented primarily to survival, and where a new set of relationships has to be constructed by the kids. For the working class, 'mobility' and disruption are two sides of the same coin, the school being implicated in both. For the ruling class, 'mobility' poses problems of class cohesion, but also provides, partly in the school, means for their solution. Let us now turn to examine the two cases separately.

RULING-CLASS EDUCATION AND THE RULING CLASS

The problem of the 'ruling class' and the 'middle class'

'I'd like to help run the country instead of it being run for me', said Marnie Paton, explaining why she might go into politics. Marnie had a firm grasp of the facts of power, and a certain youthful candour. The parents are more wary. Mrs Middleton, for example, is married to a man who is the managing director of a firm employing several thousand people and making a significant contribution to Australian industrial production and export; who is on the boards of a number of other companies; a leader in various industry organizations; and influential in a large welfare organization and in the shaping of welfare policy in his state. When asked how she would describe her social position, Mrs Middleton defined it as 'not of the establishment'. Nor is it only people like Mrs Middleton who do not see social relations in terms of class or power. When we have given talks to parents and teachers about our research, our use of the term 'ruling class' has given offence, raised eyebrows, and caused confusion.

Mrs Middleton thinks of her husband as 'not of the establishment', and we think of him as a member of a ruling class. The key difference is that Mrs Middleton is referring to what her husband *has* and we are referring to what he *does* and the circumstances in which he does it. What counts about Mr Middleton is the way in which he shapes the lives of others — his employees, and welfare clients, directly; all those affected by the condition of Australian manufacturing, and the mood and outlook of employers as a group, indirectly. That is, all of us.

But can we call this 'ruling'? As Mr Middleton tells it, no. From his point of view *he* is the one who feels the pressure. He worries that he cannot fit enough into the day, keep in touch with enough people and events, make judgments and decisions well or quickly enough. 'The market place is really boss', he says. All this is true. If by 'ruling' we mean giving orders and having them instantly obeyed, or being free of constraint, or self-indulgent, or carrying on like a parade-ground martinet — then Mr Middleton does not rule. But if we attend, rather, to the energy and creativity with which Mr Middleton responds to the constraints of his situation, and to his success in doing so (he takes justifiable pride in the survival of his firm where others have sunk); if we notice that he acts in the context of an extended network of people doing the same kind of thing; and if we see that the net result of that pattern of activity is the regeneration of a general set of relations of power and privilege — and that Mr Middleton has both — then he does indeed 'help to run the country'. It makes good sense to think of him as a member of a ruling class.

But Mr Middleton makes our case easy. What of the professionals in what we call our 'ruling class' sample? Or of their wives and children? Perhaps most awkward of all, what of the people like Harold Elliss, a carpenter who rose to a modest management position and whose daughter goes to St Margaret's College? Or George Midland, a salesman who now directs the sales section of a sizeable firm, whose son goes to Rockwell High?

There is a single source of the difficulties posed by these examples: the habit of thinking about the relations between individuals and class as a 'location'. We have examined the effects of this mentality in our discussion of 'mobility'. The mistake is in thinking of people as passive, or mere markers of a geometrical spot, and in thinking of the places they occupy as points on a scale or boxes in a pile. As we have seen, the connection between individuals and class is, in fact, an active relation to complex processes. That relation is only partly captured by the question: 'In which class is this person?'. It is more fully grasped by asking: 'Into which class relations does this person enter?'.

Take Marnie Paton's family, for example. Her father is a barrister with a prosperous city practice, and a visiting lecturer in law at a university. He is a member of a number of a professional bodies and president of the state tennis association. He and his wife have been important in restoring the fortunes of their daughters' school, which had fallen on hard times. Mrs Paton is a member of the Liberal Party. Both parents play at a prestigious golf club. They own a farm in the country, to which Marnie and her myriad school friends repair for holidays and weekends.

There is no need to expand this catalogue in order to make several points. First, there are important differences between the situation of the Middletons and the Patons, most notably (as we saw in Chapter Two) in the kind of work done by the fathers. Mr Paton's work and work situation are organized primarily around a particular body of expert knowledge, which is the exclusive possession of a particular group, and certified by the state. He is scarcely at all involved in the direction of other people's work. He is not the recipient of a flow of income generated by others; he earns only when he himself is working. Second, the Paton's class relations are by no means confined to those of the father's work. They extend to embrace the political, social and economic activity of all members of the family, including Marnie. In this way the differences between those who are members of the paid workforce and those who are not are expanded and compounded. There is a great variety in the situation of the eleven members of the two families.

There is, however, unity in diversity, and this is our third point. There are many mechanisms, including the school, which strive to express what is common in their interests and situations, and to subordinate differences and conflicts. More, these institutions and practices have their necessity and take their energy not only from people like the Patons and the Middletons but also from people in very different situations and relations. A class exists only in and through its relations with other classes. It is a complex association of activity, situation, and structure. When we speak of people as being 'in' a class, we do so as a shorthand way of referring to this complex pattern of relations. When we speak of the Middletons and the Patons as being 'in' the ruling class, we are referring to their access to power and privilege, and their dependence on and contribution to an order of things which sustain it.

Can we speak of a 'middle class'? We are in no doubt that the situation and experience of people like the Ellisses and Midlands is very different from the Middletons and the Patons (on the one hand) and most of our working-class parents (on the other). Their relation to the schooling system sums it up nicely. Peter Midland is much better off than most of the kids at Rockwell. Annie Ellis is much poorer than most of her friends at St Margaret's, and her father feels badly out of place when he goes to parents' meetings. They seem to belong somewhere in, yes, the middle.

Many of the age-mates of these students are to be found in schools like Rockwell High, and a few in schools like St Margaret's. However, there are also considerable numbers to be found in the state schools of suburbs more affluent than Rockwell or in the more modest Catholic schools. Students in such schools are more likely than our working-class sample to go on to higher education or the career-structured end of the labour market, and less likely to do so than our ruling-class group. In short, the educational situation and experience of these people speaks of quite particular economic and social circumstances which mark them off from most of the kids and parents we talked with. Different, yes. But a *class*? In our view, no.

Certainly not by numbers alone — contrary to much popular and academic myth, we are speaking here of a minority, not a majority, of the population. In any event, numbers are not what is really at stake in defining classes. Our basic argument is that Australia's middle managers, humbler professionals, technical experts and small business people do not have the stable interests which characterise both working and ruling class, and lack a developed set of cultural institutions devoted to the expression and defence of fundamentally shared interests. The distinctiveness of the groups commonly and loosely referred to as 'middle class' is best appreciated, we believe, as an example of the diversity and conflict which exist within classes. We turn now to look at one of those 'cultural institutions', the ruling-class school.

Shared space and the problem of autonomy

One of the most striking class contrasts to emerge from the study is the degree to which the secondary school, foreign territory to most working-class families, is possessed by the ruling-class families. They feel at home there; they feel, in a more than economic sense, that it is theirs.

The old-boy and old-girl networks, for instance, don't just function to the benefit of the old scholars. They are actively cultivated, and made to function, for the benefit of the school. A number of the parents we interviewed had been active in fund-raising, and in doing that had mainly sought out old scholars, parents and relatives. The fruits of this activity can be seen in any Independent school, in plaques commemorating gifts for the library, the swimming pool, the assembly hall, or whatever — which are usually named after the principal donors. The schoolchild lives in an aura of generous donation and symbolic ownership.

Fund-raising and finance committees are only one form of parental involvement. In fact each school is surrounded by a small swarm of peripheral institutions and activities: mothers' clubs, old scholars' associations, finance committees, parent/teacher meetings, fete committees, canteen committees, uniform exchange shops, sports days. . . . This is also true to a limited extent of state schools, and the contrast is instructive. Whereas working-class parents tend to fade out of these activities after their kids go up to the secondary school, ruling-class mothers seem to be quite as active in secondary schools, and fathers distinctly more so.

Further, the school staff is drawn into the social network of the families. Consider, for instance, this passage from the interview with Andrew Wilson, a history teacher at one of the ruling-class schools. He is speaking of a girl from a 'very very wealthy' family:

> I make jokes to her about 'tonight when you get home, walk across the polo field, around the heated pool and turn on the air conditioner and do your homework, you know, switch off the colour TV' — Sort of send her up, because I know in fact she's got a very ordinary home and her parents are very nice.
> *How do you know that?*
> I've met the parents.
> *When you say 'very ordinary home'?*
> Very ordinary-looking home, with nothing luxurious about it.
> *You've been there?*
> Yes.
> *How did you come to be there?*
> I was invited.
> *Why was that?*
> Well, I mean the parents met me, and I know the girl. Just friendly with her, and the girl's been around to our place, dropped us off a present for Christmas.

Where teachers are themselves old scholars of the same school, the contacts are already to some degree established. More than classroom teachers, the principal is drawn into the social networks of her constituents-and-customers. The principal of Andrew Wilson's school laments that she gets invited to dinner parties by more parents than she has days to spare; she simply can't keep up with the demand. The principal of another does it in groups, by appearing as an after-dinner speaker at Rotary, at fund-raising for other causes, and so on.

In a number of ways, then, the ruling-class school is a focus in a dense and extensive network of relationships. Far more than with the working-class school, it is the *shared space* of parents, teachers and students. As another of the teachers in the school just discussed put it,

> Well, here you get the feeling more that it's all a big family, everyone knows everyone, than in the state schools I've been in.

Now, all this has certain dangers. The school is *not* a family, and its functioning can be compromised if it begins to operate too much like one. If the parents move in too closely, they tread on ground that can also be claimed as the professional province of the teacher, and that will produce friction. While we were told stories of successful pressure by parents to remove teachers they disapproved of, we also heard of moments like this:

> I rang up the headmistress, Mrs Smith at the time, who really had a shot at me. She told me I was a malicious gossip, and how dare I say anything about a member of her staff!

On the other hand, if relations among all the parties get too cosy, the technical performance of the school can suffer, as pressure from parents for academic achievement wanes.

Most important, if the school gets too closely bound up in the surrounding networks, it loses the power to perform a crucial service for its constituency — to modernize ruling-class education. Earlier in this chapter we argued that the market in educational services provides the key mechanism by which renovation is achieved. The corollary to this is that the school must have enough autonomy to operate in that market, to conceive and carry through stategies of its own. There is a considerable job to be done in transforming expressed and implicit needs into a viable educational practice. This task has to be performed in the face of constantly changing circumstances and conflicting demands, and within powerful institutional constraints (such as the shape of matriculation exams). A school can't do that if it is simply an extension of existing social networks.

The school is thus simultaneously embedded in a market and in a network, and a complex dialectic arises from this. The network is crucial in making it possible for the school to operate at all; but the autonomy given it by the market is also essential. It is true that the ruling-class school is the instrument of a class; we can also say now that it is *an active part of the class*. This is so, not just in the sense of providing the conditions in which class advantages can be handed from one generation to another; but also in the larger sense of organizing the class, and providing part of the means by which it is renewed and reconstituted in the face of changing circumstances.

The school as class organizer

The most immediate way in which the school organizes the class, and by no means the least important, is in organizing kinship and friendship. Parents like Mr Middleton explained how they had kept up their contacts with the like-minded people they first met at school. A vivid description of the earlier stages of this process is given by Tricia Williamson:

> *What about the boys around your way, what schools do they go to?*
> Well most of the boys go to St Peter's and a couple go to Milton or Scotch or Churchill or Loyola, you know just all these sort of schools, private schools. Some used to go to high school in Smith Street.
> *Any of the kids stay there?*
> I don't really have any friends going to high school. Just a bit slack and horrible.
> *What type of people are they?*
> Oh, they don't care about anything, you know. They don't know what they are going to do when they get older, and they're terribly slack. I suppose some people really do work there, but it depends on the person; most kids left by themselves and they just slack off completely . . .
> *Do you have much contact with the boys in the private schools?*
> Yes, because they all travel from Jones Street wharf on the ferry, and they sort of all catch the bus. Like the whole ferry knows, each kid knows the other one, sort of not like trains, they come sort of every half hour or hourly. All the kids just get on one ferry, scream and yell around together. I think most of the kids that go to a private school, you know, St Peter's and Auburn or Milton and St Margaret's sort of go to parties together, but they don't really invite any outsiders. They don't invite kids from public schools all that much, because I think you know each other better.

In these remarks, Tricia condenses themes that come through in a whole string of other interviews; we have every reason to believe her ethnography is accurate. Let us try to systematize these points. First, the school establishes contacts and builds networks. Tricia meets and makes friends with people in her school, and then collectively with boys and girls in other private schools, and this begins to define the circle within which she will probably marry and from which she will draw adult friends.

Second, the network of acceptable people is defined not only positively, by making contacts on that ferry-load of ruling-class fun, but also negatively, by excluding kids who aren't on it because they're at the high school. 'They don't really invite any outsiders. The ruling-class school is a means of drawing social lines, of defining 'Us' as against 'Them', and is very clearly seen that way by many of our respondents.

Third, this sense of social difference is expressed in an imagery of order and tautness. Tricia's key word for 'Them' — repeatedly used by other kids discussing the same point — is 'slack'. Its implications range from laziness (apparently Tricia's main theme) to disorder, misbehaviour, untidy clothes, not wearing uniforms, poor speech habits, bad manners, and not caring about one's future. Not all the kids, however, accept as naively as Tricia the approved view that slack is horrible. Chris Legrange, one of our resisters, is more sceptical; he would rather be in a slack old state school and enjoy himself.

Finally, it is clear in Tricia's account that it isn't just the one school that is doing this organizing, it is a whole group of schools. She names, in fact, half the elite Independent schools in the city among her contacts. In the construction of the class as a network of friendship, kinship and acquaintance — as in the construction of the ruling-class schooling market — it is the *system* of private schools that is crucial. 'Independent' doesn't mean 'isolated', socially speaking. Marnie Paton puts it beautifully, talking about Regatta Day when she and her friends turn out to watch the boys' schools battle for rowing honours:

> I think that's the greatest gathering of private schools, because everybody goes there . . . and you just see so many people you know. That's what I meant by 'united' . . . Most of our parents' friends have children that go to private schools, and so we know lots and lots of people.

All of this seems to obey the rules: drawing lines, knotting networks, defining 'Them' and 'Us'. The ruling-class school creates ruling-class solidarity. But it isn't as simple as that. Why, for instance, is there the *need* for all this network-construction and solidarity-formation? And what are we to make of the official self-image of these schools, which typically reject social exclusiveness and stress that they draw families 'from all walks of life'?

We have spoken several times of diversity and change within the ruling class. New groups are recruited or force their way in, as pastoralism declines, manufacturing rises and falls, multinational corporations appear and expand, new professions develop and old ones are transformed. The 'catchment' for any Independent school registers much of this. The 'all walks of life' theme in the schools' official self-image is, clearly enough, a response to this heterogeneity and change. And another theme, that the schools take no account of social differences among the pupils, treat the child of a plutocrat and a shopkeeper just the same, exactly defines the schools' task in the face of this heterogeneity. It is to override it, to *create a unity* where only narrow common ground and a fragile common interest was before.

Nor is this a transient problem. The turbulent process of capital accumulation pits different kinds of wealth and power against each other. Pastoralists have interests opposed to manufacturers, capitalists to professionals, multinational capital to local, large capital to small, and so on. Internal conflicts of interest, ideology, and outlook are a permanent, necessary feature of the ruling class; and overcoming their effects by evolving and imposing a common educational practice is a permanent, necessary task of the ruling-class school. Hence the heavy stress on the *school's identity* that in other respects seems so anachronistic: the badges, the songs, flags, sporting colours, the out-of-date but insisted-upon uniforms, and so on — all the manifestions of 'school spirit' that so irritate resisters like Chris Legrange and Millie Hailey.

It is not only the school officials who grapple with the problem of class mixing within the school. The kids do too. We have already discussed Colleen Rossner's sketch of three kinds of girls at Auburn College. It is notable that her description is mainly organized on class lines. The core of the 'snobs' are the daughters of old-established pastoral wealth and their friends, the 'down group' are pretty firmly associated in Colleen's mind with crudity and lower-classness, the 'more intellectual' tend to come from professional families. This is not an oddity of Colleen's perceptions; a number of other pupils, and teachers, gave us similar observations of this and other schools.

The question of the internal order of the ruling-class school that we raised in Chapter Three now has to be seen in this light, as a question of the hegemony of one class, or section of a class, over others within the social mixture of the school. A group who are a minority among the pupils may still be dominant in this sense — in the old phrase, they give the school its 'tone'. And one of the things that matters for others is coming into contact with them in and through the school. Jane Brownlee, for instance, has taken on establishment styles from her schoolmates — her father being newly-rich. Those who can't participate, for instance Joanne Carpenter because of her fundamentalist religion, are likely to be pushed to the social margins.

The heterogeneity of class is expressed not only within one school but also among a group of them. Megan Ryder mordantly comments on the contrast between her school — mostly 'upper middle class, professional people' — and the *really* rich one up the road, in the context of a discussion of the drug problem:

> The kids at St Margaret's, most of their parents are pushing to keep them there. I can't think of a kid in our class whose parents are finding it easy to keep them here. So we don't have a [drug] problem of schools like St Anne's, where there is too much money, and the kids have the money. [With a laugh] I can't think of anybody who has the *money* to buy drugs.

In this context the network-construction *between* the schools takes on more significance, as does the range of ways these schools officially interact — in sporting competitions, in dances, dramatic productions, music, and so on. Once again, a unifying practice is generated in response to the centrifugal effects of diversity and competition.

This is not to imply that the schools' efforts always succeed. If they do, it is in the face of dilemmas and difficulties. Two seem particularly important.

The first is that there are always different ways of doing the job, and these differentially affect the interests of different groups or sections of the class. There are, then, chronic problems of policy. If the school makes a serious mistake in its choices, it may offend sufficient of its clientele to be at risk in the marketplace: we have mentioned the principal who went too far and too fast in the direction of liberalization. We have noted the dilemma of 'marriage or a career' that faces ruling-class girls, and the different policy options created for the school. How far to organize the school's life around religion, how deeply to go into technical subjects and hard science, how tight to screw down 'discipline' on physically-adult teenagers, are all relevant policy questions whose resolution varies as the market changes, and the principal and teachers try to thrash out the right combination of choices.

The second is the question of how far the job can be done at all. In the very broad perspective, there is a contradiction between the ruling class's need for class organization and its need to maintain hegemony over other classes. This is an issue which people who, like Mr Middleton, occupy positions of leadership and responsibility in the ruling class, are sharply aware of.

This creates problems for the Independent schools, particularly about social exclusiveness. The more clearly they draw lines and stress social distinction, the more they serve their clients' demands for class identity and the class's need for solidarity. But in so doing they may offend those excluded, create resentment against privilege, and erode the hegemony of their clientele in the society at large. In earlier periods of history this was the least of their concerns; but it is a very real one now. A reputation for privilege can damage the school. It is noteworthy that under the first proposals for 'needs-based' funding of schools by the Whitlam government, a whole category of the wealthiest schools was to get nothing at all. A quick ruling-class mobilization altered that, and under the Fraser government private schools have been in a much happier position; but the underlying issue remains. Indeed it is institutionalized by the rivalry that has developed with the elite state high schools in the Matriculation exams.

It is interesting, then, to see the new defence of private schooling that has emerged in the last few years. It is not based on the old conceptions of 'leadership' and 'service', but purely and simply on the notion of an educational market and the 'rights' of parents to buy the product they like best. On this kind of notion it is private-school parents who are 'disadvantaged', since they also have to support state schools via taxation. We can expect to hear a good deal more of this; though as it conflicts so markedly with these schools' traditional self-images, the claims of teacher professionalism, and the reluctance to make inequality too naked, it will meet considerable resistance even in the ruling class.

The private school principal

To speak of 'strategies' and 'resolutions' implies people in a position to conceive of them and carry them through; and this mainly means the school principals.

We have noted already two significant points about the principals in ruling-class schools: first, that they are essential in the process of educational change through the market, a change of regime being the ultimate stake of market pressures; second, that they are personally a focus of the social networks surrounding the school. These should be related to the points just made about the role of the school. The process of class formation involves a number of different kinds of work — political organization, economic mobilization, and so on. One important kind is cultural: articulating views of the world, organizing and conveying ideas, managing cultural institutions, persuading, explaining, teaching. The private school principal is a key figure in the cultural labour of class formation.

To put it another way: the Independent school principal is an 'organic intellectual' (in Gramsci's famous phrase) of the ruling class, someone whose work gives identity and form to the social group they are embedded in; and a fairly important one, at that. It's no accident that the Speech Day addresses of Independent school principals are prominently reported in the capitalist press.

Coming from careers in teaching, they are hardly likely to be personally wealthy; but in terms of position, function, and social relations, must be regarded as part of the ruling class. We have mentioned how they figure in the social circles of the school's families. And the schools they run are significant businesses in anyone's terms. In relation to the market, the principal is an entrepreneur; in relation to the staff, an employer (*de facto* — the council usually is *de jure*); and in relation to the operation of the school, a manager. As the principal of Auburn College put it, when meeting the fathers of her girls, she finds herself talking 'as one executive to another'; they understand each others' problems.

This general position admits of a number of strategies for handling the tasks. There are, in the first place, alternatives that concern the general orientation of the school and its 'positioning' in the market. One is implicit in the issue we have seen come up a number of times, between academic performance and network construction. No private school principal can afford to neglect either, but it is certainly possible to stress one. The principal's main strategy, that is to say, may revolve around the renovation of curricula, the attracting of high-powered staff and the encouragement of their professionalism, the creation of an internal order in the school focussed on academic competition; with just enough cultivation of networks to provide the sinews of war. Or it may revolve around the cultivation of the school's identity and traditions, building up prestige through sport (for boys' schools especially) and the generous donations of old scholars, laying stress on the character, social skills and moral outlook of the pupils; with just enough attention to the academic side to perform well in Matriculation results and make sure the school doesn't slide in the market. Another issue on which strategies may divide is that of modernization and liberalism, the attempt to create a relatively relaxed and pupil-centred school or a taut and teacher-centred one.

There are also alternative styles of Headship in relation to the staff of the school. Mr Legrange recalls from his childhood the classic figure of the charismatic Head, stalking the school like 'a great regal spectre', and notes that he was held in utter awe by most of his staff. Personal authority has plainly been extremely important in Australia's private schools in the past, across a spectrum from Dorothy Ross on the progressive side to James Darling on the establishment.[12] But charisma is now at a discount. In more than one of the schools in our study, a principal who depended heavily on it had been found wanting, and had been replaced. A Head who still tries to operate this way can be regarded as an anachronism, and something of an embarrassment, by the parents. The practicable options now have to do with the different forms of rational authority, and the different uses of technical expertise.

A principal may try to maximize the efficiency of the school by centralizing strategic decisions, or may try to maximize the involvement of the staff through delegation and decentralization. These choices have a complex relation to the strategies the principal is pursuing in relation to the school's clientele. If, for instance, the school is engaged in a 'standards' campaign to tighten discipline and beef up academic performance, centralization of control may be helpful in enforcing uniform discipline but counter-productive in terms of enlisting the classroom teachers in a stronger academic effort.

Though these are real options, they don't imply that the principals are free to construct their job just as they please. The constraints are strong, and the principal personally is subject to all the pressures that define and redefine the role of the school.

We have every reason to think that these pressures have intensified in the recent past. Among them the increased, and now entrenched, academic competition from state high schools; the increased pressure from parents for academic performance, and their increased willingness to intervene in school affairs (especially ruling-class fathers, with their belief in 'going to the top' to get something done); the problems of financial management in a period of rapid wage escalation; and the rise of teacher professionalism and teacher unionism. Put these together with the irreducible demands of routine management, getting to know the kids, keeping up networks, and having some involvement in the academic life of the school, and it is not hard to see sharply-increased personal strain on the principal.

Delegation can do something, but much of this load will still come back to the principal's desk. So we find one of our principals working from nine a.m. to midnight, seven days a week, confessing that the strain is 'incredible'; and, despite all those efforts, still losing touch with the students. As one student observed:

> She's good with the school and everything, but I sometimes think that she doesn't really care about the girls. I suppose she does, but I just get the impression sometimes that she doesn't care as much about the girls as she does about the name of the school.

It is arguable, indeed, that the Headship is becoming an untenable job; and that these developments will force some change in the pattern of management in these schools before too long.

WORKING-CLASS SCHOOLING AND THE WORKING CLASS

The working class and the labour market

A connection between schooling and qualification for work is now so generally assumed that it is worth recalling that, as recently as the early 1950s when most of our working-class parents left school, the position was very different. We have already discussed their experiences of school, which on the whole had not been inviting; some escaped from it the day they were legally able to, and not many stayed very long after that. At a certain point, Mr Arlott recalls,

> the Brothers used to tell you . . . sort of hint to you that it was about time you left, and you just worked it out from there.

Others got the hint from their parents. When Mr Roberts was 14, his father, a sleeper-cutter for the railways, told him he had got to the age where he should earn a wage, so he left. Or from friends, or brothers and sisters, or they just worked it out for themselves. Mrs Roberts left school on the Friday before she turned 15, and on the following Monday, her birthday, walked into a factory job that had been arranged by her sister. With Mrs Wilkins,

> I don't really think I would have gained any more if I'd have stayed at school . . . I think I'd had enough of school. Too I thought, I can buy my own things, save Mum and Dad [from the expense of her upkeep] . . . Independence, really, that I could have some money of my own to do what I wanted to do with it; I think too most of my friends were leaving, to get jobs . . .

What these reminiscences are saying is that there usually wasn't any highly specific reason for leaving school at this age; it was just that there wasn't any good reason for doing anything else. Going on to the labour market about one's fifteenth birthday was the settled practice, the thing almost everybody in this milieu did. Boredom with school, economic need, desire to be independent and adult, all combined to make it a positive step. On the school's side, it didn't normally involve any specific training or preparation for the jobs their pupils mostly went into — working in shops and factories. Getting *qualified* had nothing to do with it.

It is striking, then, that these same people *as parents* are taking a very different view of the school. Most of them (not all, but a considerable majority) want their kids to go on in school as long as they can; and a number have already said that they are prepared to take on the financial strain, for instance by taking a second job. Further, they see schooling as *useful* for the kids, economically, in a way their own schooling was plainly not. So they are putting across a line to their kids that is very different from what they got from their own parents.

Why the change? Most obviously, it has to do with economic trends since the 1940s: the 'long boom', and the structural changes in the workforce that came with it. But it's not economic change alone — it's that in interaction with a selective education system. While most of our parents were having the kind of experience just mentioned, the schools *did* give vocational training to two significant groups of working-class youth who were to be lifted above the ruck: girls intended to go into secretarial work, boys intended to go into a trade. Those who were trained in these ways in the early days of the postwar boom were in an excellent position to prosper with it, as clerical jobs multiplied enormously, and there was a strong and steady demand for tradesmen.

In the period in which the parents in our study have been in the workforce, there has been a great boom in 'credentialism', and an expansion of the education industry to supply more credentials — either more years of regular schooling, or new specialized tickets. The key point is that this growth of credentialism occured in a period of expansion: the number of jobs was also growing at a rapid rate, and people who got the credentials *did* get ahead. Our parents saw them, often enough, get ahead of them. Mr Grey can virtually do a surveyor's job in practice, but can't get a ticket; so he remains an estimating foreman. Mr McArthur reckons that if he'd had better schooling, and was able to spell and write better, he'd probably have his own firm by now; he remains an employee.

In understanding this, it is important to recognize that the working class in Australia is a diverse and divided group; if anything, more so than the ruling class. By 'working class' we mean, broadly, people who have common interests because they are dependent for their living on a wage or a wage substitute (such as a pension), and don't have means of gaining larger shares of the social product through ownership of capital, power in organizations, or professional monopolies. As with the ruling class, the notion of class also refers to the institutions and practices that give expression to common interests or shape a common identity — unions, political parties, self-help organizations and so on; and to the family and neighbourhood networks that tend to construct working-class 'communities'.

Such institutions and networks are always working against counter-tendencies to fragment and divide the class — such as wage differentials and terms of employment that divide more skilled and privileged workers from less. It is clear that in this period of Australian history, the tendencies towards division were becoming stronger. A massive inflow of new ethnic groups, industrial diversification, and increasing economic inequalities, were all part of this process; as was the growth of credentialism — which hooked up a competitive organization of education with a more finely differentiated workforce.

The parents have drawn the obvious, and oft-repeated, lesson from this experience: more schooling means better jobs. They apply this retrospectively, often criticizing themselves (wrongly, we think) for thoughtlessness in leaving school when they did, and lamenting lost opportunities in their working lives. And they apply it prospectively, to their kids. It's not just a matter of what they say in questionnaires or interviews — a lot of them are very firm in practice. The school would be glad to be rid of Bill Poulos, and he would be glad to be quit of school, but

> Dad won't let me leave.

The trouble is, the kids now suspect this will not work. They are often better informed about the local labour markets than their parents are; and the news is bad. (What the kids are often unaware of are the changes taking place in work itself; for instance, the effect of computerized technology on skilled trades.) When official statistics give overall youth unemployment rates of 17 per cent (to take

November 1978, about the end of our fieldwork), the situation in working-class areas like the western suburbs of Sydney and Melbourne and the northern fringes of Adelaide is markedly worse.

It is clear to many of the kids that if they stay at school a bit longer hoping for a better job, there is now no guarantee that the job will be there when they have finished. There may even be an advantage in leaving early to grab whatever jobs are going. The balance may be tipped towards non-economic reasons for leaving school, such as the fact that it mean assuming adult social status. On the other hand, as competition for the few 'better' jobs stiffens, it may lead kids who think they have a change of academic success to cling more anxiously to the school. In all, under conditions of youth unemployment, the relationship between the school and the labour market has become more ambiguous and complex, and the kids more divided in their reactions.

This has a disturbing effect on the schools though again the patterns are complex. Some teachers think the trouble is that many of the bright kids who would formerly have gone on after Year 10, seeing their age-mates leaving and knowing the state of unemployment, look for jobs, are more likely to get them, and don't come back. Those who do come back are the ones who couldn't get jobs. How far this is true we can't say, but if there is even a tendency in that direction it will seriously disrupt the meritocratic school's project of academic selection. The situation is also inflaming the school's chronic problem of keeping order. Higher retention rates than in the past means larger numbers of older kids whom these schools aren't set up to handle and often don't really want. They are not compliant and also not easily marginalized; therefore can be a lot of trouble. A good deal of effort in such schools is currently going into the attempt to devise 'non-academic' Year 11/12 curricula to meet this situation.

The breakdown of the boom-time relationship between school and labour market is also having a disturbing effect on many families. The Poulos family, as we have mentioned, is locked in conflict over how long Bill should stay at school. His father insists, with all the patriarchal authority he can muster, that Bill shall stay to Year 12 and get his Matriculation; his mother, too, is keen on this. Mr Poulos sees a future for Bill in a 'nice and clean' white collar job — a draughtsman perhaps, or an architect, at all events something better than his own job driving a truck. Bill wants to get out now. He's fed up with school, irritated by the teachers, and has good relations with only one. He wants to get a job as a builder. His father pans that as a dead-end job — 'a builder stays a builder' — but it's the best thing Bill can see around. Not only is school knowledge useless for this purpose; staying longer at school means he will miss out on the chance of an apprenticeship with a builder he knows. And apprenticeships don't grow on trees nowadays; even Mr Poulos admits that there were 31 applications for one apprenticeship at his firm recently. The conflict is at the moment irreconcilable. Bill *knows* his father is wrong about the job situation, Mr Poulos is quite committed to the idea of improvement through education, and the main effect of it all is to add domestic tension to Bill's battles with the school.

Of course that isn't the whole story. Mr Poulos' insistence on Bill having a chance at white-collar employment can hardly be separated from his own experience as a skilled manual worker. He had been a pattern-maker for fifteen years with a particular company, where he was an active unionist; he then had to have an operation which left him unable to do that particular job, and the boss seized the chance and got rid of him. He was unemployed for a year, and then could only get a job washing cars and trucks. Manual workers do have vulnerabilities — including the risk of something happening to their bodies — that clerical workers normally don't. So there is a real point to what Mr Poulos wants for his son; it isn't just a matter of adult obtuseness. At the same time there is real point to Bill's resistance.

The details, of course, vary from family to family; but it is clear that there is a great deal of tension about this kind of issue. We could multiply examples, and have already talked about the Owens family; here, briefly, is one more. In Jeff Warnock's family his parents are divided. Mr Warnock argues to Jeff that his ambitions (to be a pilot or a civil engineer) are unrealistic, that he'll be on the dole anyway, and look how I got on without education. Mrs Warnock is scathing about this attitude, calls it jealousy, and urges Jeff on:

> Digging ditches for the Water Board — you won't be doing that, mate!

But he nearly did leave from Year 9 — had all the documents ready, was only turning up at school once or twice a week, and stopped only when he realized he wasn't old enough to get a licence and wouldn't get a decent job. (It's worth noting that he didn't tell the teachers any of this was going on; it was all argued out within the family.) His theory now is that though more education won't necessarily get you a job, it will at least put you at the head of the queue.

The state of the labour market, then, has forced a great deal of debate about the kids' schooling, a considerable amount of conflict and painful reassessment of what had been taken for granted. General opinion among the parents still was more favourable to schooling than opinion among the kids, but, in some cases like the Owens, it is plainly being revised. We think there is a real possibility that the tacit alliance between working-class parents and the schools is at risk; and that, if retention rates hold up, it will increasingly be as a result of the pressure of youth unemployment alone.

Peer life and 'youth culture'

One of the reasons why the kids can sustain a conflict with their parents' views on schooling is that youth now has a group identity, and a kind of support, that the parents did not have at the same age.

In Chapter Three we suggested that within the physical setting of the school grounds and buildings there are in a sense two schools — the one paid for by the government and controlled by the teachers, and the one that grows up in the crannies and corners of the first, controlled by the kids. The second is part of a larger complex of peer networks in and out of school, street life and beach life, and events in and around amusement parlours and the like, that is sometimes called 'youth culture'. The main interests in this complex are music, clothing, food, conversation, and sex; and it is crucial, both to the kids and to anyone dealing with them, that it is very largely outside adult control.

The high school has played an important part in the emergence of this sphere of life, if only by bringing large numbers of teenagers together and making them interact with each other. The rise of 'adolescence' as a social category has closely paralleled the rise of mass secondary schooling. The school plays a more intimate organizing role, too, especially by the way its streaming practices throw particular groups of teenagers together and start the process of attaching labels to them. The kids don't accept labels passively; they process them, and much of the processing happens outside the teachers' observation, 'out in the yard', or outside the school. We have seen already how important peer support is to school resisters as classroom 'troublemakers'. What we see now is what lies behind this support: the extended network of interactions and tensions, groupings, fads and fashions, loyalties and rivalries that make up peer life.

When we say that peer life is a space very largely outside adult control, that isn't to say that adults don't influence it or even try to control it. In fact the most important single organizing force in this sphere is the branch of business that supplies the youth market: the pop music industry (radio, records, concert promotion), amusement arcades and discos, clothing and cosmetic manufacturing and retailing, the car and motorbike business, and those parts of publishing, film and TV targeted on youth. 'Commercial youth culture', as we may term this, is hardly oppositional — it is closely connected with mainstream capitalism. No self-respecting department store lacks its teen boutique; no major record company lacks its saccharine-rock, pseudo-punk, and programmed disco lists; the new fast food stores attract congregations of teenagers. Commercial youth culture treats the separateness of youth merely as a way of segmenting the market to maximize sales, and, within the youth market, age group differentiations are very important. But in doing that, it can't help but supply materials that the kids can turn to their own uses.

Among them, making differentiations among themselves. Tastes in music and styles of dress are among the ways groupings within peer life distinguish themselves — the kinds of groupings identified for public consumption as punks, surfies, mods, bikies, and so forth. This diversity of groupings has been labelled youth 'sub-cultures' by some of the research literature, especially in England. We have some reservations about that concept. For one thing we are dealing here, for the most part, with simply one aspect of teenagers' lives — not the global way-of-life that is normally implied by the term 'culture'. So talk about youth cultures or sub-cultures is in danger of exaggerating their coherence and totality; and thereby missing the *specific* role peer life plays in the lives of the great majority of teenagers, and the intricate way it interacts, sometimes in conflict but sometimes not, with their family life and participation in the formal life of the school.

Perhaps more importantly, the state of being a teenager, as we argued in Chapter Two, is a constantly dissolving one, and dissolves in the direction of adulthood. When the kids come into conflict with their elders, at home or at school, it isn't around a demand to be treated like an adolescent, but around a demand to be treated as an adult.

Peer life and commercial youth culture support this demand, and constitute teenagers as adults, in two main ways. First, as consumers. A child consumes mainly through purchases made by her parents. The youth industry now puts out a range of products which (by and large) only teenagers buy, and thus has constructed a zone of freedom where the teenager is an economic adult — forming preferences and exercizing them by spending money. Since these are capitalist enterprises the commodities can be costly, and a lot of teenagers in consequence have to take jobs. In one inner-city school in Sydney it was recently found that about 40 per cent of the kids had part-time jobs.

Second, as sexual beings. The child in the family is more-or-less officially supposed to be sexless, as is the student in school: sex-play with other kids on school premises is forbidden, and girls who get pregnant normally leave. Even jewellery is often forbidden. Commercial youth culture recognizes their sexuality, indeed celebrates it. 'Rock-and-roll is sex', Chuck Berry long ago remarked, and he spoke no more than the truth. Erotic Coca-Cola ads, disco-dancing competitions for nymphets in jeans stores, magazine competitions for boys to design the ideal 'fuck-truck', are only a few of thousands of examples. Much of the sex is pretty watery, but it's also constant; and thus the commercial output supports and legitimizes the exploration of sexuality that is a constant preoccupation of adolescent peer life.

A complex of institutions and informal networks that is able to do these rather important things for teenagers, which offers freedom, pleasure, and responsibility, is capable of providing very significant support for the struggle almost all of them wage, at some level or other, with the institutions that fundamentally define them as children — the family and the school. We see the growth of this complex over the past twenty years or so as an important element in the deepening problems of authority in the working-class school. This should not be seen, as some teachers and parents tend to, as teenagers getting out of control because they are mindlessly following fads. If there was a 'Kiss Army' when the American rock group *Kiss* came to town, there were also kids who turned up to demonstrate against it. Rather, there is an appropriation of materials that the society offers, and often a very selective appropriation.

We say "in the working-class school" because the growth of an oppositional peer life has been mainly a working-class phenomenon. The class dimension is acidly expressed by Annie Ellis, commenting on the 'stereotype' (her word) the other girls at her local high school expected her to conform to:

> Oh, stupid things, like getting my hair cut the same as theirs. Not wearing school shoes, because everyone else wore sandshoes. Shaving my legs because they all shaved their legs. Plucking my eyebrows because they had to pluck their eyebrows. Watching 'Little House on the Prairie'. Things like that. I just hated it, you know, and I didn't go along with any of it, and they didn't like me . . .
> *What about the boys?*
> They felt the same. Most of them, anyway. Like, they used to say [exaggerated pommie accent]: 'Ooh deah, Annie's coming'.

Annie eventually solved the problem by getting her parents to send her to St Margaret's College, where she felt at home.

Her observation is, we think, accurate; and in places like St Margaret's and Churchill College these aspects of teenage life are very muted indeed. But though they are far stronger in our working-class schools, they very rarely identify themselves as working-class or tend towards a working-class identity. (Punk styles and 'new wave' rock are the main exception: some new wave bands have an explicitly radical and working-class politics.) The capitalists engaged in youth marketing have every interest in preventing this, after all. Their intervention in this sphere of life is profoundly divisive, in two ways.

First, by pushing kids away from parents. The derisive attitude towards older people implicit in a lot of the youth media content precisely cuts the kids off from the knowledge, traditions, and wisdom of their parents. There is a rupture in working-class experience being produced here. It's far from absolute, but it is real.

Second, by separating girls from boys. Commercial youth culture is not only sexual; it is profoundly, viciously sexist. In the endless stream of quasi-erotic advertising and advice directed to teenagers, there is hardly a suggestion that there is any way of being a girl other than by being acceptable to boys. Apart from not recognizing other kinds of sexuality, such as the homosexual affections that many teenagers are in fact experiencing and exploring, commercial youth culture actively enforces patriarchal norms. And though the kids might be critical of bits of it, the authors have rarely come across so unrelieved male-supremacist propaganda as is found in magazines like *Van Wheels*, directed mainly to teenage boys. About the only exception would be the rigorous training in triviality and self-immolation for girls conducted through the pages of *Dolly*.

State education and cultural intervention

It is clear that the school is not the only cultural institution impinging on working-class life; but it is probably the most important. A high school is often the biggest *thing*, physical or financial, in a new working-class suburb; and it and its feeder primary schools the only community facility with which virtually all the families in the district are connected. School is comparable with television and radio in the amount of kids' time it occupies, and enormously more important in organizing their peer relationships and their lives generally. Just as an institution, then, and regardless of what its staff and policy-makers are trying to do with it, the school represents a massive intervention by the state into working-class lives. In this and the next section we will try to grasp some of the dimensions of this intervention, first in terms of its cultural and psychological effects, then in terms of its impact on the process of class formation.

In Chapter Two, discussing parents' experiences in their own schooling, we saw how often these were alienating and intimidating. Working-class people are often injured, insulted and disempowered by their experience with schools. This is not a pleasant thing for educators to have to recognize; but it is a basic fact of the situation and has to be reckoned with.

It comes through in three main ways in our interviews. First, in parents' accounts of their own schooling and what it has meant to them since — which, as we have seen, is often a feeling of being diminished as a person. Mrs Midland, whose experience was by no means as abrasive as some already quoted, still feels reduced by the inadequate education that she got:

> I feel sometimes that I am unable to communicate with people of a much higher education.

Mr McArthur, who left school still unable to write or spell very well, puts it less delicately:

> I want Kate to go to school for longer than me, because I don't want her to be dumb like me.

These are common observations. Among the main effects of education for that generation were that it made people feel stupid, it made them feel inferior to others who had more of it, and it showed them, at a vulnerable age, that they were despised.

Second, in the fullness of time they came back to the schools as parents. And the schools, it seemed, remembered them. Pleased to use their voluntary time and labour, the schools didn't want to know about their educational ideas — the aims of parent/teacher nights aside. They don't have any way of participating in the teaching/learning process except by helping the kids with homework; and, as we have seen, that soon gets beyond what *their* schooling covered. When something goes wrong and they go up to the school with a protest or proposal, the school often just fends them off. The criticism most often voiced of bad teachers or principals by working-class parents is this: they don't *care* about our kids. And in that is embedded a class insult: they don't think *our* kids are worth caring about.

Third, injury comes out in the interviews with many of the kids. In Chapter Three we noted how often they protest about uncivil and unfair treatment by teachers. Getting yelled at is not an ego-building experience, and kids in working-class schools get yelled at a lot. Teachers — especially when tired and under pressure — can be offensive and insulting, and the kids register and resent it.

Nor is it only a question of the style in which they are treated. The streaming and selective structure of the school convinces lots of these kids, just as schooling convinced their parents, that they are 'dumb'. When you 'fail' an exam, or when you get put in the 'E' or the 'G' stream, the school is doing something to you that has a very clear message about your inferiority. And the kids, building on cues such as streaming and gender, can and do insult and injure each other. The 'A' stream looks down on the 'hoods', and the hoods resent the privileges and prestige accorded the 'brains'; boys resent privileges they think are given to girls, and sexist attitudes abound.

That these things count, and hurt, implies that the school has credibility. Partly this is because it has real powers — it is the gateway to higher training, and decides who can in fact get access to qualifications. But most kids in working-class schools aren't headed that way. The school's wider credibility rests, we would suggest, on two other things.

One is that the put-downs of working-class people just surveyed, though widespread and systematic, are not the whole story. For each story of insults from teachers, working-class parents would tell another of a teacher who had been really good to them, who was remembered with affection and gratitude. A vignette from Mr Bailey's apprenticeship:

> We had a guy who worked there, he was an ex-schoolteacher, and he was a beaut guy. He was twice my age you know; and this fellow used

to spend all his lunchtimes and morning tea breaks and everything, teaching me maths.

Again, we could multiply examples. And the parents see similar things happening now: teachers who 'go out of their way' to help their kids, teachers who really concentrate and bring them on, principals who do listen to their complaints, and so on. Similarly the kids distinguish good teachers, those who are civil and fair, those whose classes are interesting. Even among the resisters, it's rare not to have had good relations with at least some teacher. And this plainly represents an important potential for something better, overall.

The second point is more abstract, but quite as important. The school stands for the offer of knowledge; and there is a great deal of respect for knowledge among working-class people. There is often ambivalence about the *form* of knowledge — for instance doubts about credentialism, among both parents and kids. But learning itself is widely respected; and education as such valued, often in a more straightforward and less calculative way than among ruling-class families. And where *education* is valued, the *school* has an enormous resource; though it may have to earn the right to tap it.

One of the key moments in cultural intervention, we would suggest, is when that respect for knowledge gets attached to what we have called the 'hegemonic curriculum', or to the arbitrary notions of correctness and competence so central to traditional pedagogy. Mr Grey, for instance, argues that the school has got sloppy about the basics:

Education should be for when they *leave* school to take a job, no matter whether it's a labourer, up to — what do you call it? — a federal minister of government, or anything like that. Whatever the level is, that's what they should be educated right for. I don't care how the kids speak, as long as you can understand them. But when you write it down, and when it's as a heading on the job that not just people in your own trade is going to see it, your boss will always want it to look presentable. And *that's* where I say it is. Like you've never seen 'Australia' spelt incorrectly in a heading: well why should it be done at school? And that's the bad thing I've got against English. I don't think they teach them right, on that subject. I don't know if that's at all schools, but I know it goes for the local ones here. They don't pull them up.

Mrs Grey does care 'how the kids speak':

> We had elocution at school, and, I don't say it's much good today, my speech, but — one night there we went out, there's a couple of kiddies from his school, and every second word the 'ing' is dropped. And I think, well how are you going to go for an interview for a job, cause I know if I was interviewing, that would go against them. I think he's too old, you know. That does worry me, the way they speak. I'll pick him up on it. Don't know if it's right or wrong but I do. 'Goin' and 'comin' and 'dunno'. Everyone's the same, girls and boys. And if you see someone on TV, someone being interviewed, and you hear a girl speak nice, I'll say 'Gee isn't that nice', and they'll say 'Oh, she's got a plum in her mouth!' But it's not a plum, it's just speaking properly . . . They're not encouraged to stand up and read anything.

The point is, Mr Grey *can't* spell correctly himself (he has to keep a dictionary by his side at work), and Mrs Grey *can't* 'speak nice', and both of them are well aware of it. So their conviction that there is one right way to spell or to speak, and that it's the school's business to teach it, and to keep the kids in line while they get it straight, necessarily confirms their own cultural exclusion.

Those who have seen schooling as a mechanism of hegemony in the society at large have usually seen it as a way in which conservative and complacent ideas are implanted in people's minds. We agree that schooling is a powerful mechanism of hegemony; but we don't think that is the main way it operates. By and large, people know when they are being thought-controlled, and resist it. Nor do people like Mr and Mrs Grey necessarily accept established authority — indeed, they are both, as these extracts show, quite critical of the school. Much more important, we would suggest, are the ways cultural intervention splits and layers working-class consciousness. The things that working-class people confidently and securely know are pushed aside or devalued as not being proper, socially-recognized knowledge. In the context of the hegemonic curriculum, respect for knowledge can only be realized as competitive individual appropriation.

The school as class disorganizer

In discussing the Independent schools we explored a number of ways in which they serve to organize the ruling class. The local comprehensive state schools also have effects on the cohesion and self-understanding of the working class, perhaps equally important, but certainly not in the same direction.

We should again stress that the comprehensive high school was not in any simple sense *imposed* on the working class, and any account of the matter that treats it as an imposition will go badly wrong. It grew in response to a powerful demand from the working class, and it represented an egalitarian reform.

The idea behind the comprehensive school was that of a common schooling for all children, a 'community school' as it was also often called, which could express the common interests that underlay diversity and conflict, and help to humanize the common life.[13] There is no doubt that at some times and places, common schooling really did provide a focus for the community life of the adults as well as the children of a particular district. Schools have long done this in country areas, where comprehensivization is a long-standing policy because it is cheaper. And in the postwar period, schools also provided important foci of social organization (and sometimes even political action) in the new working-class suburbs which were spreading with such astonishing speed around the major cities. After all, as we have remarked before, schools were often the *only* important 'community' facility in these suburbs. The primary schools were perhaps more important in this respect, as a focus of informal contacts, friendship, and shared voluntary work within walking distance for women who worked full-time at home. Still, the area-based comprehensive high school also played its part.

But the ideal of a common schooling *for the whole society* was not within the reach of these reforms. The Independent school system remained, the Catholic school system remained, a number of selective state high schools remained — and still do. In any case city space was strongly class-segregated, and the typical new high school was thus created as a working-class comprehensive rather than the truly common school of the comprehensive ideal.

Indeed, at this point we can see that the internal diversity of the working class reacted on the schools as they were being created. Two important aspects of the postwar Australian working class, the fact that it includes a wide range of incomes and resources from the very poor to the very comfortable, and the fact that it was increasingly diverse ethnically as a result of mass immigration, strongly affected the 'catchments' of different schools. Ethnic clustering in certain suburbs, and the division of the city between cheap, middling, and expensive suburbs, didn't just mean that the new comprehensives were pleasingly diverse. It meant that they got sorted out into an academic hierarchy, well known to teachers, with those with a heavy admixture of semi-professional and 'white-collar' Anglo families being very different places to teach in from those with heavy concentrations of Mediterranean migrants and households in poverty. Every school is to some extent a class mixture; but the way it works depends a good deal on the balance of the ingredients and the history of their interactions with each other.

Further, the reform that created a new organization of secondary schooling did not extend to the thorough renovation of curricula or teaching practices that progressive educators were also arguing for at the time. A curriculum derived from the private schools and the old selective highs was installed in the hegemonic place in the new comprehensives. A reform based on working-class demand, but achieved on these very restricted and conservative conditions, brought with it deeply divisive consequences for working-class families.

The most important of these, we would suggest, have to do with compliance and resistance to the hegemonic curriculum. At a number of points in the evidence we have quoted, a strong sense of class division is clear in people's handling of these themes. School resisters are connected by the Greys with the 'hoods' who menace the peace of their streets; and a good many other parents of academically successful kids, and teachers, offer equally pointed sketches of the 'no-hoper' families they assume lie behind the exam-failing, trouble-making, early-leaving kids. Reciprocally, some of the non-academic kids' families are scathing about snobbery, pretentiousness and claims to moral superiority by others in the neighbourhood; and some of their kids produce the same sort of reaction to the compliers at school.

A division between 'rough' and 'respectable' sections of the working class is of course a very old one and operates in many spheres of life. The school didn't create it; but, when organized in this way, the school provides a very important expression and legitimation for it. This reinforcement is particularly potent both because it operates intimately *within* the neighbourhood, *inside* the residential community, and because it gives social meanings and definitions to kids before they even enter the labour market.

The divisive effect of such social practices has to be set alongside what was discussed in the last section, the marginalization of working-class knowledge and intimidation of the school's clientele, to get some idea of what the school as a cultural institution is actually doing to working-class solidarity, consciousness, and morale as a social force.

We may add the effects of the school as an agency of selection.

Secondary schools have long seen their role as that of training the future 'leaders' of society. To the extent that working-class comprehensives do this, through their academic programme or by other ways of identifying student leaders (student councils, prefects), they tend to divide them from their class. This effect is strongest with social promotion through academic success, but is also a problem with student representatives, who are invited to operate in a structure created by the adults and starkly different in its forms of organization from the peer life around them. Nor should we think of such things as only affecting the 'successful'. Few may be upwardly mobile, but many are afraid of being downwardly mobile. Where the means offered to prevent it is a form of individual competition, we have division and distrust being built into working-class experience at a very basic level. Competition is *always* divisive, always opposed to the sense of solidarity, of common fate, and the need for collective response, that is basic to the self-organization of oppressed or exploited groups.

At a deeper level again, the school sets up contradictions around the very idea of intelligence. The intellectual culture to which the school system is attached (via the university training of teachers and the academic derivation of syllabuses) presupposes a connection between intelligence and dissent. Universities often don't work this way in practice, but the principle of their life in constant dissent, debate, challenges to received ideas, scepticism of all authority not derived from rational argument. The way the working-class school works drives a wedge between intelligence and dissent.

The main form of dissent that occurs in it, as we have suggested, is the bearer of an important working-class tradition of resistance to power and authority. But in this milieu it is pitted *against* the bearers of knowledge. It becomes anti-intellectual, and, partly for that reason, open to commercial exploitation. Everyone comes to agree that the resisters are 'stupid' — that's even a word they use themselves for what they do in classrooms and outside school with their friends ('Oh, just stupid things . . .'). Conversely, to the extent that the school does succeed in identifying lively minds among its pupils, its system of selection labours to attach them to constituted authority, hierarchy and orthodox thinking as represented in the streaming system and the hegemonic curriculum. It gives them a social identity defined by the contrast with the mass of the kids, and especially with the resisters. It treats intelligence as a badge of apartness, not as a tool of participation, conviviality, solidarity. On both sides the fruitful connection of intellect and dissent is broken. They become the badges of distinct and sometimes opposed groups. The school, and the working class as a whole, are the losers.

We have stressed that the mass secondary school grew in response to demand from the working class; and we should stress again, having said these hard things, that the school is not a villain intervening to break up an otherwise pure and united class. There are many other institutions and forces producing similar effects; and, for its part, many features of the school are responses to features of the working class — the shaping goes both ways. Above all, this shaping has a history, grew in a specific set of circumstances, has changed, and can be changed again. After a discussion of the school's role in gender relations, we will try to suggest what some of those changes could be.

SCHOOLING AND GENDER RELATIONS

The discussion of gender and schooling, like the older literature on class, has been mainly concerned with the issue of unequal opportunities for boys and girls. There is now a formidable pile of research evidence showing that these inequalities continue to exist, though their character has changed. In recent years there has been a development rather like the 'Reproduction Approach' in the case of class, a focus on the way schools reproduce the subordination of women. This has mainly been seen as a process of imposing sex stereotypes on children. Both perspectives can be clearly seen in the excellent Schools Commission report of 1975, *Girls, School and Society*, which summarizes the Australian evidence and proposes ways to make opportunity more equal and assumptions about sex roles less rigid.

As with the parallel literature on class, we would argue that these two approaches are incomplete, and, by themselves, misleading. Relationships between the sexes are not just a matter of distinctions leading to inequalities. They are also relations of power. When we talk about gender we are talking about ways in which social relations get organized in the interests of some groups, over-riding the interests of others. Nor do the schools just reproduce sex stereotypes or confirm girls in a subordinate position. They do that some of the time; but they also subvert conventions and restructure gender relations. It is not just a little of one and a little of the other. We have to see the schools as involved, to a degree, in the very constitution of gender relations. They are not the main influence doing this, but are certainly one of the parties to the process — helping to construct and reconstruct that whole aspect of social life.

The assumption we make is that being masculine and feminine is not a simple consequence of being biologically male or female. In this we are supported by contemporary research on sex and gender, which demonstrates that what is taken to be masculine and feminine, and the characteristic ways men and women interact with each other, are *socially* constructed above all. Where we differ from most of the literature on 'sex roles' is in stressing that these social relations also are *historical*. To understand the state they are in at any given time, we must understand how they have come into being, how they have been produced. Gender relations change historically. When they are changing quickly (as they have among some groups in Australia recently), the question of how they are produced becomes very obvious. But it is just as important in understanding what goes on when they are changing very slowly, or appear not to be changing at all.

The construction and reconstruction of gender

The Schools Commission report observed that 'throughout its curriculum and organization the school differentiates between male and female students in ways which reinforce sex stereotyped expectations'. This is true, to a limited extent, of what we have seen in our interviews. One can point to school uniforms, modes of punishment, and some differences in curriculum, where boys are differentiated from girls in this way. But this is hardly the main point. As we saw in Chapter Three, some schools at least are very pointedly involved in practices directed towards constructing masculinity and femininity. That football, for instance, is often played by boys and rarely by girls is a trivial point; what counts is the way it serves as a focus for a whole programme of constructing masculinity, and subordinating some forms of it to others.

We have already registered that there is a whole range of masculinities and femininities; stemming from different family patterns, courses of growth and personal choices, and reflected in different kinds of emotional attachments (for instance, homosexual and heterosexual), different traits of character, and different ways of participating in social life.

The high school enters the picture at a very important stage of psychosexual development, and its impact on the construction of gender has to be understood in this light. The masculinizing and feminizing practices within it, such as the cult of football at Milton College, are in important respects responses to psychosexual diversity and its fluidity in early adolescence. The school certainly doesn't brainwash kids into a stereotype — the 'Cyrils', after all, remain. But its intervention has a lot to do with the hierarchy constructed among different kinds of masculinity and femininity; and, at the same time, the relations that are constructed between boys and girls.

It follows from this that different school policies or structures may go some way to *change* the hierarchy of kinds of masculinity or femininity at any one time, and hence affect the overall patterns of gender relations. The clearest example of this in our research was in some of the girls' private schools; the changing balance between different kinds of femininity there has been discussed in Chapter Three. We have also called attention to the much more ambiguous impact of the academic curriculum on working-class femininity. There is an effect, but a selective one: on the academically-successful girls involved in a project of social mobility, who with the aid of the teachers can be shifted out of their present milieu by educational promotion. The tendency here is not to reconstruct gender relations in the working-class milieu, but to split certain kinds of women away from that milieu.

Yet there are changes going on in gender relations in the working class; most importantly to do with women's work.

Women's and men's work

The most dramatic change in the Australian labour market in the last generation has been the massive increase in the employment of married women, about 5 per cent of whom had paid jobs before World War II, about 40 per cent at the end of the 1970s. Women have increasingly moved into higher education and the professions. But it hasn't all been progress up the tree. Management has remained largely closed to them; and new industries such as computing, and newly-reconstructed industries such as banking, have grown new forms of sexual division, creating dead-end jobs for women such as key-punch operating. And as employers have found part-time work a useful option, overwhelmingly it has been women who have filled the bill — with resulting low incomes and low promotion prospects.

At the top end of the labour market, the education system has plainly been important for entry into the professions. Not that this has always been quick or easy. Mrs Somerset, for instance, entered a profession in the early 1950s; her career was aborted when its demands conflicted with her husband's. Yet that experience fed into her concern for her daughters, and is a powerful force behind *their* trajectory towards the professions and a new model of marriage. The school, in situations like this, is not acting alone. Rather it is the means through which pressure for change in the sexual division of labour finally takes effect.

In this kind of process it is important to reckon with the teachers themselves. Forty-six per cent of secondary school teachers in Australia are women, probably half of them are under thirty, and the younger teachers are better trained. Teachers are themselves involved in a changed sexual division of labour; and a significant number of the younger women teachers have been influenced by feminism. They, with sympathetic male teachers, support the project of careers for girls, and provide a base for counter-sexist campaigns in schools: in careers advising, in the reading matter supplied to young children, in removing promotional barriers for women in their profession, and in teacher organizations.

Yet there is little mutual influence between teachers and working-class families; so this activity goes on in isolation from changes in the sexual division of labour that are occurring beyond the school fence. The massive change in women's employment has not been in the professions alone. There has been a major redefinition of work and responsibility in working-class families too, where married women by the thousands have taken jobs as office cleaners, chicken packers, checkout operators, sandwich makers, label stickers, and the like. Enough of the traditional definition of 'woman's place' remains, especially among the men and boys, to make the conventional house-bound wife-and-mother role still a goal for many families. But fewer and fewer households can actually afford it; and two vital changes have occurred.

The rise in workforce participation has meant vastly increased numbers of women who earn a wage, and thus have a measure of financial power of their own. That can mean a real change in power relations in the family. Second, increasing numbers of working-class women, in their own ways, are contesting male control and insisting on independence or equality. This rarely takes the form of a conscious feminism. No working-class mother we interviewed had any contact with the women's movement. But there is here a real and conscious shift from conventional models of womanhood. Sometimes this stems from the failure of a husband to provide adequate support, forcing the wife to get a job of her own. Sometimes there is outright resistance to husbands' attempts to enforce male privileges. Their education has given them no help whatever in understanding and working through these changes; and their daughters seem to be getting a roughly equal amount of preparation to face them. There are educational tasks here — for adult education as much as the schools — which urgently need to be tackled.

School organization

So far we have been dealing with more or less conscious educational policies. There are also ways in which schooling affects gender without any very conscious purpose being involved, by virtue of the way schools are organized and function.

The aspect of school organization where gender relations have been most clearly the object of policy is coeducation. In Chapter Three we noted that there were few signs that this had led to any relaxation of sexism. The research evidence is ambiguous as to whether it depresses girls' academic performance. But there can be no doubt at all that coeducation has had a major impact on gender relations through its effects on teenagers' informal social life. For all the sexism that is still rampant there, encounters between boys and girls in the coeducational comprehensives are enormously freer and easier than they used to be for teenagers incarcerated in the old segregated schools. High school students now are sexual beings in a much more open and obvious way. Here the reorganization of schooling has interacted with the changes in peer life, and the growth of commercial youth culture, to produce a relaxation of prohibitions that is a constant worry to parents and a chronic problem for schools — which can do little to stop a process their own structure has accelerated.

In other respects, the structure of the high school is conservative in the extreme. Almost all retain a decidedly hierarchical form of administration: principal and deputy at the top have very wide powers, and there is a delegation of limited and specific responsibilities to heads of departments. It is not at all exceptional to find state school principals making rules and carrying through policies which are incomprehensible to kids and parents, or even actively opposed by them. Classroom teachers for the most part have a say in general school policy only by courtesy of the principal. It is this kind of authority that ruling-class fathers usually exert in their households, and many working-class men wish they could. It is not surprising that 88 per cent of state secondary school principals in New South Wales, South Australia and Victoria are men (even more in Western Australia and Queensland). Those who are women are commonly in single-sex girls' schools; and, whether there or in coeducational schools, they too are working within patriarchal structures that constitute power and authority as the major axis of relations among people.

Yet in terms of the school's authority structure, the most striking unintended effects occur right at the bottom. In Chapter Three we noted that resistance to school discipline and academic teaching is generated among both boys and girls, and in both ruling-class and working-class schools (though much more widely in the latter). For boys, the typical forms of resistance affirm conventional masculinity, even amplify it. Among girls, there is a form of passive resistance to schooling which is common enough; but there is also an active resistance very like the boys', which undermines femininity. In the past, female 'delinquency' normally was assumed to mean becoming a sexually available marginal member of a gang of delinquent boys. But sexual freedom isn't so deviant now; and, anyway, most of the active school resisters are strong young women who are not about to become doormats for the local boys if they can stand up to their parents and schools. So their resistance genuinely does challenge their subordination as women. But the school gives them no help in understanding this difficult and puzzling aspect of their lives, since they won't take advice from teachers, and teachers are by and large exasperated with them anyway.

Extent of the school's role

We have described three main ways in which the school is implicated in the construction of gender and gender relations. The inequalities of educational opportunity and the reproduction of 'sex-roles' spoken of in the literature are, we would suggest, aspects of this larger process. And they are aspects liable to change, because the production of gender is complex and tension-ridden, as well as being the subject of social struggles. Thus the change in high school retention rates — which only a few years ago produced a clear differential in favour of boys and now shows a slight margin in favour of girls — does not in itself mean a fundamental change in the relation of gender and schooling. (It may, for instance, mainly reflect the squeeze on the female youth labour market, and the new conditions under which an old division of labour is being maintained.)

The other reason for caution here is that in some respects the school seems to have very little impact on gender relations. The main institutional site of gender relations in Australian society is the household and family, and we have seen that the school is held, or holds itself, at a distance from what goes on inside most households. The next most important site is the labour market and workplace; and, for the great majority of working women, the school doesn't have a great deal to do with steering them into or away from mass occupations like factory work, retailing, and routine clerical work. (Though, as some of our working-class mothers say, the school can have an effect by doing nothing.) It is notable, too, how quite a major institutional change in schooling, the advent of general coeducation, has made little difference to the depth of sexism, or even to opportunities for educational promotion.

In some other respects, however, the school seems to have a powerful effect. Coeducation did reorganize the social life of teenagers. The school is important in the construction of masculinity and femininity during adolescence, and in ordering the relationships among different kinds of masculinity and femininity. So it isn't a matter of the school being only loosely connected with gender relations in general. We can conclude that its effects in organizing them have been strong but highly specific. If that is correct, it is important in understanding both the potentials and the limits of counter-sexist educational practices.

We also have clear indications that the connection between gender and schooling is not static, but historical, and responds to the class milieu and the state of class relations. Let us now turn briefly to this three-way relationship.

SCHOOLING, CLASS AND PATRIARCHY

Understanding the interplay of class relations and gender relations is one of the most difficult problems in the social sciences. There are deep differences of opinion about how to pose the problem in the first place, and what a solution might even look like.[14] Though there have been a good many attempts, no-one can claim to have a satisfactory solution at present, and we don't pretend to either. But the issue has come up so persistently in this project that we have had to wrestle with it, and try to get some bearings on the way this interaction affects, and is affected by, schooling.

The first thing to be clear about is that they *do* interact, and that means all the time. Sometimes people think of class relations as confined to the factory and gender relations to the family (or perhaps the drive-in); more formally, that class and gender are complementary social systems, each operating in its own sphere. This, we would suggest, is mistaken. There are gender relations inside factories, and there are class relations inside families and in the upbringing of children. Schooling is a very important case in point, where both class and gender relations are present in the same sphere, and, more importantly, within the same practices.

We would make two other general points, the reasons for which should be obvious from our material. First, both class and gender are, in their different ways, structures of power. They involve control by some people over others, and the ability of some groups to organize social life to their own advantage. As power is exercized and contested, social relations are organized, and come to be in some degree a system. So an important corollary about class and gender relations is that they are systematic rather than random.

But, and this is our second general point, this does not mean being systematic in a mechanical sense, like an air-conditioning system. Both class and gender are *historical* systems, riddled with tension and contradiction, and always subject to change. Indeed it may be better to think of them as *structuring processes* rather than 'systems', that is, ways in which social life is constantly being organized (and ruptured and disorganized) through time. What is most important to grasp about them is their dynamics, the ways in which they exert pressures, produce reactions, intensify contradictions and generate change.

The simplest form of their combined influence is where they simply intersect, and jointly shape some aspect of schooling. To understand what goes on at St Helen's College it is rarely sufficient to know just that it is a ruling-class school or just that it is a girls' school; the fact that it is both is important in understanding most facets of it. The situation of a working-class schoolboy is always different from the situation of a working-class schoolgirl; they cannot (except for very summary purposes and at the cost of sloppiness) be lumped together as if there were just *a* working-class situation. We hope our material has shown this fairly fully; and we stress it particularly because there are teachers who have become sensitive to one structure but not the other. It is important to think about educational situations and processes in terms of both.

Complications arise because gender and class are not the same kind of structure. Obviously enough, gender has something to do with biology that class doesn't, and class has something to do with wealth and accumulation that gender doesn't. Unfortunately a good many discussions of educational inequality do treat them in the same way, just as little boxes. This is not what we mean by 'intersection', nor is it a very fruitful way of understanding a relation between social structures.

The joint presence of gender and class, say for a working-class boy, means *a relationship between processes*. It means that the construction of his masculinity goes on in a context of economic insecurity, or hard-won and cherished security, rather than economic confidence and expansiveness. It means that his father's masculinity and authority is diminished by being at the bottom of the heap in his workplace, and being exploited without being able to control it; and that his mother has to handle the tensions, and sometimes the violence, that result. It means that his own entry into work and the class relations of production is conditioned by the gender relations that direct him to male jobs, and construct for him an imagined future as breadwinner for a new family. And so on.

Because they are different kinds of structures, with different dynamics, their relationship with schooling often works in different ways. We still lack a good social history of Australian education; but, even in the fragments we have, it is clear that the history of the two relationships is often divergent. It was, for instance, problems of class relations that led to the construction of mass elementary schooling in the nineteenth century. The school system then tended to segregate children along both class and sex lines (especially after the elementary years) and to have separate curricula too (domestic science *vs* manual arts, etc.). In that respect the two relationships appear similar. But it is clear that what the schools were actually doing for class and gender relations was very different; for the subordinate class got less secondary education while the subordinate sex got more. In the early twentieth century, school participation rates for teenage girls were higher than for teenage boys.

After World War II the schools were again reconstructed in response to a class dynamic, but also in response to the shift in gender relations that had built up steam during the war. So coeducation came in about the same time as urban high schools became comprehensives; both kinds of formal segregation, that is, were dismantled at much the same time. Coeducational comprehensives did not get very far in mixing social classes, but did mix the sexes and reconstruct peer relations. And while class differentials in secondary and higher education remained wide, the sex differential which had been re-established in the 1920s now began to close.

These points are simply indicators of a problem, not a serious sketch of a history. But it is clear enough that in grasping the intersection of class and gender in contemporary schooling, we have to pay close attention to their different dynamics.

Thinking about 'intersection', however, is not enough. Class and gender don't just occur jointly in a situation. They abrade, inflame, amplify, twist, negate, dampen and complicate each other. In short, they interact vigorously, often through the schools, and often with significant consequences for schooling.

The reconstruction of gender relations that is going on at Auburn College, for instance, crucially depends on the class situation of the girls and the school — the kind of teaching force it has, the degree of autonomy it has, the parental strategies that make professionalism an acceptable programme for the girls. In a very different setting, teachers like Arlette Anderson at Rockwell High see a way for some Rockwell girls to escape sexual subordination in an ocker-dominated, patriarchal milieu, by using the class mechanism of social promotion via meritocratic schooling and entry into semi-professional jobs. On a larger scale, we can see that it was in response to class dynamics that the education system as a whole was organized as a system of academic competition. But once it was organized that way, it became available to women to improve their position vis-a-vis men.

It is important, then, that class processes can abrade or erode patriarchal social arrangements, and vice versa. To put this more generally, the two sets of relations can come into contradiction. We would propose as a hypothesis, suggested but not proven by our material, that this is a fruitful source of aberrant educational careers. We have, for instance, already discussed a ruling-class school resister, Chris Legrange, who comes from a family that is virtually the scene of a small class war, where patriarchal authority has been eroded, and where Chris uses the threat of downward class mobility via school failure as a weapon in the war with his mother. Yvonne Crisp, an academic high-flyer in a working-class school, has a father who failed as a small farmer and failed to get promotion as a railwayman, and a mother who succeeded as a schoolteacher. Mr Crisp has attempted, and failed, to establish patriarchal authority in the family and a subordinated definition of women's place. The fight between husband and wife has been long and evidently bitter; the emotions and energy involved have fuelled Yvonne's desire to escape from her milieu, and her attachment to academic success as the means; though her real attachment to her father is also holding her back from a full-blooded commitment to professionalism.

Schooling, then, can serve as a means of resolving conflicts that arise from the clash of patriarchal and class relations. It is also possible for it to exacerbate them. This has probably happened in the school's relationship to the labour market. The downturn of the mid 1970s and rising youth unemployment was followed by calls for Mums to get out of the workforce, i.e. to solve the problem by reversion to an older sexual division of labour. That this hasn't happened is partly due to the need of working-class families for two wages to support their children at school for the longer periods that have become customary, and also partly to the demand for equal economic rights that has been fostered by equal provision of schooling.

Complex and open-ended social dynamics don't lend themselves to neat formulae or simple practical solutions. In raising the issues touched on in this section, we are conscious of muddying the water more than clearing it — we seem to be feeding in complications at a faster rate than ideas that might sort them out. The point is that however poorly understood in theory, these questions can't be avoided as questions of practice. If we want to do anything about changing either class relations or gender relations in education, we must realize that we are also acting in the field of play of the other structure; we need to grasp the ways they each work on, reinforce, and subvert each other. Both barriers to change and potentials for reform arise in this interaction. We suspect that some of the conceptual difficulties may begin to sort themselves out as practical experience accumulates. The main thing is to try.

5
Inequality and what to do about it

CAUSES AND CONCEPTS

The teachers, parents, policymakers and political movements who have wanted to do something about the problem of educational inequality have naturally looked to academic research to tell them about the causes of it. Once the causes were known, something effective might be done towards a cure.

The research literature, however, has spoken with many voices and suggested unfortunately conflicting cures. We can't go through this literature in fine detail here. But we think it is important, in working towards practical conclusions, at least to reckon with the main arguments and register what our material has to say about them. Four main types of answer have been given to the question 'what causes educational inequality?': answers stressing differences between individuals; the characteristics of schools and families; the relationships between home and school, and class lifestyles; and the place of schooling in the social structure.[15]

Differences between individuals

This is without doubt the most popular explanation: many of the students, teachers and parents we talked to hold it. Among researchers it comes in two main forms, 'soft' and 'hard'. The soft version emphasises attitudes and dispositions — liking for school, need for achievement, ability to postpone gratification. The cure it suggests is to stimulate poor performers' taste for the fare the school offers them, to motivate them to do more learning.

The hard version stresses differences in ability, usually conceived in the form of intelligence or IQ. When the touching faith in IQ tests as a scientific measure is combined with the rather less touching but also widespread belief that levels of basic human abilities are inherited, the only possible cure for poor performance is to stop low scorers from breeding and try to get high scorers to breed more. Where it is thought that environment counts, the cure is to beef up its educational supportiveness by enrichment programmes.

There are good reasons why such ideas should appeal to teachers. In doing their jobs, they are constantly required to put pupils in rank-orders of merit (marking, assigning students to streams or sets), while, as we have seen repeatedly, remaining largely ignorant of the social circumstances of their lives. Those teachers who know most about their pupils' backgrounds, the experienced private-school staff, work in an environment where ideas of competition and individual merit are very deeply entrenched. In effect, the individual-differences explanation of unequal outcomes is institutionalized in the education system itself. Competitive, hierarchically-organized schooling produces its own explanation of its own effects.

To point this out isn't to deny that people differ, and differ markedly, in outlooks, personal styles, interests, bodily development, and skills. And these differences do count in education — as everyone who has ever stood in front of a class will agree. What's wrong with the individual-difference model is not that it stresses diversity, but that it misinterprets diversity. It sees differences in skills, interests and outlooks as things fixed in each individual, which can be measured and put on a scale in abstraction from the circumstances of the person's life. This may look scientific, but it is really not good science. As we have seen in this study, the closer we get to particular people, the more conscious we become of the extent to which their skills, interests and outlooks are developed in response to the circumstances in which they live, and cannot be understood if seen apart from that context. A true appreciation of individuality pushes one towards, not away from, a reckoning with social context.

And that, too, is required even within the individual-difference model by the unavoidable fact that many of the 'differences' have social correlates. IQ is correlated consistently with social status measures, for instance; and expectations, interests and levels of confidence seem to differ as between boys and girls. To explain this is the point of the 'Inequality Approach' we introduced in Chapter One, and we must now turn to its typical explanations.

Characteristics of families and schools

Families are thought to shape the educational careers of their young members in a wide range of ways: the extent to which parents care about schooling, the manner in which family members relate to each other (meal-time discussions, methods of discipline), their material provision (for example, of a quiet place to study), and their internal structure (especially the state of the parents' marriage). It's some combination of these factors that teachers have in mind when they refer to a pupil as having a 'good' or a 'bad' family background. Translated into research, this approach produces deficit theory: the idea that certain family variables correlate with school success, and that school failure grows from families that are deficient in the desired qualities. The cure, plainly, is intervention in those families to bring them up to scratch.

A sound instinct to reject that totalitarian conclusion leads some people to deny the factual premises — for instance, teachers who insist that children can and should be treated as individuals in the classroom regardless of what occurs outside it. We would argue against this. The evidence from our study is perfectly clear: families are very powerful institutions, and their influence over their young members registers in every part of their lives, including schooling. No sound educational strategy can ignore it.

That doesn't, however, commit us to deficit theory in any shape or form. One very obvious argument against it is that the same family can produce quite different educational careers for different children. We have numbers of cases where a younger child has reacted in anger against the school success of an older one or set herself to outdo the first. Relationships within the family are vital; and children are active in the business, from the start. The family doesn't just print its mark on the child like a rubber stamp; and attempts to understand educational outcomes via the overall attributes of families, the 'family variables' of much questionnaire research, are bound to fail.

It is interesting that the school has figured much less prominently than the family in writings on the causes of educational inequality. Sometimes it is simply assigned fewer variables in a multivariate study, sometimes it is marginalized by theories that treat all schools as if they were the same, just transmission belts from Social Forces in the great outdoors. Yet there are several traditions of thought which hold that the state and characteristics of schools do count, including the 'school effects' literature which we mentioned in Chapter Four. The calculations by ruling-class parents which lead to choice of a private school also assume that schools count, somehow. If this is a major cause of educational inequality, the cure lies in making school provision more equal.

On the general issue, our evidence is clear: schools are active and influential producers of educational outcomes. We have found large differences between them, and a range of powerful mechanisms at work within them: teachers' strategies, streaming and creaming, the impact of different curricula and changing catchments, the pattern of peer group life. We see in the case studies the massive impact of these processes on school pupils; most dramatically in the contrast between the schooling of our working-class parents and that of their children.

It is also quite clear that the school is not a sealed unit whose output can be measured and understood in isolation from its context. Educational 'choices' only make sense in terms of the relationship between a pupil's experience at school and her experience elsewhere. The organization of the school itself is profoundly affected by its relationship to its catchment or clientele, as we see very clearly in comparing our two main groups of schools. No more than with the family do we find here the ultimate cause of educational inequality.

The characteristics-of-institutions, then, do not provide us with an explanation of educational inequality any more adequate than the characteristics-of-individuals. The problem is fundamentally the same: in both cases the question is set up as a search for the factors (conceived of as discretely measurable entities) whose influences carry the most weight. Sophistication is sought by adding to the research more and more variables, more refined and abstract measures of them, and using more and more elaborate statistical techniques to model their covariation. It is not surprising that an approach so much at odds with the reality of the situation should lead to the appalling intellectual muddle we find in recent books written within the Inequality Approach, and should lead to no useful advice for teachers. What is perhaps surprising is that academics keep on doing it.

Home/school relationships and class lifestyles

When we push beyond the attributes of school and home to the relationship between them, the first question we confront is how they match. A familiar argument explains school success and failure by the degree to which the 'culture' of the home and of the school correspond. Here we begin to enter the territory of the Reproduction Approach, for the notion of 'cultural capital' used by Bourdieu and his followers is essentially a development of this idea. 'Cultural capital', like money capital, is the birthright of the privileged classes and the means by which they reproduce their privilege from generation to generation.

There are, we would suggest, severe difficulties with this account of the matter. It practically obliterates the person who is actually the main constructor of the home/school relationship. The student is treated merely as the bearer of cultural capital, a bundle of abilities, knowledges and attitudes furnished by the parents. On our evidence, this is wrong. What children actually bring to the school is their relationship to their parents' educational experiences and strategies; and that relationship may involve rejection, ambivalence, misunderstanding or selection, as much as endorsement or duplication. The idea of home/school relationship in this model is drastically impoverished and static. It is clear from our material that the reality is dynamic — the interactions among kids, parents and teachers are constantly being renegotiated and reconstructed, at times quite dramatically mutated in crises of the pupil's school life. Finally, the plain facts are that privilege is not always passed on and under-privilege is not always perpetuated.

Yet the notion of 'cultural capital' isn't entirely absurd; it exaggerates a good insight. There is often a lot to be learned by investigating such points as parents' familiarity with the academic curriculum, their endorsement of or opposition to the school's authority relations, and their ideas of competition and advancement.

In fact there have been many suggestions that there are differences in the way of life between social groups that make them more or less likely to generate educational 'success'. The most influential has been the idea of deep-rooted social class differences in approaches to schooling — what are called 'attitudes', 'values', 'expectations'. Another important argument, coming mainly from Bernstein's work, suggests class differences in language use stemming from differences in their patterns of child-rearing and family interaction. The 'culture of poverty' idea — that poor people adapt to poverty by developing a way of life which then confirms them in poverty — is another that has appealed to some educators dealing with working-class children.

The great strength of these arguments is that they confront the problem of educational inequality on the right scale, the scale of whole social classes. They are weakest when, in the style of the Inequality Approach, they treat classes simply as sets of individuals defined by their prestige or possessions. They are strongest when, as in Bernstein's work, they ask questions about the characteristics of classes in terms of *activity*, what people actually do in daily life.

Some arguments about class lifestyles are factually wrong — notably the quite widespread view that working-class ways of life lead to a lower value being placed on knowledge or education. Among the working-class people we talked to, that is simply not true. They valued it highly, despite often having had bad experiences with it, and often being sharply critical of the particular version of education on offer. Working-class schools have an important resource here, that must not be lost because of derogatory stereotypes of the working class.

Our sample is, of course, from only one segment of a deeply divided class, and it is possible things are different elsewhere — though research with the Mediterranean migrants who have made up a large part of the post-war Australian working class suggests very strong support for education among them too. Nevertheless this points to the fallacy of assuming any class to be a homogeneous group of people with the same character or culture or class being, from which we can read off educational consequences. Classes are always complex and internally-divided groupings, composed into a class by a dialectic between their own activity and its circumstances. And that, of course, never goes on in isolation; it proceeds in the context of a class system. To understand the relation between class and schooling we have to understand the ways in which the education system shapes, and is shaped by, the processes of class construction and division. We need to look at the way in which a specific schooling system was produced. This brings us right into the territory of the Reproduction Approach.

The place of schooling in social structures

The simplest, and not the silliest, answer to the question 'why educational inequality?' is that the schools are designed to produce it. They are set up to 'sort and sift', to give elite training to the children of the rich, to prepare others for the assembly line, and to legitimate the results. That is why we have a testing programme, selective promotion to upper levels of education, privileged private schools, and so on. To produce educational inequality is the proper business of schools performing their function of reproducing an unequal social order.

The evidence of our study is not consistent with the functionalist elements in this account. Certainly the school system does all these things; but it also does many other things that contradict them. Schools promote kids without testing them, the state system challenges the private schools, schools have ideologies that value people for other things than competitive achievement, they produce radical students as well as complacent ones, they make working-class kids dissatisfied with the prospect of factory work, and so on. If 'reproduction' predominates in a given case, it is because that side of things has won out in a contest with other tendencies, not because it is guaranteed by some sociological law. More, it is clear, as in the case of the elite private girls' schools and the challenge to ruling-class patriarchy, that the schools can be the vehicle for significant *changes* in established social relationships.

We must look, then, at the historically-developed structure of relationships between the schools and their catchments to understand how inequality is produced. This has been done in some of the better social histories of education, and there is some awareness of it in teacher unions' campaigns against State Aid to private schools on the grounds that it reinforces privilege; but it remains undeveloped as a research and theoretical perspective.

Our material suggests that these relationships have developed in ways that give different social groups radically different capacities to fashion educational arrangements that are favourable to them. As we saw in Chapter Four, the connection of the ruling-class school with its clientele is principally through a network and market, while in the case of the working-class school the key institutions are state compulsion and a centralized bureaucracy. Ruling-class educational aspirations are thus able to construct a form of schooling that is organic to the class, while working-class educational aspirations meet a process of cultural intervention that is inevitably disruptive.

Up to a point, it is sufficient to notice that there is a direct connection between schools and social classes. The connection is easiest to understand when classes are clearcut groups with a strong sense of their own identity and when schools are directly attached to them. The design of our study tends to produce that impression because of the two sub-samples. But we know that classes in contemporary Australia are not as clearcut as that; we also know that classes were more like that in earlier periods of Australian history. In short, the nature of the relationship between classes changes historically; and schooling is deeply implicated in those changes. Schooling changes its size, organization, scope and tasks in response to changes in class relations — as we saw in the 1940s and 1950s, and as we are seeing again now.

Further, schooling is one of the battlegrounds where changes in class relations are fought out, and also one of the participants in the battle. In the 1940s and 1950s there was a profound shift from what is sometimes called a 'corporate' form of class relations to a hegemonic one, with a working class much less conscious of a distinct identity and interests, and more profoundly divided than before. One of the key ways in which a new pattern of class relations was instituted was developments in schooling. In particular, the combination of a great expansion of secondary schooling and the dominance within it of a curriculum organized around the individual appropriation of academic knowledge.

We have touched on this story several times already; here we shall try to state its theoretical significance, as it sums up a good deal of our work. In trying to understand educational inequality today, one is trying to grasp the impact of that new mechanism, mass meritocratic schooling. The fact that radically different views of it are taken in the research literature — that it gave opportunity to all, and that it made no real difference to inequality — is a pointer to its own contradictory nature.

More and more working-class kids did enter, and were shaped by, the new-model secondary system. But they came to it from circumstances that were at odds with its characteristic practices. Further, it was constructed by a distant authority, which had been responsible for generations of a mostly bitter experience of schooling. Ruling-class kids found themselves in changed circumstances too, in a genuinely mass competition for advancement through education. But they came from families to whom competition was congenial, and through schools that were able to reform themselves to embrace the new circumstances.

Thus the egalitarian impulse behind meritocratic secondary schooling came up against the historically-constructed character and divergent interests of the different groups that participated in it. The new schools were both 'above' social division *and* firmly attached to the lives of particular classes. Out of this contradiction flowed the contrary effects which different parts of the research literature latch on to. Meritocratic schooling contains, in its very foundations, impulses towards both the inheritance of social position and the disruption of that inheritance. Schooling reproduces *and* transforms.

We have formed something like the same conclusion about the connection between schooling and gender relations; though, as the research on this link is thinner, and historical research practically non-existent, we can only raise it as a hypothesis. As with class relations, though for different reasons, there was something of a crisis in gender relations in the 1940s, especially in connection with mobilization for war. A determined post-war campaign got large numbers of adult women out of the workforce and into full-time housework and childcare, but didn't kill the aspiration for equality. The education of their children became one of its vehicles, indeed one of its few legitimate expressions. Coeducation was the means by which the authorities could respond to a demand for equal provision for girls. But the egalitarian impulse here came into contradiction with the powerful impulses in family organization and the labour market towards sexual segregation, and in consequence coeducation hasn't even begun to end sexism in schooling. Indeed it has provided a means by which sexist practices in teenagers' peer life can find freer expression.

For some time we have been talking about 'causes' of inequality in a very different sense from that of individual-difference or even class-difference explanations. In full-blown Reproduction Approach arguments the 'cause' is, if anything, the structure of the social system as a whole; and it is difficult to see any 'cure' apart from a general social revolution — which, by and large, is not Departmental policy.

There are, we now think, good grounds for considering that the intellectual tangle we have been tracing in the last few pages is so confused, and the lessons for practice so obscure, because the problem has usually been set up the wrong way.

An analogy may help. A concern with inequalities of income may lead us to investigate why Joe Bloggs is rich while Mary Stojanovic is poor, and often we can tell that with reasonable precision — Joe cornered the Queensland market in used Kelvinators just before a heatwave, while Mary, who can't speak English, works as a cleaner and has five kids, was abandoned by her husband who ran off to make his pile working for Joe. But we don't understand the causes in the sense of knowing what to do about it, unless we understand how our economic and political system keeps Mary poor, keeps producing situations like his and hers, and enables Joe to evade the taxation that is intended to redistribute some of his money to Mary.

Similarly with educational inequality: a search for particular factors and principal causes makes some sense when we want to understand what has happened to particular people or families. Though even that has its limits, for the system produces exceptions to its own rules. The same schools generate upward mobility, and downward mobility, and no mobility at all.

The problem, again, is that we need a somewhat different notion of 'cause'. Educational inequality isn't a matter of factor piling upon factor, and cannot be understood by a kind of arithmetic of advantage and disadvantage. If anything, the analogy should be with chemical compounding rather than with addition and subtraction. We need tools with which to think about qualitative changes, leaps and discontinuities, as our means of penetrating to the *essence* of the system.

In the same way, the concept of 'inequality' grasps only a very limited part of the reality. Of course some people have more money, more education, than others. But equally plainly there is a larger reality underneath and all around those differences — the social relations and practices in which they arise. Notions like 'inequality' are not much use when we try to grasp how people enter those relations, what they do to them, where they come from, and how they might be changed.

In short: the search for 'causes' of 'inequalities' has been, and is bound to remain, fruitless so long as the terms in which the search is carried on are fundamentally at odds with its object.

The notion of cause in social analysis has little purchase unless it is linked with social action. What we need for an assault on injustices that exists in, and work through, the education system, is knowledge about how a given pattern of social relationships has come into being, how the people in the situation relate to it, and what are its tensions and contradictions. It is simply not helpful to think about it as an array of causal factors that can be manipulated to produce a cure. Rather, we need to think in terms of the *potentials* that a given situation has for the people in it, and the *constraints* on what they can do with it. Both potentials and constraints are constructed by the history of the social relationships involved, and they also change as social structures change. What it is possible to do in Australian working-class schools in 1981, for instance, is distinctly different from what was possible ten, or even five, years ago.

Enough of theory. Though we hope this discussion may have been useful in clearing the air, it is time to try spelling out what some of the potentials and constraints in the present situation are.

A DEMOCRATIC STRATEGY FOR SCHOOLING

Equal opportunity

For more than a century, the main thrust of democrats concerned with education has been to open it up to the people. The battle-cry has been access, transforming educational privileges held by the dominant class, race, or sex into educational rights enjoyed by all. The traditional mileposts of progress in countries like Australia have been moments like the opening of the universities to women, and the Education Acts that established state-funded schools open to all. And UNESCO now charts progress in world education by the statistics of access, the growing provision of school places, and the rising percentages of populations who get advanced schooling.

The struggle for access to education has been a radical and democratic movement in two main ways. The first concerns the fact of exclusion itself, the sense that one of the more important measures of social injustice was the monopolization of good education by a privileged group. This still counts. One of the facts that really drives home to people what is happening in South Africa, for instance, is the highly unequal provision of schooling for the blacks and the whites there. The other point has to do with the content of education. Knowledge is power; and the demand for more education by the workers' movements in capitalist countries was very clearly intended to increase workers' power to shape their future, and not have it dictated to them. The workers' movements in many countries undertook a major educational effort of their own; though in the course of time that was killed by political defeat (as in Germany) or the expansion of the state school systems.

The evidence recited in Chapter One makes clear that opportunity in education is still far from being equal, that massive class differences in educational access are still found in almost every country in which the issue has been studied. Do we, then, gird ourselves for another round in the century-long battle for equal opportunity? — our goal a universal system of well-staffed, well-equipped schools, properly supported with technical services, curriculum advice, and sociological research reports like this, which will enable them at last to give every child a genuinely fair start in the race, selecting on talent alone for higher education and scholarships. To achieve that, in present conditions, would be a mighty task. Is that where we should be putting our energies?

We should be clear, first, that while the struggle for equal opportunity has been pushed ahead by working-class and socialist parties, it does have important negative consequences for the working class. A number of them have come into focus in this research.

From the point of view of the student and her family, what 'equal opportunity' means is the opportunity to seek individual promotion in the school system and, through the school system, in economic and social life. The material from our working-class schools shows vividly what this already means: streaming and creaming in the organization of the school; discrediting of parents' knowledge and judgments; teacher-student relationships that rarely involve real trust. A heavier stress on equality of opportunity could be expected to intensify these effects, not mitigate them.

Similarly with the effects of the equal-opportunity strategy on the structure of the working class as a whole; which can be summed up in a phrase, deeper division. It has long been familiar from research on schools, and is clear in our material, how the process of selection helps to generate a social dichotomy, stereotyping, and hostility between the 'brains' and the 'dumbos', those who can 'use their heads' and those who 'are good with their hands', the rough and the respectable. This is only one aspect of the divisions that develop or are deepened by the competitive organization of schooling around the hegemonic curriculum. Among others are the different relationship of boys and girls to academic knowledge and the process of competition; and the regional and ethnic divisions that make different schools very different places to work in, but which can't become the focus of learning because they are marginalized by conventional subject-matter.

Above all, we find division arising around the position and practices of teachers. All the processes just mentioned work via teachers' relationships with their students. Many of the differences between ruling-class and working-class schools mapped in this study come to a head in the fact that most teachers find the former stimulating and encouraging places to teach in, and the latter disruptive and wearing. The equal-opportunity strategy would place even more emphasis on the teachers' role as guardians of legitimate knowledge and gatekeepers for advancement. Hence it would normally intensify the character of teacher-student relationships we have so often seen in working-class schools — a contest for control with the 'less able' groups, a relationship with the 'more able' based on wary calculation. And what, most of all, these pupil/teacher relationships signify is the social separation between teachers as a group and the working class as a group, which embodies a profound disconnection between knowledge and social life. Here is the ultimate trap in the 'equal opportunity' strategy: it reinforces a distinctive and disempowering tendency in Western culture.

Given its importance in educational thought and policy, it is notable that equal opportunity is not a central issue for the working class itself. So far as our evidence goes (and on this point we think our sample would if anything be biassed towards people concerned with this issue) parents are little concerned with the question, and the students not at all. Many of the kids have no knowledge whatever of other kinds of schools. Those who are aware of the elite private schools are much more likely to think of them in terms of useless (and harmless) snobbery than in terms of privilege; and, therefore, respond by insisting that we and our school are just as good.

Parents defend the general principle that every kid should have a fair go through education, and are likely to know that the rich can get a fairer go than most. But they are also likely to say 'good luck to them' or 'if they have the money they have the right to spend it on their kids'; and to express disdain for the 'social climbers' who try to join them. In the matter of their own kids' education, working-class parents are concerned that schooling should be a means of protection rather than advancement, and this concern exists within a larger claim for a decent education which respects their kids and their right to know.

'Equality of opportunity', then, does speak to some working-class concerns, and that is one reason why it will remain a significant slogan in education politics. But it deflects attention from broader working-class needs and interests, and there is no prospect that equality of opportunity will become an issue around which working-class concerns with education can be mobilized on a large scale.

The goal of equal opportunity owes its very significant place in the history of Australian education not to its being a working-class demand but to its place in class relations as a whole. As we have suggested, equality of opportunity is a formula expressing the reconciliation of a genuinely radical and popular demand for more, and empowering, education, with a stratified and competitive social order and the interests which are dominant within it. The organization of mass education as individual competition is a mechanism of hegemony in class relations: it divides the working class, undermines its self-confidence, attaches part of its energy and talent to a process of competition. More: the establishment of a link between meritocratic schooling and the labour market, whereby the school became a 'sorter and sifter' and credentialling became a major form of labour market differentiation, can be seen as one of the major achievements of the ruling class in the postwar decades. No longer did economic inequality stem obviously from an unequal pattern of ownership. Now it appeared to follow from an unequal distribution of talent, duly measured and certified by the schools.

That achievement was, in various ways, fragile. Not all educators were content with the role in which the new conservatism cast them, as priests of the meritocracy. Not all working-class people bought the ideology of talent; though most (on our evidence) have been sufficiently influenced by it to be very unconfident about articulating opposed views about knowledge, skill and merit. The capitalist economy was not, as the 1970s have shown, able to deliver on the promise of having economic opportunity open to all. Perhaps the most corrosive effect was that while it became necessary to have consumed more and more schooling to get a job, most jobs actually needed less school knowledge to do. Equal opportunity served as a powerful legitimation of an unequal schooling and society but became in due course the focus of questioning and criticism. The debate on 'equal opportunity' in the early 1970s, centering on the Karmel reports, popularized the term but certainly did not originate the policy. These debates registered the crisis of a policy which had been implicit in the secondary education boom for twenty years.

But to recognize that is only the first step towards developing another strategy. One of the biggest obstacles to any other strategy is that it means abandoning the thrust of a century of campaigning for equality through common schooling. It involves accepting the idea of a divided education system, at least in the medium term; and, even in the shortest of short terms, that is no light matter.

We hold no brief for either segregation or comprehensivization *as such*. As we have seen, gender-segregation in ruling-class girls' schools has been a condition of subordination in one historical circumstance and of insurgency in another. It seems likely that the decline of the technical school system in the postwar period destroyed a working-class foothold in the state education system. And the emergence of a particular form of comprehensive schooling has done great damage to working-class kids and working-class interests. It is always a matter for judgment as to how the interests of particular groups will be best served, and it is a judgment full of dilemmas (not only for reformers).

In our judgment a class-divided educational system is what we now have and what we will have for some time to come. Even before we take into account social selection within any school, the state (and Catholic) system is divided because of the geographical class division of the cities, one of the most entrenched and resistant forms of social inequality. The segregated ruling-class education system in the Independent schools has, if anything, been reinforced by conservative governments in recent years. At least one state conservative party (the NSW Liberal Party) has promised to expand the number of state selective high schools. And a Labor government in Canberra would probably lack the will, even if it had the strength, to abolish either private or selective schools — if Labor ministers of education in the States are anything to go by.

In short, the reform movement founded on the goal of 'equality of opportunity' and the tradition of academic work which has been associated with it, which we have called the Inequality Approach, has failed. The question is, what do we do instead? We would suggest that what we have to do is accept the fact of class division in the school system as the price of a broader strategy in which the schools can again become the means for democratic purposes.

Good schooling

The democratic tradition in education, even in its worst moments, has never been completely reduced to the idea that the reform of schooling is simply about getting more and getting on. The failure of a tradition which focusses on access and individual opportunity has opened the way to a reconsideration of the content and purposes of schooling. The trouble is that this reconsideration has been dominated by conservative 'back to basics' campaigns which, to the extent that they are successful, will compound the difficulties of working-class schooling. A starting point for a different approach is furnished by earlier education movements which were, significantly enough, conducted by working-class people: the idea that knowledge should be really useful; and that knowledge is power.

What, in the practical situation of under-financed departmental high schools in country towns and working-class suburbs, can be done to make knowledge really useful and empowering? Quite a lot, we would suggest; though none of it is very easy. In this section and the next we want to sketch a line of march we think is possible in that situation, some of the constraints on it, and some features of the current situation that must shape it. We don't pretend that this is any sort of panacea for the current troubles of these schools; and we certainly don't claim that it is an approach that will eliminate conflict.

Three kinds of answer to the question 'what do working-class kids need to know?' have appeared in postwar secondary education. The first is that they need to know what the academic disciplines teach, because that gives access to a general culture and to the most developed account of the wider world. Anything else is second best. This view of things was associated with one of the strands of opinion which supported comprehensive schooling, and has recently enjoyed a renaissance among some radical thinkers. The problem is, as we have seen, that the attempt to get most kids to swallow academic knowledge produces insurmountable problems of motivation and control. Not only because of the abstractness of the content, but also as a consequence of the formal authority relations of its teaching.

Teachers have borne the brunt of the kids' reaction to the academic curriculum, and many have, in consequence, looked for knowledge which their students will find 'relevant and meaningful'. But in practice the syllabuses developed around this idea have been contained by the hegemony of the academic curriculum in almost all state schools. They have turned out to be ways of handling 'difficult' students, and compound the divisions introduced to schooling by the hegemonic curriculum. Their content is often a matter of personal preference, reflecting the kids' immediate world rather than explaining and expanding it.

A third notion is now emerging which draws on each of these earlier answers to the question. It proposes that working-class kids get access to formal knowledge via learning which begins with their own experience and the circumstances which shape it, but does not stop there. This approach neither accepts the existing organization of academic knowledge nor simply inverts it. It draws on existing school knowledge and on what working-class people already know, and organizes this selection of information around problems such as economic survival and collective action, handling the disruption of households by unemployment, responding to the impact of new technology, managing problems of personal identity and association, understanding how schools work, and why.

This is not to suggest that the school can be simply an agent of present working-class purposes; it must have a critical relationship with its clientele and their experience, and be free to oppose those aspects of working-class life which are themselves oppressive. There is always something uncomfortable about teachers, or researchers for that matter, telling the masses what's wrong with them as if there were nothing wrong with us. But given an equal willingness to recognize the beams in our own eyes, we can recognize the fact that living in an exploitative society, and being exploited and pushed around, does some pretty nasty things to people.

We see this, in our study, in the ugly sexism of some of the boys and their fathers; in the aimless hitting-out of some of our school resisters, especially the girls whose angry rejection of all control and direction in the present is slashing their options for the future; in the cultural desert that many of the parents inhabit and the kids are being locked into by commercial domination of youth culture. The school must be prepared to tackle such problems (if only because nobody else is, usually). Above all it must be prepared to struggle constantly against sexism and patriarchy, however deeply embedded they are in the school's clientele, given the crucial importance of adolescence in the cycle of oppressive gender relations.

This implies a different relation between what is learned and the person learning it, not in the obvious sense of 'being relevant' but rather in the learner's involvement in its selection and organization. It also requires a different way of measuring and controlling what is learned. That is, a form of assessment which has learning — not competitive ranking — as its object. 'What we want from a democratic education system', argues the most imaginative Australian writer on working-class schooling,

> is a planned improvement in everybody's standards of work, which is to say that we need courses which will help each person improve their work, and assessments that make it clear where they are in the course and what they can do next.[16]

None of this is consistent with the present academic curriculum. It would be different from, and in conflict with, the way of combining knowledge, people and resources now dominant in state schools. But we do not propose that every state school should abandon that curriculum, although many undoubtedly should. What we do suggest is that the place of the two kinds of curriculum in the school, the allocation of resources, prestige and energy to them, and the relations between them (including the provision of easy movement by students from one to the other) — these should be the central questions for every working-class school. In short, schools need to argue their priorities out.

What guarantee is there that they will get them straight? None. But it is certain that schools will not get their priorities straight except through a reconstruction of the relationships through which the school works. It is easy enough to state what is needed: a closer connection with the knowledge and resources of working-class people, most notably parents; an opening of the school's policy-making to their influence and the kids', and (for that matter) the teachers'; sufficient independence from Departmental control to allow this to happen, though close enough connection with the rest of the education system to be able to draw on resources that aren't available locally.

But that only begins to list the problems. One cannot rely on opening the school to 'the community', because most of the time there is no community. The working class is fragmented and divided against itself in the present state of class relations; and as other 'community-based' programmes have found, what 'community control' is likely to mean in such circumstances is handing power from a departmental bureaucracy over to the local bourgeoisie — local business people, doctors, clergy, and the like.

Further, there is a problem peculiar to schools: the age relationships on which they are constructed in the first place. This has always been an awkward set of relationship in high schools, since their students are neither fish nor fowl. No longer children, they cannot act as adults either. Teachers are placed in the contradictory position of relating to people who are their equals and also their responsibility. The tensions focussing here have, in the past decade or so, been sharpened by the development of a commercialized youth culture which has increased the kids' confidence in relation to adults, but has also offered them an illusory conception of freedom as the absence of constraint. In this context, many schools have sought to reassert their particular kind of authority while their students have tried to escape authority altogether. The problem, for both sides, is to reconstitute it.

The general course which we suggest, then, is one of making

working-class schools organic to their class. We have said that this path is not likely to be short of conflict, and we have no illusions that there is likely to be anything like consensus within the working class about what an organic school should do. Nor, we emphasize, should the school follow the line uncritically even if there were a consensus. What we envisage is not a day when the conflict which is now endemic in the relations between schools and their working-class clientele will disappear, but ways in which that conflict can be made educationally constructive rather than destructive.

We should not forget, in reckoning with these difficulties, that we have a working model of that relationship in very good order. The ruling-class schools studied in this project are organic to their class in exactly the sense we are talking about here. They help to organize it as a social force; they help to give it its sense of identity and purpose; they form an integral part of its networks; they induct the young into its characteristic practices; they express common purposes and an agreed (for the most part) division of labour between teachers and parents. As we have seen, they are far from conflict-free; and as we have also seen, they are far from being the direct and immediate agents of the parents' wishes. Being organic to the class in this case means having a reasonable degree of independence, that makes possible the invention of new strategies and the management of conflicting interests.

We are certainly not suggesting that the form of the ruling-class school system is appropriate to the working class, though current right-wing ideology does suggest that. Since Departmental control does produce a bruising experience of bureaucracy for many parents, the 'freedom to choose' represented by 'voucher' schemes and 'private enterprise' in schooling may temporarily appear attractive. But it's not a hard calculation to recognize that for the working class this would mean a thinner spreading of already inadequate resources, a futile multiplication of efforts, and, above all, not the organization and empowering of the working class but its greater vulnerability and deeper internal division. Under any conceivable practical conditions, an educational market will advantage the rich, and no-one else.

A public education system, then, is the only option; but we certainly have to contemplate a substantially different organization of public education to make it organic to the working class. In various places around Australia, and particularly in Victoria, there have been important and encouraging experiments in this direction. The schools of the Brunswick district of Melbourne, for example, have gone on from winning a good deal of autonomy from central control to forming a confederation through which they are organizing to defend their gains, to share resources and ideas, to establish links with local working-class organizations, and to build a coordinated educational programme for the area. A wide sharing of this kind of experience is very important.

The present moment in Australian education

Much of this book has been an attempt to develop an analysis of social structures and processes that lie 'behind' the immediate problems that parents, teachers and kids face in everyday life. This understanding will only be relevant to action if it can be put to use in analyzing the practical situations people face. Since situations constantly change, this can never be done once and for all. In this final section we offer a sketch of the general situation faced by Australian educators (particularly in state high schools) in 1981. It will in some respects be out of date by the time it is published; but we hope it may encourage other people to try their hand at the same kind of thing.

We began the book with the assertion that an era in Australian secondary schooling has ended. We hope the broad outlines of the turning-point are clear: the end of growth; the exhaustion of the drive for equal opportunity through a common schooling; the transformation of the working-class high school from a solution to social problems into a major difficulty for social policy.

In the short term, this situation has resulted in confusion and dismay among educators who had come to rely on continuing growth almost as a natural law. When conservative ideologues tried to capitalize on working-class dissatisfaction with education by blaming the schools for youth unemployment (by failing to 'teach the basics' and make kids properly employable), teachers reacted indignantly because they sensed this was wrong, but had no alternative reasons to offer.

Nor did educational policy-makers have any effective counter to the unfolding strategy of the conservative government in Canberra. The second half of the 1970s saw the running-down of a range of programs concerned to enliven and support public schooling, such as the Disadvantaged Schools Program, and the abolition of others, such as the Schools Commission's Innovations Program and the Education Research and Development Committee. Funding to universities has been squeezed, with actual contraction in staff numbers in most, and particular pressure on teacher education programs.

Yet a squeeze is not a strategy. We would suggest that after a period in which confusion on the Right was as deep as elsewhere, the broad outlines of a conservative consensus on what to do with mass education have now emerged. A key sign of this is the transformation of the Schools Commission from an agency giving substantial support to public schooling and its improvement, into an instrument which — particularly by its underwriting a rapidly-increasing percentage of the costs of private schools — has the capacity (and it would seem the intention) of driving deeper the wedge between public and private schooling.

Though this is important in itself, as our analysis of the social meaning of the private school system indicates, it is only part of a larger strategy. The central thrust of this strategy is consistent with the overall economic policy of the conservative coalition, to seek economic revival by widening inequalities of wealth and income, and increasing incentives to capitalists. It is to confirm and expand a division within the school system which thirty years' attempts at reform failed to eliminate: between those who have sufficient hope of entering the career-structured end of the labour market to encourage them to study, and those who have not. For the former the recipe is: compete harder. For the latter: better training for being employees.

The most publicized aspect of this is 'transition education' for working-class kids. This program has had a mixed reception among teachers, for good reasons. In the hopes of its conservative promoters, it would re-establish the damaged links between the working-class school and the lower end of the labour market. Schooling would be turned into training relevant to particular kinds of jobs, and in the process, the kids would learn that they get what they deserve. Being aimed at the collapse of the high school's legitimacy in the face of youth unemployment and disenchantment with credentials, 'transition education' is a powerful idea. It speaks to real concerns of parents, students, and teachers. But it also cuts across other strategies that schools have been developing in response to the same problems. It has some difficulty holding the kids' allegiance; it does not create decent jobs for them. And it is difficult to control. Some teachers have found here a point of purchase for the kind of curriculum we sketched in the last section.

A combination of inegalitarian policies and changed economic circumstances also threatens the usefulness of schooling to women

— just at the time when principles of sexual equality and the promotion of non-sexist curricula and career counselling have become reasonably widespread. Married women have, on the whole, held on to their place in the paid workforce during the recession. For women involved in the reorientation of ruling-class schools towards the professions, there is no going back. But in occupations that have traditionally provided channels of advancement for women, like teaching, nursing and social work, there are now fewer job openings. The highly selective boom that is now under way concentrates opportunities in fields like accountancy, management, mining, and the heavy trades — where employment is dominated by men. These shifts in the labour market could reduce the pressure on schools to sponsor a changed social position for women, and compound the school's tendency to divide those who cannot compete in the 'career' end of the labour market from those who can.

Where can we look for pressure of a different kind? Not, it would seem, from the current round of official enquiries and reports on education policy. The Williams report, the latest in the series of attempts to formulate a central policy on working-class education, has given no clear lead, and certainly provided no alternative to the drift of federal government policy. At the State level, a preoccupation with evaluation and 'accountability', such as we see in the setting-up of the Keeves enquiry in South Australia, certainly responds to working-class families' concern about what the schools are doing for their kids. But it does so in a way that is likely to encourage standardization of curricula and tighter central control of schools — and thus benefit technocrats rather than workers.

The people who are in the gun, in the campaigns for 'accountability' and tighter central control, are classroom teachers. Our argument must ultimately focus on their situation and their problems. It is the curriculum over which they have professional control that is the key to many of the social issues in education which we have been mapping. Teachers on their own are certainly not able to carry through the whole of the reforms we have been talking about, which depend also on the involvement of parents, administrators, unions — and researchers. But these other groups, without the involvement of classroom teachers, can do precisely nothing.

It becomes very important, then, to get accurate bearings on the social situation of teachers, the constraints they work under, and the possibilities open to them. We have sketched some of the conflicting pressures earlier in this book, and hope to explore them in more depth in follow-up research. Clearly, some aspects of teachers' work and professional ideology make them vulnerable to conservative responses in the current transition. The isolation and stress of classroom work in working-class schools make some willing to support authoritarian responses to 'discipline problems' — getting rid of resistance by getting rid of resisters, or reasserting the right to use physical violence ('corporal punishment'). The sense that teachers rightly have, that they are bearers of important cultural resources for the whole society, makes some vulnerable to cultural elitism, and to deficit-theory explanations of why working-class kids are hard to teach.

But there are also elements in the situation of teachers that can lead in quite different directions, and the changes of recent years have thrown several of them into relief. The classroom situation may isolate teachers from each other but they are thrown into extended contact with another group of people from whom they can learn a lot. The recent, sudden reality of teacher unemployment is putting teachers as employees into closer touch with the experiences of other groups of workers, and with the prospects of their own students. Professionalism, conservative in some respects, also encourages autonomy and innovation on the job. Potentially, it is a powerful opponent of bureaucratic control. One of the most important gains in the 1970s has been the assertion of a significant degree of autonomy by state schools, especially in curriculum matters. It is no accident that this is currently under attack in the name of 'accountability'. Teacher unions, usually preoccupied with economistic 'wages and conditions of service' issues, have been showing increasing interest in the content and purposes of schooling; and, especially in Victoria, have lent weight to the push for school autonomy.

Perhaps most important of all is a fact so obvious that it is easy to overlook: state school teachers are public servants. State education is under pressure now mainly because it is part of the state, in a period when ruling-class strategy is to squeeze the 'public sector' and reduce the scope of the state's activity. In much recent conservative rhetoric, 'public' is made synonymous with inefficiency, stagnation and waste; 'private' with efficiency, innovation and drive. The current transfer of federal funds to the private schools is often justified in just those terms.

Yet being a 'public servant' has an older and larger meaning, which is highly relevant to teachers' views of themselves. However battered the professional ego may get, however cynical the old hand in the staffroom may profess to be, it still remains true that most teachers went into teaching not because of the chance it gave them to become a millionaire, but because it was a job where they thought they could actually do some good. Serving the people continues to be a muted but significant part of what they think they are about. This is a fact about teachers that should be known — and cherished — by people who have to deal with them, including sceptical parents. Public education should be defended precisely because it is a public service, our only chance of asserting the common good as the highest principle of educational policy, in the face of rampant private interest.

In arguing that view of teaching, we would stress that it remains an abstract ideal unless it can be embodied in social relations that expand the *emancipatory* possibilities of education. We would like to close by raising several points about those relations.

First, it is important that state school teachers should come to see themselves for what they really are: the teachers of the working class. Not the only ones (given the Catholic system), and not all of them (given the state schools in ruling-class suburbs). By and large, however, that is what they are, and long will be. Until teachers recognize it, and indeed take pride in it, the real character of the problems they face will remain obscure.

Second, as we have already observed, teachers cannot do it all alone. The potentials for a progressive educational response that are certainly present in their situation, have to meet with encouragement and support from other groups who influence the situation in the schools, and influence people's ways of thinking about it. This includes parents, kids, school administrators, intellectuals, the women's movement, and the labour movement generally. All have a responsibility for the way the social struggle about education turns out, and whether the conservative hegemony recently established can be reversed.

Finally, the education we are speaking of is plainly more than a mere reflection of existing social life; it bears on its reconstitution. There is a great defensiveness and timidity among people who work in education, founded on the belief that schooling is on the margins of social life, or is strictly bound by other forces. Our evidence suggests that this is a misapprehension. Schooling is a powerful institution through which people and their relationships are produced. That is not a matter of choice; schools *do* that, one way or another. The choices are about *how* they do it. Schools have the capacity to shape the way they do that work and determine which social interests will be advanced by their labours.

In making such choices, we would argue, educators should look to the deepest roots of their trade. Education has fundamental connections with the idea of human emancipation, though it is constantly in danger of being captured for other interests. In a society disfigured by class exploitation, sexual and racial oppression, and in chronic danger of war and environmental destruction, the only education worth the name is one that forms people capable of taking part in their own liberation. The business of the school is not propaganda; it is equipping people with the knowledge and skills and concepts relevant to remaking a dangerous and disordered world. In the most basic sense, the process of education and the process of liberation are the same. They are aspects of the painful growth of the human species' collective wisdom and self-control. At the beginning of the 1980s it is plain that the forces opposed to that growth, here and on the world scale, are not only powerful but have become increasingly militant. In such circumstances education becomes a risky enterprise. Teachers too have to decide whose side they are on.

Appendix
Details of method

In Chapter One we gave a general account of our methods; this appendix is to give technical details to help in the evaluation of our study, and some advice to other researchers who may be contemplating similar work.

The research plan

Our original scheme was to interview two age groups, around 9 years old and around 14 years old, and for each student, to interview all the important people in the immediate circle — friends, family members and teachers. Interviews with friends, and family members other than parents, were dropped at an early stage, partly because of cost, partly because this sort of task is best done by other methods. The 9 year olds were dropped because funding was only available to study one age-group. (Luckily: we vastly underestimated the richness of the interviews and the time it would take to analyze them.) We chose the teenagers in order to focus on school leaving.

From the start, we proposed to use a highly flexible interviewing technique, based on a definite set of issues to be raised in each interview but leaving it to the interviewer to judge how best to do it each time. This was of course only possible with a small group of interviewers who were all very familiar with the aims and concepts of the project. The main areas to be covered were: current school performance and relationships with teachers; past school history; occupational plans and ideas about school leaving; family and peer relationships, and influences on the above; parents' working lives and the social relations of work; teachers' views of, and expectations about, the pupils; teachers' relations with the families; teachers' views of teaching, professional backgrounds, and views of the schools they had worked in, including their present one.

Considerations of time, money, and available people converged on a 'sample' of about 100 as the largest we could possibly get, and still have a good understanding of each. Two other considerations shaped the sample.

(*a*) We decided to carry out the research in Sydney and Adelaide — both to check whether there were major regional variations in the relationships we were studying (answer: no), and because one of the two 'principal investigators' lived in each city and it was cheaper and easier to interview without going interstate.

(*b*) Most of the research on these questions studies either girls or boys but not both. We considered doing the same, on the grounds that it would simplify the research and throw the class patterns into relief, but rejected the idea. That also was a fortunate decision as the issue of the relationship between the sexes, and the connection of gender patterns and class patterns, have come more and more into focus in our work.

Our sample plan thus took on its final shape. The following table shows the numbers of interview 'clusters' initially intended (in brackets) and actually done.

Clusters based on:	Girls		Boys	
	Sydney	*Adelaide*	*Sydney*	*Adelaide*
In Independent schools:	13(12)	12(12)	13(12)	12(12)
In State comprehensives:	11(12)	11(12)	13(12)	15(12)

Choosing the families

As explained in Chapter One, we did not seek a random sample that ranged across the whole spectrum of class situations, but a purposive sample that would locate people in quite specific and well-understood situations. We still needed a way of defining these for the purpose of fieldwork. With some misgivings, we adapted a scheme developed in North America by Wright.[17]

Wright defines 'class locations' by three dimensions of social relations in the workplace, identifying individuals' relationships to (a) the production of surplus-value, (b) authority and control in the workplace, (c) the mental/manual division of labour. We devised the following questionnaire items, intended to tap these points:

FATHER'S WORK / MOTHER'S WORK (if she has a job outside the home)

1 What kind of job? (Please describe the work briefly, e.g. stores clerk, maintenance fitter, truck driver, journalist.)
2 Where is the job? (e.g. car manufacturing plant, government department, own business.)
3 Does it involve any *supervision* of other workers? YES/NO
(e.g. foreman, office manager, or employer. Please give any details you think might be helpful.)

We then laid down a series of criteria for the families to be interviewed: the father's job should be at one or the other end of all three of Wright's dimensions; parents should be Australian-born, so we didn't have to wrestle with the migrant experience too; the family should be intact and nuclear, so we didn't have to deal with complicated household structures; no parents older than 45, so we had a reasonably homogeneous generation; wives at home rather than in jobs, so we didn't have to contend with differences between 'latchkey children' and those with full-time mothers. These restrictions, we thought, should produce neatly-defined subsamples.

In the screening phase of the study we gave out 1005 questionnaires, and found perhaps half-a-dozen families that met all our criteria. We had ignored some important facts. Most mothers of teenage children in the working-class suburbs we were studying do have jobs — they have to. Top professionals like barristers and surgeons don't necessarily supervise a workforce in the course of their practice. On the other hand, a good many manual workers do. It is in fact rare to find an Australian-born father working for a company and old enough to have teenage children, who hasn't risen to leading hand or foreman. Having no authority at all is usually the lot of workers who are younger, foreign-born, or female. As these and other issues became clear, it was obvious that our sampling system had to be revised.

This was done by abandoning some criteria (working mothers and age) and relaxing others (we included migrant families where English was the main language used). We gave up rigid use of the Wright scheme (e.g. admitting government employees), but tried to devise new ways of holding to its principles. Thus, on the 'authority' dimension, we included in the one group people like barristers and physicians with no supervisory role in the workplace but with a great deal of professional authority, and in the other leading hands and foremen (but not supervisors above that); and we included families who were involved with organizations that articulate class interests

— unions, Rotary, parties, professional associations. Where numbers in these now-expanded catchments permitted, we introduced an academic criterion, attempting to maximize the 'spread' across streams in each school. In various ways, then, we increased variety within each subsample while attempting to hold to the general principles by which we had originally defined it.

A note on 'class locations' and the relationship of our sampling to the concept of class

The sample plan above suggests that we are taking the two subsamples as samples of classes, which implies a concept of class as a category from which one can sample (more or less imperfectly). This is plainly at odds with the argument we have repeatedly made that 'class' is not a system of categories but a system of relationships between people.

The Wright schema, although a highly sophisticated one, still is an example of categorical definitions of class. The 'class locations' Wright defines are basically abstractly-defined categories of workers. The difficulties arose in our application of those categories because we were trying to study a system of relationships with a categorical tool.

There is, then, an ambiguity about our method which arises because we could not think of a way of sampling relationships without first sampling people. We should make it very clear, then, that we do not take our sampling categories as defining classes. The object of our study was class relations and class processes; we wished to reach through the categories, which had to be used to get the research going, to the relations and processes behind them. We wished to make contact with situations where certain kinds of class processes could be expected to cluster thickly. Where we find that is really so, we can then reasonably talk about people who are in the working class or in the ruling class; and for most of the families we interviewed that is indeed appropriate. But not all — for some of the families it isn't clearcut. Accordingly, when we talk about the 'working-class families' in our research, we are referring to numbers a little less than the numbers in the rows of the table above. We have tried to keep that complexity in mind in our presentation of the material.

Field procedure

We approached schools we thought would have high proportions of the kinds of families we sought to interview. With one exception each, out of eight Independent schools and six state schools approached, the principals agreed to the study going ahead, put us in contact with the relevant staff and provided us with space and other facilities. We have already expressed our thanks to the many people in the schools who made the project possible. Though it often doesn't appear so from the published reports, research of this kind is utterly dependent on the goodwill and active help of teachers. Although our results aren't always comforting, we hope to have given a fair return for the help received.

We approached the students and their parents by a letter home (accompanied by a covering note from the principal) briefly explaining the project and seeking cooperation in the first step, the administration of a screening questionnaire to all willing pupils in Year 9 or 10. In one state the Department of Education refused to accept the part of our standard screening questionnaire that asked for a description of parents' jobs, on the stated grounds that this was confidential information. We were therefore obliged to seek this information in a small questionnaire to the parents that went with the initial letter. There was a very high loss rate in this part of the sample, which we did not entirely understand at the time. We later found out that with the arrival of our letters some hair-raising rumours had flown around: one that it was an attempt by the Taxation Office to catch families who actually had two jobs but were only declaring income from one; another that it was an attempt by Department of Education inspectors to prove that the school and its community were better off than appeared, and therefore justify a cutback in funding.

The student questionnaires were administered in class by one of the research group; and, after the rethinking already described, the sample for interview was chosen. The parents were then contacted by letter or telephone, and a member of the research group went to visit them, explained the project in more detail, and, if they were willing, left a questionnaire for each parent. A week or so later we called back for the completed questionnaires, and (if still willing) got permission to interview the student and arranged times to interview each of the parents. These interviews were done at home, usually separately. The interviews with students were done at school, during class time, in spaces such as career advisers' and counsellors' offices, unused meeting rooms or classrooms. After these interviews were done, or when they were nearly finished in a particular school, we invited the teachers who taught that particular form to be interviewed also. Most agreed, and most of these interviews were done individually at the school. At one school, however, when time was very short right at the end of term, we held group discussions with teachers in their staffroom.

With a selection process of this complexity there are many chances of losing people. We have no simple way of calculating an overall 'response rate', but the following figures will give the key points. (These exclude the two 'pilot' schools which account for eight of our clusters.)

The total number of students enrolled in the relevant Years was 1,282, and the number of student questionnaires completed was 857, or 67 per cent. This includes students affected by the screening-questionnaire debacle described above, where the rate was 31 per cent. Without this the rate was 75 per cent. We approached 142 families for the next stage, and 92 clusters were finally interviewed, a rate of 65 per cent. This figure varies with method of contact: where the first request was by letter, the rate was 54 per cent; where (from shortage of time) it was by visit or telephone, the rate was 84 per cent. Here, as elsewhere in the project, the importance of personal contact is obvious.

Some reflections on method

Our rather elaborate field procedure was time-consuming, but it also had positive effects. Because we had to explain ourselves and get other people's agreement at each major step, we were under pressure to be sensitive to their interests and concerns. It also meant that they became fairly familiar with us and the project. By the time we taped an interview with a parent, he or she would normally have seen two or three of our pieces of paper, and we would have visited the house two or three times. We showed ourselves willing to put time and effort into understanding their kids; and we think that is a major reason for the very good rapport with the parents that most of the interviews show. Ironically, the people who had least chance to familiarize themselves with us and the project were the kids, as we realized afterwards; this was a mistake which is reflected in their interviews being on the whole less rich.

We had several reasons for using questionnaires as well as interviews: to make selection quicker, to get some basic information in advance of interviewing, to compare the methods, and to calibrate our findings against those of other research (by using their questionnaire items). We think the questionnaires were useful for the first two purposes. On the third and fourth purposes, the interview data is so much better than the questionnaire data that we now rely on the latter hardly at all. It is clear in many cases that answers to questionnaire items were entirely misleading. Questionnaires have another cost: some people told us afterwards that they had been quite anxious about the prospect of filling in a hefty form, and no doubt many of our refusals were due to that reason. Our advice to other researchers is, if you have to use questionnaires, keep them short and straightforward; and explain the research personally.

This is not to imply that the interview is a bland and neutral research tool. Like any other conversation, it is affected by the social character of the participants — shaped by the social forces we are trying to research. The kinds of things a female research assistant from a working-class background can talk freely about with (a) a multinational company director and (b) a mother of three with a job in the local cannery, are rather different in both cases from what a male professor with a background in the professional bourgeoisie can. We tried to deal with this by making sure that each of the four of us did all kinds of interviewing, but have still had to take careful account of who was interviewing, and in what kind of situation, when analyzing the results.

Interviews of this kind produce a vast amount of complex information. Most time spent on this project has occurred since the fieldwork, in digesting the results and trying to order and account for what we found. Two and a half years after the fieldwork, we are still very far from having this process complete; and we expect to be working on it, in one way or another, for years to come. The problem is that the information becomes staler as we get to understand it better, and hence less and less relevant as a basis of practical advice. The decision to publish our findings now is inevitably a compromise, and Chapter Five reflects a state of play in our own thinking rather than a definitive statement.

At another level, though, this research could never lead to practical advice. Though we were able to identify, explore, and understand a good many problems that working-class families were facing, we couldn't offer them any help in solving them: our knowledge wasn't organized in a form that would individually be of use to them. The suggestions in Chapter Five are of no use to a mother worrying whether to go back to work to support her elder daughter in high school, at the cost of leaving no-one at home to take care of her younger son; or any other of the thousand and one problems of practice which families confront. We are a bit closer to having something to say about the practical dilemmas of teachers (partly because that is our own trade), but it's still fairly abstract.

We would suggest, then, that there is a real problem about research, whatever its techniques, which remains an academic intervention from outside the situations it studies. We would hope to see future research being organized in a fundamentally different way — by or with the people it is ultimately supposed to benefit. There are severe problems with this, not least that research funds are normally available only to professional researchers. Even among them, current federal government research policy is to concentrate more of the available money on fewer and bigger projects.

Nevertheless, the goal of a different model of research is clear. It should empower the people who are normally just the objects of research, to develop their capacity to research their own situations and evolve their own solutions. It should embody a relationship where expertise is a resource available to all rather than a form of power for a few. In short, social research can become more democratic, and we would suggest that is the way, rather than funding elite super-scientists, to produce really useful knowledge.

Notes

1 Statistics in this paragraph are from J.I. Martin and P. Meade, *The Educational Experience of Sydney High School Students*, Canberra, AGPS, 1979, 31; Australian Government Commission of Enquiry into Poverty, Poverty and Education Series, *Outcomes of Schooling*, Canberra, AGPS, 1978, 12; Schools Commission and Australian Bureau of Statistics, *Australian Students and their Schools*, Canberra, 1979, 52. Note that the last set of statistics gives '*apparent* retention rates', which will be affected, though not grossly, by pupils shifting between systems during secondary schooling.

2 A useful introduction to the research on industrialized countries is W. Tyler, *Sociology of Educational Inequality*, London, Methuen, 1977. For the third world, see P. Foster, 'Education and social inequality in sub-Saharan Africa', *Journal of Modern African Studies*, 1980, vol. 18, 201 – 236.

3 We desperately lack a good social history of Australian education; even a short history of comprehensive high schools. The statistics in the first paragraph below are drawn from rather fragmentary official sources and the rest of the story is pieced together from sources such as those mentioned in section B2 of the Reading Guide. The South Australian statistics quoted come from J.A. La Nauze, *Education for Some*, Melbourne, ACER Future of Education Series, 1943.

4 D. Bennett, 'Comments on Michael Pusey's paper "The legitimation of state education systems" ', Macquarie University seminar on Current Crisis in Education, September 1979, 7.

5 See section A of the Reading Guide for recent contributions to this debate. On the expansion of intelligence testing, see W.F. Connell, *The Australian Council for Educational Research 1930 – 80*, Melbourne, ACER, 1980, 71 – 5, 89, 169 – 174.

6 D. McCallum, 'The educational inequality problematic: a note on Australian education intellectuals, 1935 – 1945', in L. Johnson and U. Ozolins, ed., *Melbourne Working Papers 1979*, Sociology Research Group, University of Melbourne, 1979, 83 – 109.

7 J. Branson and D.B. Miller, *Class, Sex and Education in Capitalist*

Society, Melbourne, Sorrett, 1979, 2.

8 The twentieth century was called 'the century of the child' by the Swedish educator Ellen Key in a book of that name published in 1900: see W.F. Connell, *A History of Education in the Twentieth Century World*, Canberra, CDC, 1980.

9 The discussion which follows draws mainly on Freud's *The Interpretation of Dreams* and *Civilization and its Discontents*, and Sartre's *Being and Nothingness* and *Critique of Dialectical Reason*. The theory of practice implied here and elsewhere in this book is developed mainly in Sartre's *Critique* and in the writings of A. Giddens, e.g. his *Central Problems in Social Theory*, London, Macmillan, 1979.

10 B. Hill, *The Schools*, Ringwood, Penguin, 1977, 57 – 71.

11 In NSW this standard pattern has recently been slightly modified by the establishment of the Education Commission as employing authority; the Department still handles recruitment.

12 See K.S. Cunningham and D.J. Ross, *An Australian School at Work*, Melbourne, ACER, 1967; J. Darling, *Richly Rewarding: An Autobiography*, Melbourne, Hill of Content, 1978.
For the concept of 'organic intellectuals', see A. Gramsci, *Selections from the Prison Notebooks*, London, Lawrence and Wishart, 1971, 71.

13 The clearest Australian statement of the ideas referred to here and in what follows is W.F. Connell, *Foundations of Secondary Education*, Melbourne, ACER, 1961, 51 – 68.

14 A useful recent review of the problem is M. Barrett, *Women's Oppression Today*, London, Verso, 1980; see also A. Tolson, *The Limits of Masculinity*, London, Tavistock, 1977.

15 Examples of the following perspectives can be found by reference to sections A and C of the Reading Guide.

16 W. Hannan, 'Goals must be attainable', *TTUV News*, Feb. 1981.

17 E.O. Wright, 'Class boundaries in advanced capitalist societies', *New Left Review*, 1976, no. 98, 3 – 41.

Reading Guide

Part A The Australian educational inequality debate

In this section we list the major contributions to research, theory and policy on educational inequality over the last decade. Further references can be found in the Schools Commission's *Educational Disadvantage: A Bibliography* (July 1979) compiled by D.M. Goodman (though note that this is not a complete listing of Australian material).

P.J. Fensham, ed., *Rights and Inequality in Australian Education* (Cheshire, 1970) and T. Roper, *The Myth of Equality* (NUAUS, 1970) are the main writings that formulated the issue at the turn of the decade. The major policy documents that attempted to formulate responses were P. Karmel and others, *Schools in Australia* (AGPS, 1973); Schools Commission, *Girls, School and Society* (1975); and R. Fitzgerald and others, *Poverty and Education in Australia* (AGPS, 1976).

The research literature on extent and causes of class inequalities was summarized and criticized in R.W. Connell, 'Class and personal socialisation', in F.J. Hunt, ed., *Socialisation in Australia* (Angus & Robertson, 1972; a revised version in R.W. Connell, *Ruling Class, Ruling Culture*, Cambridge UP, 1977). Criticisms of this view, and alternative explanations, were then offered by various authors, including D. Toomey, 'What causes educational inequality?', *Australian and New Zealand Journal of Sociology*, vol. 10, 1974, pp. 31–37; and D. Edgar, whose views are now set out in 'Education as cultural reproducer', chapter 8 of his *Introduction to Australian Society* (Prentice-Hall, 1980). The debate was reviewed by B. Abbey and D. Ashenden, 'Explaining inequality', *Australian and New Zealand Journal of Sociology*, vol. 14, 1978, pp. 5–13. (See also the replies by Toomey, Edgar, and Abbey and Ashenden in the following issue of this journal.)

Meanwhile empirical research in the stratificationist vein continued to accumulate; significant examples are M.J. Rosier, *Early School Leavers in Australia* (Almqvist & Wiksell, 1978); and J.I. Martin and P. Meade, *The Educational Experience of Sydney High School Students* (Commonwealth Department of Education, 1979). P. Gilmour and R. Lansbury, *Ticket to Nowhere* (Penguin, 1978) attempted to relate this evidence to changes in the labour market. The growth of a 'reproduction' approach can be seen in the journal *Radical Education Dossier*, and most clearly in J. Branson and D.B. Miller, *Class, Sex and Education in Capitalist Society* (Sorrett, 1979). R. Sharp, *The Culture of the Disadvantaged* (DSP Discussion Paper No. 5, Schools Commission, 1980) is a brief and elegant discussion of contending points of view.

Part B Background material, Australian

1 Class and gender relations beyond the school

The historical development of these aspects of Australian life is documented in K. Daniels and M. Murnane, *Uphill All the Way* (University of Queensland Press, 1980); R.W. Connell and T.H. Irving, *Class Structure in Australian History* (Longman Cheshire, 1980); and E. Windschuttle, ed., *Women, Class and History* (Fontana, 1980).

There is a large, and very uneven, literature on contemporary Australian society. For insights into the issues that form the background to this book we would particularly recommend: D. Storer and others, *'But I Wouldn't Want My Wife to Work Here . . .'* (Centre for Urban Research and Action, c. 1976), on migrant women at work; N. Grieve and P. Grimshaw, *Australian Women* (Oxford University Press, 1981); R.J. Kriegler, *Working for the Company* (Oxford University Press, 1980); A. Game and R. Pringle, 'The making of the Australian family', *Intervention*, no. 12, 1979, pp. 63–83; and P. Sheehan, *Crisis in Abundance* (Penguin, 1980) on economic changes.

2 The history and sociology of schooling

J. Burnswoods and J. Fletcher, *Sydney and the Bush* (NSW Department of Education, 1980) is a delightful, and insightful, pictorial history of state schooling. The social history of Australian education is still very underdeveloped; an overview can be gained from P.H. Partridge, *Society, Schools and Progress in Australia* (Pergamon, 1968); B.K. Hyams and B. Bessant, *Schools for the People?*

(Longman, 1972); B. Bessant and A. Spaull, *Politics of Schooling* (Pitman, 1976); and R.T. Fitzgerald, *Through a Rear Vision Mirror* (ACER, 1975).

P.W. Musgrave, *Society and the Curriculum in Australia* (Allen & Unwin, 1979) is the first sustained attempt at a fundamental problem; and L.E. Foster, *Australian Education, a Sociological Perspective* (Prentice-Hall, 1981) is the first attempt to pull together a scattered literature. A very useful, and readable, compendium of the relevant figures is *Australian Students and their Schools* (Schools Commission and Australian Bureau of Statistics, 1979).

3 Schools, teachers, and curricula

There are several lively books describing school life and kids' experience: D. Humphreys and K. Newcombe, *Schools Out* (Penguin, 1975); H. Schoenheimer, *Good Schools* (National Press, 1970); B. Hill, *The Schools* (Penguin, 1977). The most interesting attempt to analyze private schooling is perhaps J.J. Smolicz and J.M. Moody, 'Independent schools as cultural systems', in S. Murray Smith, ed., *Melbourne Studies in Education* (Melbourne University Press, 1978) pp. 1–67.

Research on teachers is still thin; recent compilations are A.D. Spaull, ed., *Australian Teachers* (Macmillan, 1977); and G.W. Bassett, *Teachers in Australian Schools* (ACER, 1980).

Notable contributions to recent social analysis of curriculum and related issues are the Schools Commission report *Schooling for 15 and 16 Year Olds* (1980); and M. Pusey and R.E. Young, eds., *Control and Knowledge* (Research School of Social Sciences, ANU, 1979). On school-community relations, see D. Pettit, *Opening Up Schools* (Penguin, 1980); and valuable practical guides by G. Andrews and others, *The School Policy Manual, Practical Techniques for Involving the Community*, and *Organizing for Participation, a Parents' Action Manual* (School and Community Interaction Trust [22 Blanche Court, East Doncaster, Victoria], 1981).

Useful papers on these issues are often found in *The Secondary Teacher* (journal of the Victorian Secondary Teachers' Association); *TTUV News* (journal of the Technical Teachers' Union of Victoria); and *Radical Education Dossier* [P.O. Box 197, Glebe 2037].

4 Teenagers and their situations

The serious literature on adolescence is surprisingly limited. The most recent comprehensive survey, now more than ten years out of date, is W.F. Connell and others, *12 to 20* (Hicks Smith, 1975). K. Lette and G. Carey, *Puberty Blues* (McPhee & Gribble, 1979) is a lively, fictionalized account of growing up in Sydney; it should be taken together with G. Hawkins, 'Reading "Puberty Blues" ', *Refractory Girl*, no. 20–21, 1980, pp. 58–64. D. Dunphy, *Cliques, Crowds and Gangs* (Cheshire, 1969) long ago showed what could be done by close-up research methods; this is now being done in more sophisticated ways by a new generation of researchers such as L. Samuel, 'The making of a school resister; a case study of Australian working-class secondary school girls', in R. Browne, L. Foster and D. Magin (eds.), *Source Book of Australian and New Zealand Studies in the Sociology of Education* (Macmillan, forthcoming).

Part C General literature

1 Overseas research on these problems which we have found particularly useful or stimulating
W. Tyler, *The Sociology of Educational Inequality* (Methuen, 1977) is an admirable review and introduction. J. Ford, *Social Class and the Comprehensive School* (Routledge & Kegan Paul, 1969) is a now somewhat neglected but very interesting discussion of a central issue. B. Jackson and D. Marsden, *Education and the Working Class* (Penguin, 1966) is the classic on social mobility; S. Bowles and H. Gintis, *Schooling in Capitalist America* (Basic Books, 1976) the most formidable study of education, class and the economy at the macro scale. The *Harvard Educational Review* ran two excellent special issues on 'Women and Education' (vol. 49 no. 4, November 1979, and vol. 50 no. 1, February 1980).

P. Willis, *Learning to Labour* (Saxon House, 1977) is now a standard text on working-class boys; less noticed, but in a number of ways better and more practical, is D. Robins and P. Cohen, *Knuckle Sandwich* (Penguin, 1978). A useful starting-point for the rapidly-growing literature in this area is G. Mungham and G. Pearson, eds., *Working Class Youth Culture* (Routledge & Kegan Paul, 1976).

G. Grace, *Teachers, Ideology and Control* (Routledge & Kegan Paul, 1978) is the best study yet of teachers and the working class; P. Woods, *The Divided School* (Routledge & Kegan Paul, 1979), is an excellent inside account of a working-class secondary school, though not very much aware of class processes.

R. Sharp and A. Green, *Education and Social Control* (Routledge & Kegan Paul, 1975) take up the theme of progressivism and its unintended consequences. M.W. Apple, *Ideology and Curriculum* (Routledge & Kegan Paul, 1979) is often difficult reading, but a useful survey of a key topic.

Finally, R. Sennett and J. Cobb, *The Hidden Injuries of Class* (Vintage, 1972), besides having well-observed material on schooling, is a highly readable classic on the effects of class relations on personal life.

2 Really useful knowledge

R. Johnson, 'Really useful knowledge — radical education and working-class culture 1790–1848' in J. Clarke, C. Critcher and R. Johnson, eds., *Working-class Culture* (Hutchinson, 1979) is a fascinating historical study of working-class people's attempts to define the content of their own education. The School of Barbiana, *Letter to a Teacher* (Penguin, 1970) and P. Freire, *Pedagogy of the Oppressed* (Penguin, 1972), are notable modern attempts to relate the content of education to the realities of poverty and social struggle. W. Hannan, *In the Name of Everyone* (VSTA, 1981) collects the essays of our most acute teacher-theorist; and J. Docker, *'Learning for Real' in the Secondary School* (Disadvantaged Schools Programme Discussion Paper No. 4, Schools Commission, 1980) describes a notable Tasmanian project. R. White, *Absent with Cause* (Routledge & Kegan Paul, 1980) shows what can be done in the education of the most 'resistant' working-class kids. J. Field and S. Sullivan, *'It isn't happening in Brunswick'*, School Work Programme, Moreland High School [25 The Avenue, Coburg 3058 Victoria], is a model study of school leavers by school leavers.

As examples of self-help approaches to knowledge and its uses, which might stimulate thinking about curricula, we would suggest *Our Bodies, Our Selves* (Boston Women's Health Collective, 1971) concerning health and sexuality; and M. Cooley, *Architect or Bee? — the Human/Technology Relationship* (Transnational Cooperative, 1980 [G.P.O. Box 161, Sydney 2001]) on industrial techniques and their social consequences.

Part D Other publications relating to this project

1 Reports of the research

D.J. Ashenden and others, 'Class and secondary schooling', *Discourse,* vol. 1 no. 1, 1980, pp.1–19.

R.W. Connell and others, 'Class and gender dynamics in a ruling-class school', *Interchange* [Canada], vol. 12 nos 2–3, 1981, pp.102–117.

G. Dowsett and others, 'Divisively to school: some evidence on class, sex and education in the 1940s and 1950s', *Australia 1939–1988, A Bicentennial History Bulletin*, no. 4, 1981, pp. 32–60.

S. Kessler and others. *Ockers and Disco-maniacs: a report on sex, gender and secondary schooling,* Sydney, Inner City Education Centre, 1982.

2 Discussions of theoretical and policy questions

D.J. Ashenden, 'Australian education: problems of a marxist practice', *Arena*, no. 54, 1979, pp. 43–58.

R.W. Connell, 'On the wings of history: a critique of social reproduction theory', *Arena*, no. 55, 1980, pp. 32–55.

R.W. Connell, 'Problems of class and schooling', in *Who Owns the Curriculum?* (Victorian teacher unions and parent organizations), 1980, pp. 27–32.

R.W. Connell, 'Class, patriarchy, and Sartre's theory of practice', *Theory and Society,* Vol II, no. 3, 1982, pp. 305-20.

Index